Using Media in
Religious Education

Other Books By Ronald A. Sarno

Achieving Sexual Maturity
Let Us Proclaim the Mystery of Faith
The Story of Hope: The Nation, The Man, The People
Liturgical Handbook for CLC's
The Cruel Caesars
Morality: How To Live It Today

USING
Media in
Religious Education

Ronald A. Sarno

Religious Education Press
Birmingham, Alabama

Copyright © 1987 by Religous Education Press
All rights reserved

No part of this publication may be reproduced, stored in a retrieval system, or transmitted, in any form or by any means, electronic, photocopying, recording, or otherwise, without the prior written permission of the publisher.

Library of Congress Cataloging-in-Publication Data

Sarno, Ronald A.
  Using media in religious education.

  Bibliography: p.
  Includes indexes.
  1. Christian education—Philosophy. 2. Communication (Theology) I. Title.
BV1464.S33   1987   268'.6   86-33844
ISBN 0-89135-058-6

Religious Education Press, Inc.
Birmingham, Alabama
10 9 8 7 6 5 4 3 2

Religious Education Press publishes books exclusively in religious education and in areas closely related to religious education. It is committed to enhancing and professionalizing religious education through the publication of serious, significant, and scholarly works.

PUBLISHER TO THE PROFESSION

Contents

Foreword vii
Preface ix
Acknowledgments xiii

PART I—BASIC CONCEPTS

Chapter 1: Religious Education as a Form of Communication 3
Chapter 2: Modern Communication Theory: An Overview 41
Chapter 3: Communication and the Teaching Act 84

PART II—VARIETIES OF MEDIA OPPORTUNITIES

Chapter 4: Audiovisual Materials 169
Chapter 5: Printed Materials 183
Chapter 6: Learner Media Productions 195
Chapter 7: Religious Broadcasting 215

PART III—MEDIA APPRECIATION

Chapter 8: The Development of Media-Literacy 235
Chapter 9: The Development of Motion Picture Appreciation
       Selected Feature Films and Television Mini-Series
       With Religious Education Themes 251
Chapter 10: The Development of Television Appreciation 271
Index of Motion Picture and Television Titles 283
Index of Names 286
Index of Subjects 292

Foreword

This text represents Dr. Sarno's long and patient study. Religious educators now have the fruit of his labor: an evaluation and a synthesis of the link between the traditional methods of catechesis and the modern media of communication.

This work meets a genuine need for the profession. It fills a void in the religious education literature because of its clarity, analysis, and extensive use of resources. This study presents us with a comprehensive but balanced view of the delicate problems that the electric age brings to the contemporary task of faith communication. The text tries to build a bridge between two worlds: the media-world and the world of religious education.

Some excellent teaching ideas flow from Sarno's discussion of seminal authors. I cite two ideas that I have especially made my own: First, a holistic, experiential approach constitutes an invitation to make a faith commitment. In this regard, Sarno is not an exponent of an abstract catechesis which remains the simple-minded repetition of the past. As the father of a family, who is responsible for the well-being of a living organism, Ronald Sarno is existentially aware of the practical steps of everyday life. So he realizes that faith does not entail a flight from daily human life but rather a dynamic insertion into that life, guided by the light of God.

The second teaching idea that I have made my own is this: Audiovisual language represents the most appropriate language for this experiential approach.

I am not speaking here of audiovisual techniques, but rather of audiovisual *language*, that is, the cluster of attitudes, of behaviors, and of words which a person uses to communicate the self via a medium. The Gutenberg language best expresses the rigor, the coherence, and the precision of doctrine. Audiovisual language best expresses the whole range of human emotions, including waking up to life, becoming excited, and being appealing. Audiovisual language surpasses all other forms of communication in its ability to touch the heart and to show the concrete experience of the journey of life.

Each morning, to get to work, Dr. Sarno takes a long, pleasant bus journey into the center of New York City. In a similar way, I believe his text will now take its place in that long file of pilgrims who for the last twenty centuries have dedicated themselves to retelling the marvelous message of Jesus in the language of their contemporaries.

PIERRE BABIN
Ecully, France

Preface

I believe the gospel call of Jesus Christ is not only a substantive content but also a structural content. Jesus not only spoke a message about God; he also said his words to specific people in a variety of ways. By his use of location, he revealed that God belongs in daily life with common people and not only in holy places with the elite at ceremonial times.

I believe the freedom of the gospel pertains to the process of teaching/learning. Jesus wisely discarded established techniques of traditional religious education to teach in a new way. He taught not only by his words but also (and more importantly) by deed, by example, and by symbol. Today his disciples need to continue this true Christian tradition, that is, to use what is new to instruct learners in the gospel.

I believe the gospel is not merely a message about God; it is a way of life and a love for a person.

I believe the church is best understood as a true community of loving and caring. Whenever church officials demand doctrinal integrity of the cognitive sort, or make sterile calls for church order and discipline, they can be most ineffectual. The faithful need to believe that their church leaders truly care for them as persons and are there to offer them solace during the anxieties and failures of daily life. Church order flourishes in those communities which exhibit authentic Christian unity. Such church order, however, is not the regimentation of an army. Rather, such order is the dynamic, complex unity of a loving, caring family.

I believe in the innate goodness of learners, young and old. I believe if we religious educators work wisely at our task the fruits of our labor will be abundant.

I believe the most vital task today is to teach/learn religion. Without a solid foundation in Judeo-Christian values, both teachers and learners flounder. Effective religious education is, on the one hand, the hardest of all tasks and, on the other hand, the easiest of all tasks. It is hardest when we—teachers and learners—resist the gospel call to be all we can be. This is the ancient battle between sin and grace. I believe sin is a misguided insistence on wanting only what we consider is best for ourselves. I believe grace is God's astute awareness of what is really in our best interest. Wisdom is knowing the difference. One of the tasks of religious education is to teach wisdom. Religious education is the easiest of all tasks when we—teachers and learners—really turn our lives over to Jesus Christ. Then everything we do becomes a teaching/learning in what we believe and value.

I believe in the value of print literacy. In fact, I believe print literacy is the key for curing poverty, because print creates the technological sophisticate who can earn his or her way in the world. Illiteracy and destitution are frequent soulmates. I refuse, however, to identify traditional print culture with the gospel of Jesus Christ. I believe that whenever religious educators make this identification, they wind up frustrating both themselves and their learners.

I believe the audiovisual media are the most effective communication tools ever developed by human ingenuity. An intelligent use of the audiovisual media is the best way to teach/learn the gospel of Jesus Christ. I believe in media literacy. Without media literacy, today's learners become passive consumers or the pawns of the politically powerful. I believe that even when a teaching/learning environment is very sophisticated about media literacy it will still fail as religious education if there is no genuine love between the teachers and the learners.

I believe the most effective way to learn media literacy is by producing media events. I believe learners of all ages are quite capable of producing quality media events if we teachers guide them and allow all of their creative energies to flow.

I believe the answer to sexually explicit media material is not censorship. Rather, the daily example of men and women who truly love one another and in turn love young learners is the most effective antidote. True eroticism does not lead away from the gospel's call to love, but rather straight to it, like an arrow in flight to its intended target. Eroticism and pornography are worlds apart.

I believe the answer to drug abuse is not stricter law enforcement. Rather, teaching the young learners self-esteem and demonstrating how meditation can provide the most powerful and exciting alternative states of consciousness imaginable is the most effective antidote.

I believe that the medium is the message, or that procedure is a true content, and that we religious educators—teachers and learners—are the media of Jesus Christ.

This book is an invitation to the religious education profession to accept the living bond between modern communication and religious education.

Acknowledgments

This text grew out of failure. Assigned to teach young learners religious education as a new teacher, I soon found out that the traditional methods of using printed materials simply did not work. I discovered that the print language often does not have a powerful impact on young learners who grow up in a media-world of instant communication.

I decided to do research on this topic, and my dissertation at New York University explored the relationship between modern communication theory and religious education during the period 1950-1980. Portions of this text are based on that research project.

Many fellow religious educators and learned colleagues have helped me to produce this text.

I want to thank Walter J. Ong of St. Louis University for his brilliant conversations which encouraged this project. I am especially grateful to Marshall McLuhan for his enthusiasm during the early stages of my work.

In its earliest form, this manuscript owes much to the guidance of Lee Belford, Norma Thompson, Neil Postman, and Paul Mattingly. I am especially indebted in this early form of the manuscript to the well-known religious educator Gabriel Moran who spent considerable time in focusing my arguments and in demanding precision of language. The world-class media specialist Pierre Babin was gracious enough to read the first draft of what was to become the final manuscript and to write a Foreword to this volume.

On a more personal note, I wish to express my deep gratitude to my wife Una who patiently proofread the entire text before it went to the publisher. She has endured far too many nights of a husband away at school, or at the library, or at the typing table. My daughter Niamh has been teaching me a great deal about nonverbal communication. I pay tribute to my late father, Anthony Vincent, who taught me an enduring love of printed books.

Over the years countless friends and work associates have provided words of encouragement, suggested contacts, or simply said, "That is a study that really needs to be done."

I hope this volume meets their expectations and provides religious educators with information on how to communicate the life of faith in a world of instant communication.

RONALD A. SARNO

Part One

Basic Concepts

1

Religious Education as a Form of Communication

INTRODUCTION

How a religious educator perceives communication theory radically affects how such a teacher approaches instruction. This book proposes that the more simple the notion of communication theory, the more simple (and the less effective in practice!) is the concomitant understanding of what religious education is all about. Conversely, the more rich and complex the notion of communication theory, the more rich, complex (and the more effective in practice!) is the understanding of what religious education is all about.

A simple notion of communication focuses on a communicator bringing a message to a recipient. A consequence of this view, as we shall see in the course of the argument of this text, is that religious education is reduced in meaning to the bringing of a message to a passive recipient. A more rich and complex comprehension of the task at hand recognizes that total communication takes place in an environment that affects the whole person.

Communication theorist Paul A. Soukup notes that communication connotes more than merely conveying a message. Rather, there are three principal effects for communication: it connects; it invents; it regulates. Communication is *connective* by relating individuals to their environment and to other individuals. Communication is *inventive* since an individual's or a society's involvement in speech or other communicative acts enhances or develops cognition. Finally, communication also *regulates* human behavior by constituting and enforcing a specific code which delimits the linguistic and behavioral options available to the users of that code.[1]

Consequently, communication varies with time, place, and social construct. It radically depends on what type of communication tools are available. In education, communication is significantly affected by the personality of the teacher and by the personality of the learner. The goal of total communication requires that the communicator must be cognizant of the *whole* effect of the act of communication. This means paying careful attention to the cognitive, the affective, the environmental, and the consequent behavioral modification of the learner. A religious education grounded on total communication recognizes that its goal involves much more than delivering a message from the past. The precise goal of religious education is to communicate in such an effective manner that its teaching re-creates the total person of the learner.

The thesis of this book is that the more a religious educator knows about communication theory, and the more that such a knowledge is applied to practice, the more effective will be the act of religious instruction.

CULTURE, COMMUNICATION, AND EDUCATION

Cultural historian Walter J. Ong describes three phases of communication, each characterized by its principal tool for communication. (1) The *oral* culture uses vocal speech as its principal means of communication. The oral culture is characterized by personalism, tribal loyalty, and an intensity of feeling. (2) The *literate* culture uses the written word as its principal means of communication. The literate culture is characterized by abstraction, disinterestedness, and a scientific approach to the physical world. (3) The *mass-media* culture uses the electric media (radio, the telegraph, cinema, television, etc.) and forms a global communication environment. The mass-media environment is characterized by empathy, global awareness, and personal involvement.[2] Although Marshall McLuhan claims that such a culture fosters individual participation, communication theorist Neil Postman retorts that the mass-media culture is really characterized by a greater passivity and a more totalitarian authoritarianism than the literate culture.

For Walter Ong, none of these communication cultures truly replaces another. Each is subsumed and co-exists with the others. Furthermore, subsocieties within a larger community can be characterized as retainers of earlier epochs. Contemporary stone-age primitives are examples of an oral people living in a mass-media world.

Today a new communication era is emerging: the world of the technological word.[3] This new era is characterized by the mutual interlocking of the personal computer with various media: the spoken word, the written word, the televised image, the telephone, the telegraph, and so on. Characteristic of this technological era is the fact that the individual learner who is able to interface with a personal computer can participate actively in the global communication matrix. It is now possible for a learner to be a living organism "talking back" to the larger mass media. This era is characterized by programed learning, individual creativity, and a scientific approach to the social construct.

Hence we can distinguish four principal communication cultures: (1) oral, (2) literate, (3) mass-media, and (4) contemporary-technological. These communication cultures form a metaphorical explanation of how a given society approaches education.

General education is a specific function of the larger culture. In an oral culture, a teacher instructs a learner through spoken aphorisms. In a literate culture, a teacher instructs a learner through the interpretation of a given text which both have read. In a mass-media culture, a teacher uses various forms of audiovisual language to create a holistic instructional environment for the learner.[4] In the contemporary-technological culture, the teacher uses mini-laboratories, social scientific methodology, and programed learning with personal computers to instruct learners who actively participate in their own educational process.

Religious instruction, like general education, is affected by the communication era. Catechetics, theology, religious education, and social-science religious instruction are to a certain extent forms of communication dependent on the historical eras in which they originate.

CATECHETICS AS A FORM OF COMMUNICATION

In the ancient church, the Greek verb *catēchein* meant to "instruct," or to "drill." Originally, catechetics was the instruction of simple adults in the rudiments of the faith. Oral forms of instruction were employed, such as memorized aphorisms, stories, parables, proverbs, and folk tales. The *kerygma* was the proclamation of the Christian faith, intended to inspire a personal response. For those who accepted the initial message, catechetics was the next step. It was a more explicit proclamation, a call to accept or to reject the message. From the beginning, church leaders controlled the substantive content of the message to insure orthodoxy.[5]

In the patristic and medieval church,[6] this format continued, although a new class of church leaders emerged as the principal teachers. These were the clergy. The root meaning of the Latin word *clerici* denotes "those who can read and write." Hence, *literate* teachers taught *oral* learners the rudiments of the faith. Manuscripts were the clergy's resources for a set form of spoken discourse. In the milieu of Christian Europe, such a catechetical enterprise was further reinforced by the pervasive culture of faith. Christian art, such as the Byzantine icons and the cathedrals, supplemented this oral instruction. St. Francis of Assisi encouraged the use of nativity scenes and the stations of the cross. These visual aids embellished the oral instruction of the laity about the significant events in the life of Jesus.

The Renaissance divided the church into Protestantism and Catholicism. Both sides used printed catechisms. Many of the Reformed churches used Martin Luther's famous catechism, while Catholics used the Tridentine Roman catechism. Catechetics became a tool for insuring confessional allegiance.[7]

Today a little child is taught a spoken language as a means of inculturation into a specific society. An American child is taught English; a French child French, and so on. In a similar way, the Catholic church's hierarchy employs catechetics as a means of intentionally inculturating a learner into a specific community of faith. Catechetics is *not* an ecumenical enterprise!

Proponents of catechetical proclamation, such as the Protestant educationist John H. Westerhoff III, describe this form of communication in positive terms. Catechetics, for him, is intentional and in many ways didactic; it connects the learner with a historical tradition; it roots the learner in a community of faith. Catechetics takes place within a living, learning, worshiping community of faith.[8] Critics, such as the Catholic educationist Pierre Babin, describe this form of communication in negative terms. For Babin, catechetics is ineffectual in the modern world. He complains that it is clerically dominated and that it reduces the learning of the Christian faith to memorizing a message from the past. Catechetics also isolates the learner from the wider community of faith by insisting on denominational adherence.[9]

Catechetics is rooted in oral education. The fundamental communication model operating in such a culture is that an active speaker (teacher) tells a passive listener (learner) what to believe and what not to believe. Such a controlled form of instruction succeeds best in an oral culture. If learners do not belong to an oral culture, it does not succeed.

THEOLOGY: FORMAL, WRITTEN COMMUNICATION

The word *theology* comes from the Greek words *theos* and *logos*. It means "the study of God." For the Protestant educationist William Clayton Bower theology is understood as an intellectual reflection of the church upon Christian experience. It is an attempt to organize these interpretations into a logically consistent system of thought.[10] Historically, theology has always depended on the concepts and concerns of contemporaneous philosophy.

It is important to recall that Western philosophy is rooted in the introduction of writing to Greece. Plato's written reflections on Socrates' oral discourse marks the transition from the dialogic teaching of philosophy to a written reflection on philosophical methodology.[11] The church's theology has two foundations: scriptural exegesis and Platonic philosophy. Hence theology is characterized as a logical and methodological reflection on the life of biblical faith. Theology utilizes the philosophical vocabulary of its contemporaries, and theology expresses its concerns in a formal, written text. Consequently, theology typically has been a *literate* form of communication, normally intended for a *select* group of scholars.

A historical survey of Christian theology demonstrates this view. In the New Testament church, the Johannine theology in the Fourth Gospel used the vocabulary and the imagery of Greek Gnosticism. In the patristic church, Augustine employed neo-Platonism to develop his theology of sin and grace. In the medieval church, Thomas Aquinas utilized Aristotelian existentialism and provided the foundation for Scholasticism. In the Renaissance, the Protestant Reformers relied on Peter Ramus' visual epistemology to challenge the Catholic church's rigid reliance on Scholasticism. In the late nineteenth century, Protestant biblical scholars based some of their critical commentaries of the sacred text on the objections to the creation story raised by Charles Darwin's biological evolutionism. Other Protestant theologians used Georg Hegel's dialectic idealism or Søren Kierkegaard's existentialism. In the first half of the twentieth century, Catholic theologians expounded on Jacques Maritain's Neo-Scholasticism or Gabriel Marcel's religious existentialism. In the post-Vatican II church, Catholic theologians are considering the hypostatic union of the secular and the sacred, a logical consequence of Pierre Teilhard de Chardin's evolutionary immanentism. Protestant liberation theologians like Ruben Alvez manage to unify St. Paul's soteriology with Marxism. For most of the history of the church these theological reflections were the work of white, educated males. New expressions of liberation theology, black theology,[12] and feminist theology,[13] are contemporary protests against this exclusivity. When women and minorities are given access to the tools of theology—namely, philosophy and published writing—a corrective argument emerges.

At one time theology was the "queen of the sciences" and ruled over the other academic disciplines in the university. In the modern world theology continues to exert a powerful influence on the life of the church and its work of education. However, its impact on the secular world has been almost nil.[14]

For a long time theology exercised a normative control over

catechetics. Indeed, the very nature of catechetics implies clerical control. Proponents of theological control over teaching religion, such as the Protestant educationist Randolph Crump Miller, claim that such control is essential for an effective instruction in the Christian faith. Theology, according to Miller, acts as an anchor and prevents a dilution of the full richness of the Christian heritage.[15] Critics of this position such as Catholic religious educationist Gabriel Moran, challenge this assumption. For Moran, whenever theology exercises a normative control over religious education there is no true break with the ancient form of catechetics regardless of whether the term catechetics or religious education is used. Religious education is not a form of confessional indoctrination. If religious education does not sever its reliance on theology it loses the very potency and flavor it has to offer, namely: diversity, criticism, and open-endedness.[16]

In summary, theology represents formal, written communication. Theology's vocabulary and concern normally center around a particular philosophical system. Theology is usually intended for a small audience of scholars. Theologically dominated catechetics (and religious education, too) represents an attempt to fuse oral teaching and written reflection. Randolph Crump Miller, on the one hand, celebrates this fusion as an effective form for instructing learners in the Christian faith. Gabriel Moran, on the other hand, protests that this fusion is really a mirage and that true religious education must function outside of the control of theology in order to achieve its full potential.

Religious Education as a Form of Modern Communication

So far we have seen that catechetics properly belongs to an oral culture and theology to a literate culture. Religious education, however, is properly a form of audiovisual communication.[17] In the nineteenth century, technology through the telegraph developed an interlinked communication system which united every world capital. This system was strengthened by newspapers, rapid transport steamship lines and, continental railways. Then came the phonograph, the telephone, and the cinema projector. Far distances melted; old barriers were torn down; international communication lit the first glimmer of global consciousness. People yearned to break out of confessional and national chains. With improved communication came also a compassionate interest in the plight of the less fortunate. One reason that slavery ended in the nineteenth century was that many people became acutely conscious of the pain and suffering it was causing. At the same time the application of scientific methodology to education arose from the optimistic conviction that the proper use of technology could improve every enterprise, including pedagogy.

With the twentieth century came new communication inventions: the radio, television, the slide projector, the cassette tape recorder, the stereophonic phonograph, laser technology, and so on. Every person in the world now lodges in a global village of constant intercommunication. Those doctrines of the past age which emphasize confessional adherence or national boundaries seem to many audiovisual learners to be quaint, even meaningless.

Religious education as we know it today began in nineteenth-century Protestant America. It blossomed in the twentieth century, the age of mass media. An initial theory for the use of religious education was expounded by the nineteenth-century Protestant educationist Horace Bushnell.[18] In the secular world, American philosopher John Dewey and, in the Protestant communion, American religious educator George Albert Coe, who helped to found the Religious Education Association in 1903, both articulated a system of instruction that argues for student freedom, purposeful activity, the substitution of personal interest instead of punishment as a tool for motivation, an awareness of the natural developmental milestones of the growing child, the use of applied science in pedagogy, the tailoring of instruction to specific classes and kinds of learners, and community involvement.[19] Dorothy Jean Furnish, a Protestant, adds that this kind of religious education is also nondenominational, is free of clerical control, and has a positive attitude toward the development of modern technology.[20]

The willingness of early religious educators like Coe to employ learning environments other than the traditional classroom eventually led to the use of audiovisual communication and "insertion experiences" as new tools for religious instruction.

Hence religious education does not limit itself to the memorized answer, to the book text, or even to intellectual reflection derived from print media. Religious education recognizes that many human experiences are intrinsically religious and educational. Like modern audiovisual communication, religious education is also universal, open-minded, compassionately concerned about the whole world of humanity, and critical of past, authoritarian forms.

Religion teaching tends to be somewhat different in mainline Protestant denominations as contrasted to Evangelical churches. The Evangelical Sunday School class relies on a fundamental adherence to confessional doctrine (oral memory), and biblical texts (literate forms). Dorothy Jean Furnish notes other distinctive characteristics of twentieth-century, mainline Protestant religious education: For the most part this religious education uses professionally unprepared lay teachers who distinguish their work from the preaching of the clergy. These religious educators often combine John Dewey's educational philosophy with a smattering of critical biblical scholarship. These religious educators also emphasize teaching as a form of character building; they avoid sectarian dogmas.[21]

Catholic religious educationist Maria Harris dates the introduction of religious education into the Catholic church at 1966-67. She claims that religious education appeared for both theoretical and practical reasons. The theoretical foundation for Catholic religious education, according to Harris, came out of the combination of the liturgical renewal, kerygmatic catechetics, and the post-Vatican II ecclesiology which emphasized lay responsibility for the Catholic church. Practical reasons for the appearance of Catholic religious education, Harris adds, include: (1) the opening of new parochial schools without any clerical or religious teachers, (2) the loss of vocations which tends to dry up the supply of clerical and religious teachers in the traditional parochial schools, (3) the availability of graduate courses in religious education at Catholic seminaries and universities, and (4) the growing pool of educated lay people who have graduated from these religious education programs.[22]

In both the Catholic and Protestant communions there is an escalating recognition of the need to define the distinct roles of catechetics, theology, and religious education. There is also the bitter awareness among many teachers that none of these forms is having any real impact on contemporary learners. A crucial question now is how can Christianity continue into the twenty-first century.

It is the contention of this book that Christianity can optimally continue into the twenty-first century when religious education uses those forms of communication most effective with contemporary, technological learners.

Social Science Religious Instruction as a Form of Holistic, Technological Communication

Contemporary technology, especially in the form of the personal computer, is radically changing the teaching/learning environment. In the past all teaching forms of communication were fundamentally active, while learning forms of communication were passive. Ironically, much of contemporary audiovisual religious education, although it claims to be a form of active student participation, frequently results in a passive role for the learner. In practice, despite rhetoric to the contrary, much religious education tends to stubbornly retain its ancient authoritarian (oral) structure even while asserting its compatibility with the mass-media (democratic) environment. Much of this type of traditional teaching remains fundamentally ineffective with contemporary learners because it does not truly allow them an active role. Experience demonstrates that instruction coupled with personal involvement facilitates the learning of personal and social behaviors.[23]

The personal computer requires learners to actively participate in their own instructional process. The computer is programed to gear itself to the interest and pace of each learner. The computer may be considered a holistic, technological communication device. It uses speech, typescript, graphics, and the kinetic image to accomplish its programed goal. Since the computer cannot function without very precise keypunching, it has tended to operate as a check on the recent decline into illiteracy caused by the audiovisual mass media. If a learner misses a semicolon during computer input, literally nothing else will occur until the error is rectified. The computer is more demanding than the frostiest schoolteacher of the past! However, once it receives complete and accurate instructions, it is a marvelous device for personalized step-by-step learning. Moreover it enables learners to contribute their own personal programs for their own interests and needs.

In the contemporary world, technology has become personalized and holistic. Communication is dual, and the teaching/learning roles have begun to merge into a new synergy: the total instructional environment.

One facet of the social-science model for religious instruction is the conscious attempt to apply this technological, holistic form of communication to the task of faith-education. Some traditional religious educators accuse this social-science model of actually being a form of deterministic behaviorism. This unwarranted criticism masks the genuine contribution that the social-science model is making to religious education. Oral and literate models, and the more recent mass-media models for religious education, do not truly touch the majority of contemporary learners who now are functioning in a technological, holistic communication environment. Successful teaching/learning has to assume this form of communication if it is to effectively accomplish its goal.

Traditional religious educators may complain that contemporary learners fail to adopt religious behaviors because they are "too secular," or even "children of the devil." It is always easier to castigate the learners rather than to face the issue head-on: Much of what passes for religious education today is the use of outmoded communication forms. These communication forms are doomed to failure because teachers opt out of the very environment of universal communication in which learning is actually taking place. This stubborn persistence is like some of the Christian missionaries in the past who foolishly tried to bring the faith to natives while refusing to learn their language or customs. After all, the natives were the *pagans*.

Social-science religious instruction is not a deterministic form of teaching. Actually it is a humanistic form of holistic, technological communication. It is in harmony with the nature of learners, of communication, and of the contemporary *Zeitgeist*.

It recognizes the enormity of the task. Holistic communication does not resort to piosity, that self-deception that maintains that religious education is merely the transmitter of a divine message from the past. Effective religious instruction necessitates holistic communication, that is, one that recognizes the importance of cognitive, affective, and environmental factors.

Traditional religious educators often use a *priori* theological assumptions. When these assumptions do not prove effective in practice, then contemporary learners are denigrated as "Godless," "selfish," "materialistic," and "irreligious." In the social-science model, both the teacher and the learner must work hard at the instructional task. The teacher must employ tested pedagogical models; the learner must accept responsibility for participating actively in the process. The lazy teacher will limit the task of religious education to the oral one-way communication of a message. If the message is not received, then the learner is "unreceptive to the work of the Holy Spirit." A holistic communicator realizes that the laws for human teaching/learning are not repealed when the subject is religion. The same laws hold for the subject of religion as they do for physics.

One reason for this ineffectiveness is that many religious educators are amateur volunteers and not trained professionals. Although both the Protestants and Catholics unequivocally affirm their institutional support for paid-trained professionals in the field of religious education, too often the real situation for most adolescent learners is that they are being taught by untrained volunteers with limited resources at their disposal.

A typical Sunday School or CCD teacher is often an amateur with little pertinent preprofessional or professional training in religious education. It is rare for such amateurs to attend professional conferences, or to participate in workshops, or to read professional journals designed to enrich their skills. Such an amateur relies on "faith and goodwill" and simply does not do the hard work which is required to become conversant in the field of religious education.

A typical amateur also concentrates primarily on the objective truths (content) to be taught and does not pay much attention to the unique needs of each learner. The typical amateur is also timid, subservient to clerical authority, afraid of new ideas, and unwilling to accept, participate in, or even understand the subcultural-lifestyle of adolescent learners. Such an amateur is often a book-person. A book-person does not know much about audiovisual media; a book-person is often unaware of what is popular in the world of audiovisual entertainment. A book-person often does not use audiovisual media tools for teaching/learning. An even greater problem is that a book-person does not know how to encourage media-wise learners to use their skills in audiovisual communication for student self-study projects in the area of religion.

In contrast, the typical teacher of so-called "secular subjects" is a paid, trained professional. Such a professional has a master's degree or doctorate in the academic field. There are adequate resources at the disposal of such a teacher. The typical professional educator tends to be in frequent professional communication with colleagues. Such a professional is normally motivated to approach each learner as a unique individual, to pay careful attention to the learner's unique needs, and to tailor the subject matter as much as possible to meet those needs.

A good professional educator tends to be keenly aware of the power of the audiovisual media in the present environment. Such a professional is typically aware of what is popular in the world of entertainment because this information tells a great deal about the needs and wants of the learners. Such an educator is frequently sophisticated about using audiovisual media for instruction in the academic subject. Most important, such an educator knows how to inspire learners to use audiovisual media in their own self-study projects.

Because of their lack of professional preparation, different communications come to learners from many religious educators, as contrasted to teachers of "secular subjects." The *explicit*, officially sanctioned verbal communication from religious educators to learners is that religion is relevant to their lives, that God is personally concerned about them, and that active participation in the life of the church leads to a fuller, more happy life. The *implicit*, nonverbal communication, which is transmitted to learners more forcefully than religious educators care to admit, is that formal religion is irrelevant, that God does not really care about persons, and that active participation in the life of the church is for those inadequate people who cannot function in the real world.

Many religious educators might find this contrast too stark. As is natural whenever anyone's complacency is challenged, the religious educator will immediately strive to deny this contrast by recalling one or another effective, charismatic religion teacher or some bumbling "secular" teachers. This avoids the basic issue: In the field of religious education most learners are taught by amateurs. Most of these amateurs are unfamiliar with how to cope with the world of audiovisual communication and consequently most religious educators simply do not have the skills to teach the present media-generation.

In both words and deeds, Jesus urged his disciples to be knowledgeable about how to communicate with their contemporaries. His complaint about their failures rings still true today: *"For the children of this world are more astute in dealing with their own kind than the children of light."*[24]

James Michael Lee has initiated a social-science approach to the task of religious instruction. His goal is to make contemporary religious educators more astute about how the present world actually makes teaching-learning communication work. For Lee, teaching deals with the way God's grace is given in this world, while learning deals with the way God's grace is received. Religion basically connotes a way of life; theology connotes one theory about this way of life. Religious activity directly leads to a person's salvation, while theological activity remains simply a cognitive reflection on religion. Hence theological instruction is *not* religious instruction. Theological instruction prepares one to think about religion in a certain way; religious instruction prepares one to be a person of active faith and love.

Lee has discovered that the religion teaching act is composed of two distinct but existentially intertwined dimensions—structural content and substantive content. Neither exists by itself in terms of religion teaching activity. Existential substantive content is the subject matter, namely religion. Structural content is the fashioning of subject matter into teaching form. This fashioning involves the deliberative interplay of four major variables: teacher, learner, subject matter, and environment. These four major variables are always present in one way or another in every teaching/learning act. Thus the structural content of religious instruction is the teaching process, an act of formal communication. The substantive content is the subject matter which is taught. Lee has discovered eight molar kinds of substantive content present in all religion teaching. These kinds of substantive content are: (1) product content, (2) process content, (3) cognitive content, (4) affective content, (5) verbal content, (6) nonverbal content, (7) unconscious content, and (8) lifestyle content. Holistic communication requires bringing all these eight subcontents into play during the religion lesson.

For Lee, the axis of religious instruction is properly described in terms of causing desired learning outcomes. If these learning outcomes have not been obtained, there has been *no* religious instruction, no matter how holy or theologically erudite the religious educator is.

The social-science approach states that the aim and goal of religious instruction is to be found in the learner as one who dynamically interacts with one's own environment. The task of religious instruction is to facilitate the learner's religious development in such a way that the learner is optimally fulfilled as a person.[25]

For social science the substantive subject matter of religious instruction is religion—religion as it is actually taught/learned in the religious instruction act. This requires paying a great deal of attention to the role of the teacher. Here the teacher has much more than a messenger or transmitter role. The teaching theory of the social-science model is derived from descriptive statements of empirically demonstrated causal relationships between the religious educator's antecedent pedagogical behaviors and the learner's consequent performance behaviors. Here the learner is more than a receptacle for memorizing past facts. The social-science approach views the learner and the learning process from the perspective of how, in fact, the learner actually learns. The role of the learner is essential if any communication is to take place, to say nothing of successful communication. For communication theorist Eric A. Havelock the essential act of communication does not take place if the speech is not heard or the writing not read. The complete communication operation requires the sharing between two or more persons in which one vocalizes or inscribes and the other receives and recognizes the product produced.[26]

Other approaches to religious education do not concentrate on the complete act of communication, or even on the dynamics of the communication act itself. They are more concerned with maintaining the intrinsic logic of the material, or following an established topical order. Thus these approaches essentially constitute a literate form of communication derived from the visual epistemology of Peter Ramus.[27] Lee denies the complete or even adequate effectiveness of this literate pedagogical method for the modern world. For example, according to Lee, a learner acquires a knowledge of the decalogue (a cognitive outcome), a love of the decalogue (an affective outcome), and an obedience to the moral law of the decalogue (lifestyle outcome) primarily according to the laws of the learner's own human development and *not* primarily according to the logical structure or eternal import of the decalogue.

The social-science approach places a great stress on the environment in the work of religious instruction. Hence it is keenly aware of the importance of the contemporary global communicative milieu in the performance of its task. Older forms of religious education believed the act of teaching sacred eternal truths to be independent of the environment. Since the learning outcome was presumed to flow directly and extrinsically from the grace of God, the older forms of religious education tended to neglect evaluation. For the social-science approach, evaluation is an integral and vital dimension of religious instruction. It is only through evaluation that we can discern whether or not total communication has taken place and religious behaviors have been obtained—that is to say, whether or not the learners have grown religiously.

In the social-science approach, method and content are not dichotomous, because both are actual bonafide contents in their own right. In the past religious educators approached method as a means for communicating content. The essential component of religious education was its content. Method was secondary. Communication theorist Marshall McLuhan's great contribution to modern education is his insistence that the medium, or the process by which we communicate (teach/learn), is itself a content. Its importance cannot be shunted aside. For Lee structural content and substantive content are now mediated existentially in a new ontic reality called "religious instruction." Apart from the religious instruction act, these two contents are simply logical beings, mental constructs which are conceptually devised primarily for the purpose of intellectual analysis.[28]

In articulating a social-science approach to religious instruction, Lee demonstrates the inadequacies of earlier forms of theological catechetics and contemporary religious education. He insists that the scientific method of behavioralism is not to be in any way equated as a materialistic, unbelieving approach to the pedagogical task. Rather, behavioralism (the concentration on what learners and teachers actually do) constitutes an effective tool for obtaining a religious way of life. Earlier forms of communication divided teaching and learning, method and content, faith and science. According to Lee, effective religious instruction unifies these supposed opposites into a conceptual whole that enables complete and effective communication to take place. Formal complete communication, in Lee's view, is the most successful means for helping learners to actually live a Christian lifestyle.

THE CONTEMPORARY ENVIRONMENT OF THE CHURCH

Religious instruction takes place in the current church environment. What is happening in ecclesiology, theology, and linguistics, that is, the contemporary understanding of how religious language works, are a few of the salient major components of the church's environment. This environment is currently characterized by much variety, debate, and confusion.

Theologian Avery Dulles distinguishes five current concepts that believers hold about the nature of the church. For Dulles, the church may be conceptualized as: (1) an institution, (2) a community, (3) a sacrament, (4) a herald, and (5) a servant.[29]

In a similar fashion, David Tracy recognizes five major concepts about theology itself. In Tracy's view, the orthodox theology has a commitment to the perennial teaching of the church. This traditionalism remains a sufficient bulwark against the onslaughts of moderinism. Neo-orthodox theology shares in the liberal agenda for accommodation with the world. Neo-orthodox theology, however, according to Tracy, is critical of theological liberalism and challenges this liberalism for being unable to account for the existence of sin and tragedy in human experience. Tracy's own agenda is an explication of revisionist theology. Revisionist theology seeks to establish a synthesis between a belief in the vitality of God, on the one hand, and a meaningful discourse with the modern technological world, on the other hand. Liberal theology fosters free and open intellectual inquiry and an autonomous judgment; it presents a reinterpretation of traditional Christianity in order to force it into reconciliation with the modern world. According to Tracy, radical theology counters that any conscience that is truly committed to the struggle for human liberation cannot be burdened with a faith in or dependence on a transcendental God.[30] John Paul II considers this radical theology a surrender to Marxism.

Religious sociologist William McSweeney distinguishes four different subgroups in the contemporary Christian church: (1) traditional Christians emphasize the values and the stability of the past; (2) charismatic Christians emphasize the importance of personal faith; (3) political Christians emphasize the need to do justice in the world; and (4) individualist Christians identify with historical Christianity but do not acknowledge any need to belong explicitly to any of the three other divisions. For Catholics this contemporary plurality is a genuine consequence of the religious freedom won at Vatican II.[31] For mainline Protestants, such plurality is an authentic expression of their historical refusal to be bound by the norms and regulations of the Catholic magisterium.

Catholic church historian George Tavard states that the plurality of Christian subgroups is rooted in two distinct theological philosophies. Following an age-old distinction, Tavard highlights the dichotomy of transcendism and immanentism. (Tavard prefers the terms transcendentalism and incarnationalism;

however, these terms denote respectively the same two positions of transcendism and immanentism.) Transcendism is the philosophical root for religious traditionalism. Transcendism emphasizes the spiritual nature of the church and its separation from the world. Immanentism is the philosophical root for incarnational church activity ranging from meditational Christianity to political involvement. Immanentism emphasizes the need for the church to insert itself in the world.[32] Charismatic Christianity has managed to synthesize a traditional theological base with an enthusiastic faith normally associated with nontraditional sects.

Transcendism begins with the fundamental assumption that God transcends humanity. This theology is akin to Platonic idealism. Augustine was a patristic exponent of neo-Platonism in Christian philosophy. Transcendism applies this Platonic idealism to the church and to the church's responsibility to continue Christ's mission in the world. For transcendism, the church and its teaching office transcend human experience. Transcendism's avowed purpose is to lift humanity into the realm of the sacred and the mystical, as the sacred and the mystical are considered to be extrinsic to the world. Hence, in this view, it is necessary for the church's religious educators to maintain this transcendence by preventing any taint of the world from affecting the teaching office. This ideological assumption tends to prevent the transcendists from accepting any substantial intrinsic assistance from social science in the task of religious education. For the transcendists, what is basically a spiritual enterprise cannot profit from association with a science that is not fundamentally involved in dealing with the validity of transcendent reality.

Immanentism begins with the fundamental assumption that God became human in Christ Jesus. (Recall that in Latin *transcends* means *being above*, while *immanens* means *dwelling with*.) Immanentist theology is akin to Aristotelian realism, or scientific experience.[33] Thomas Aquinas was a medieval exponent of Aristotelianism as a philosophical basis for Catholic theology. Immanentism applies this experiential realism to the church and to the church's responsibility to continue Christ's mission in the world. Immanentism holds that if God can ally his divine nature with human nature in order to communicate with humanity, then the church, which cannot be greater than its own Lord, can become allied to the age in which it finds itself. This ideological assumption affects the way in which immanentism approaches the task of religious education. An immanentist is more likely to be open to contributions from social science. Yet it is also true that theologians from *both* camps often exercise theological imperialism, holding that theology will and ought to still exercise full control over the content and methodology of religious instruction.

In the Catholic church, transcendism is usually associated with conservative clergymen and laity, while immanentism is usually associated with liberal clergymen and laity. In the Protestant churches, transcendism is common among the conservative, Evangelical and especially Fundamentalist congregations, while immanentism is common among liberal, mainline congregations.

A religious educator today does well to make learners aware of the diversity of opinion in the current church. To present the church as a monolithic community with all believers saying and thinking the same thing is to do a disservice. Honesty compels us to admit that we live in a family characterized by heated arguments about the nature of the church, the meaning of theology, the task of religious education, and the expected lifestyle activities of true Christians.

Linguistics is also contributing significantly to contemporary religious education by making us more aware of the verbal environment in which we communicate. Contemporary scholars note that verbal language constitutes a paradox. Verbal language is an important means to communicate the self to the other. Yet verbal language is also basically inadequate, since total communication never actually takes place. Religious verbal language constitutes a double paradox: Religious verbal language claims to speak for a mystery (God), which is incommunicable; and religious verbal language also uses a tool (verbal language) which is inadequate for the task.[34]

Linguistics is contributing to a growing comprehension about the nature and effect of verbal language. Verbal language is part and parcel of the very thought patterns which we use, because language establishes what questions we ask and what answers we look for. Each language, or message-system, forms its own unique symbolic environment for information, which in turn produces its own peculiar psychological and social effects.[35]

If we conceptualize language as verbal behavior, certain determining factors apply to spoken communication. In order for spoken communication to have an effect on human behavior, three factors are required in order for the contingencies of reinforcement to generate an operant. A speaker must respond to the setting, and then the listener must engage in the behavior and be affected by the consequences. The requested behavior will only occur if the verbal behaviors of the speaker and the listener are supported by the additional contingencies arranged by the verbal community.[36] A cry for help in English among tribal people who speak only Swahili is not heard; the unintelligible cry does not cause any behavioral modification on the part of the hearers. Closer to home, the use of theological language does not have any direct effect on the religious behaviors of the listeners. Religious language is basically different and distinct from theological language. Theological language is objective and scientific verbalization about God. Religious language, on the other hand, has a deeply existential character and thus tends to be intensely subjective and personalistic. Much of the Bible is written in religious language. Verbal language is a symbol which points to some particular reality.[37] Theological language points to the reality of God, but religious language points to the reality of living a Christian lifestyle. A learner will only produce the behaviors of a Christian lifestyle if the teacher uses religious language because, like religious language, the Christian lifestyle is personal and subjective. Religious language is a summons to respond as a person and to change one's behavior. Theological language is necessarily a scientific statement about an objective truth that does not inherently require either a personal response or a change in behavior.

Summary: Different Types of Religious Education Constitute Different Forms of Communication

Linguistic analyst Roman Jakobson provides a conceptual tool for an interpretation of how different types of religious education constitute different forms of communication and offers an explanatory model for defining how message-systems are transmitted from the communicator to the recipient.[38] He postulates six basic elements in communication: (1) the *context* to which reference is made; (2) the *code* or system of signs which are used; (3) the message or *content* of what is said; (4) the *transmitter* who speaks; (5) the *receiver* who is spoken to; and (6) the *contact*, or type of communication which is established. I will now apply Jakobson's six elements of communication to the four major historical forms of religious education as delineated by Harold Burgess in his classic category system.[39]

A. Traditional Theological Approach

The traditional theological approach to religious education has the characteristics of formal, written communication. The *context* for this approach is that the Christian is not truly at home in the world. There should always be, for the traditionalists, a fundamental irreconcilable tension between the Christian and the environment (i.e., the world). Rather than actually use environmental effects, traditionalists strive to ameliorate them—especially since the environment is regarded as hostile to genuine Christian values. The *code* for this traditional approach is formal theological language grounded in transcendist philosophy. For the traditional school of thought, the *content* of religious education is an authoritative, biblically and theologically accurate message to be presented to the student by that kind of a teacher who, having accepted the message and experienced its benefits, is an authentic witness to it. The major source of content for Protestants is the Bible and for Catholics, the doctrines of the magisterium. The central theme of the religious message is the person of Christ. The *transmitter* is the religion teacher who is an agent of the Christian message and the central human instrument in the religious educational endeavor, following the typical formulations of the traditional approach. The primary personal requisite for such a religion teacher is authentic Christian character. Fidelity to the message is crucial. Training programs for traditional religion teachers concentrate upon the faithful understanding of the message. There is an emphasis on clear and distinct ideas. In this view, the student is the *recipient* of an authoritative, divinely ordained salvific message. In the Catholic church this is further developed because of traditional theological and philosophical views which portray humanity as the favored recipient of a divine message. *Contact* in the traditional approach is normally limited to the formal lecture or to cognitive verbal devices which place heavy stress on teacher talk. Traditional religious educators rely almost exclusively upon verbal and cognitive formulations of the Christian message.[40]

Representative Protestant exponents of the traditional approach include Frank Gaebelein and Lois LeBar.[41] A representative Catholic exponent is Johannes Hofinger, who did much to establish kerygmatic catechetics in Europe and America.[42]

B. The Social-Cultural Approach

The social-cultural approach to religious education has some of the character of informal, oral communication and also of global, audiovisual communication. The axis of this approach is to place religious education squarely in the flow of present existence. The social-cultural approach seeks to stimulate creative thought, to restructure traditional concepts of God, to redefine spiritual objectives, and to reorganize outmoded religious education programs. This approach involves the processes of questioning and of experimenting, both in thought and in conduct. Grounded in late nineteenth-and twentieth-century liberal theology, this approach conceptualizes God as still active in the world and engaged in continuous creation. Hence those Christians who have assumed the burden and the risks of re-creating their Christian faith maintain a vital link with Christ by following him on the pilgrim path of discovery and creation. In the view of this new social gospel, the secular order is in a constant state of becoming. The church is not exempt from this dynamic flux. Hence the young Christian should be initiated into a community that is also creative, personal, and social.

For an early exponent of this view, George Albert Coe, the redemption of Christ includes the transformation of the social order into the family of God. Social-cultural religious education is an expression of the democratic ideal. This approach contends that individual destinies and the destiny of society are interdependent. Hence the social-cultural approach is a corollary of incipient global audiovisual communication.

In the social-cultural approach, moral character is totally a matter of a human being's relationship to society, a relationship that can be promoted by a creative religious education that is rooted in a concrete social situation. For George Albert Coe, this kind of education is one which seeks social welfare, social justice, and a world society. The basic context for religious education is that the student shall (1) acquire the tools of social intercourse: language, number, social forms, and so on; (2) be introduced to society through the sciences, arts, literature, and most especially, through participation in the social life; (3) be trained for an occupation; and (4) be intelligently socialized by the shaping of the motives of the learner's conduct.[43]

The *code* of the social-cultural approach is not limited to verbal and cognitive expressions. Rather, all verbal and nonverbal communication is utilized and this polycommunicative method enables the teacher and student to involve themselves together in the venture of re-creating Christianity itself.[44]

Coe decries content-oriented education for the following reasons: (1) It uses force, including psychological force, to achieve its aims; (2) it subjects some human beings to the control of other human beings, even though it purports to promote obedience to God; and (3) its achievements can run counter to its own objectives, because it does not, by vigorous analysis, keep abreast of changing conditions.[45] For the social-cultural approach, the *content* of religious education is guided experience in living the Christian life. In Coe's view, a socially grounded religious education might well include the involvement of students with those who really love both them and others. Radicating religious educational content in present social interaction makes it possible to fuse love and faith. This dual content unites the voice of God and the voice of human need, even in early childhood.[46]

The content of religious education in this approach is social experience, not printed facts. For William Clayton Bower, the content of religious education is comprised of the following elements: (1) the situation as it is being lived; (2) the past experience which the learner brings to the learning situation and which is the first recourse in interpreting and dealing with new experiences; and (3) the experience of the race itself as it is communicated in many ways to individual students—this eliminates the need to begin totally anew each time the same situation recurs.[47]

Proponents of the socio-cultural approach believe the content should be ordered psychologically instead of logically. Consequently, the biblical text or magisterial doctrine should be a recourse for comprehending present human experience. God's divine life is communicated to humanity only by here-and-now living itself, that is, by an engagement in the social process.

In the social-cultural approach the teacher is a *transmitter* who participates with the students in the creation of the new world. The teacher's task is to promote individual personal growth through skillfully guided participation in a group, thus freeing each and every student to acquire full and active membership in the "democracy of God."[48] This approach requires that a teacher be endowed with a wholesome and winning personality. The teacher should recognize that the content and the method of religious education remain inseparable realities. When the teacher unites the substantive content and the method of religious education, then religious beliefs, attitudes, and overt behaviors are seen as more influenced by the shape of the experience itself than by the biblical or doctrinal subject matter that may be used to expound on the experience. In this approach, the teacher functions democratically as a guide to venturesome students rather than to passive students.

In the social-cultural approach, the *recipient* is a learner who is conceived as a living organism, a human being who develops religiously and socially out of his or her own resources. Instead of viewing the learner as another victim of original sin, this approach holds the view that the heritage of the human race leaves the learner's instinctive religious capabilities intact. However, the learner still retains a limitless capacity for good or evil. For the recipient, religious education is intended to: (1) bring about the fullest possible development of the whole person; and (2) promote social righteousness within a society of growing persons. The basic task of religious education is accordingly to help growing persons bring their experience under the control of ideas and values.[49] Hence the learner actively participates in the reconstruction of the ideal society.

Contact for this approach is not limited to delivering a message. The contact remains after the concrete communication or teaching-learning act has taken place. Since social-cultural religious educators believe that the church is responsible to society they consider the church accountable for the results obtained by its educational efforts. An evaluation of the type of contact which has taken place determines how much effect the teaching had upon the life, character, and conduct of the student. A successful contact is one which changes the student's lifestyle, not one which merely imparts a message.[50]

C. The Contemporary Theological Approach

The contemporary theological approach is a modern development of the immanentist philosophy. It is grounded in the *literate* form of contemporary theology, yet it also draws on the *oral* tradition of communal adherence and the *audiovisual* tradition of social concern. While it is a corrective of traditional theology, nonetheless the contemporary theological approach still maintains the validity of historical Christian values. To a certain extent, contemporary theology opposes the optimistic, liberal theology of the social-cultural exponents. In the contemporary theological approach there is the acute recognition that human beings are still in need of redemption. In this view, the Christian community is the locus for religious life and education. This approach usually expects some form of insertion experience by the learners into the living community of Christians.

In the contemporary theological approach, the *context* is the recognition of cultural changes accompanied by the wholehearted recognition of the validity of the biblical and doctrinal tradition. The Bible, the church's life, the culture, and the human situation, in this view, constitute an interactive organic whole. Revelation, for the contemporary theological approach, is not merely a divine content communicated in the past to be treasured and sustained exactly as received. Revelation, rather, is a continual process in which God keeps communicating personally with human beings. While the focus of the traditional theological approach is on the transmission of a salvific message, and while the focus of the social-cultural approach is on the development of an idealized social order, the focus of the contemporary theological approach is on the church in its corporate life. Hence the objectives of this approach are many: personal growth, intellectual growth, biblical understanding, and training for effective participation in the life of the church. This context strives for an understanding of the Bible in terms of its continually relevant message. The Bible, in this view, remains a written witness to revelation. More significant than what the Bible has to say about past revelation is that the scriptures provide a criteria by which present revelatory communication can be evaluated and acted upon. The goal of this approach is to educate and train persons within the church to be truly the church. For Lewis Sherrill, a Protestant exponent of the contemporary theological approach, the primary educational act is the revelation-encounter which takes place within the learner as one who is confronted with the self-revealing God.[51] For Gabriel Moran, a Catholic proponent of the contemporary theological approach, freedom can no longer remain a side issue in the aim of religious education because of the rising consciousness which has become a major fact of modern life.[52] This rising consciousness is primarily due to the global matrix of intercommunication which has heightened each person's awareness of both self and other.

For Moran, the moral anchor is no longer a list of the "do's and don'ts" from the past but rather one's personal appreciation of the life, death, and resurrection of Jesus—and especially on his continual world church today.[53] For James Smart, a Protestant theologian with an interest in religious education, the context for contemporary religious education is: (1) enabling God to work in the hearts of the students, making them into committed disciples; (2) producing that kind of understanding and personal faith which is adequate for learners to maintain a vital Christian witness in the midst of an unbelieving world; (3) enabling God to bring into being a church marked by the divine presence and committed to the service of Jesus Christ as an earthly body through which he may continue his redemption of the world; and (4) enabling learners to grow into full life and active faith in the church, thus sharing in its mission.[54]

The *code* for the contemporary theological approach consists of all of those verbal and symbolic forms which the Christian community uses to nourish and maintain its faith life. The code is meant to facilitate an effective, spiritually uplifting two-way communication between selves.

The *content* of contemporary theological approach unites objective truth with human experience. Randolph Crump Miller, a Protestant religious educationist, states that the task of religious education is not to teach theology solely for the sake of theology. The task is to use theology as a basic tool for bringing hearers into the right relationship with God in the fellowship of the church, a fellowship which is grounded in and pervaded by relational theology.[55] D. Campbell Wyckoff, another Protestant, advances an experiential position with three component principles: (1) human experience for any person is continuous; (2) the human personality develops through experience, and (3) that experience requires guidance and enrichment.[56] For religious educationists like Lewis Sherrill and Howard Grimes, both Protestants, the content of religious education is fundamentally a constellation of those inner changes in persons that grow out of the interactions that take place within the Christian community. Sherrill is most concerned with the deeper levels of communication that occur within the Christian community, the levels at which God redemptively reveals himself to human beings and at which human beings influence one another as they make their response to God.[57] For Gabriel Moran, present experience is the pivotal point for those religious educational practices which successfully lead to a revelationally vital knowledge of God. Subject matter content in the contemporary theological approach includes the Bible, Christian theology, church history, and the stories about the church today. Biblical subject matter is introduced into the experience of the student as a means of precipitating the learner's personal encounter with, and response to, God.

In the contemporary theological approach, the *transmitter* is the teacher who acts as a representative of the church broadly or ecclesially considered. Here the religion teacher is neither the transmitter of an unchanging message nor the aspiring creator of a new social order. Rather, the teacher is both promoter and participant in a process through which God is revealing himself to humanity today. For Gabriel Moran, the religious educator should not seek guidance so much *from above* as *from within*. It is within that the teacher will discover both content and teaching methods in communion with students who are together with the teacher in participating in God's *present* revelatory activity.[58] For these religious educationists, God through the Holy Spirit is revelationally present and actively involved in making the religion teaching process effective.

In the contemporary theological approach, the *recipient* is a learner who is both a child of God and at the same time, in some sense, a sinner[59] in need of redemption. This approach seeks the growth and development of the student as a person. The goal is to enable the learner to become a knowledgeable, responsible, adult Christian.

In the contemporary theological approach, the *contact* occurs in the Christian community, especially in Christian homes. Adult Christians are responsible for creating those communal conditions whereby the Spirit of God may work most fruitfully in the lives of human beings. Christian fellowship establishes a type of faith-communication in which God is a participant and which takes place as truly in the home as it does in the church. Most exponents of this approach do not concentrate on the need for an evaluation. If they do accept the value of an evaluation, they prefer to have theology establish the normative guidelines for determining success or failure.[60]

D. *The Social-Science Approach*

James Michael Lee has articulated a fundamentally new *context* for religious education. He contends that religious education is a mode of social science and not a mode of theological science. Lee distinguishes three distinct views of the context for religious education. (1) The *intellectualist* position seeks the mental development of the student in matters of religion. This is intended to teach/learn the knowledge of Christian doctrine and an understanding of Christian values. (2) The *moralist* position is geared toward making the learner in some way more virtuous by bringing that person closer to Christ. (3) The *integralist* position aims at the fusion of one's personal experience of Christian understanding, action, and love coequally. Lee favors the integralist position. For him, religious instruction should aim for that total cluster of religious behaviors which constitute religious living in its entirety. This means the modification of the entire complex of the learner's molar behavior including cognition, affect, and lifestyle. Cognitive behavior connotes the acquisition of appropriate knowledge, understanding, and wisdom. Affective behavior connotes feeling, together with appropriate values, attitudes, and love. Lifestyle behavior constitutes a concrete living out of a religious pattern of activity. Lee advances empirical evidence which shows that religious behaviors are learned in much the same complex way as all other human behaviors are learned.

For Lee, the total teaching structure requires: (1) specification of instructional objectives in operational terms; (2) design of the instructional system which is based on the best available empirical research data about those kinds of experiences that are likely to produce the desired objective; (3) the use of the instructional system in a try-out which is as close to normal as possible; (4) after making the necessary adjustments, putting the system into operation, and; (5) an evaluation of the system's effectiveness by measuring the progress toward instructional goals.

The *code* for the social-science approach is the admission that all of human life can be a form of religious instruction, provided that teacher and learner approach each experience as a mini-laboratory for producing the full cluster of behaviors associated with the Christian way of life. No form of communication, no type of human experience is incapable of being part of the code by which Christian behavior is taught/learned.

According to Lee, the proper *content* of religious instruction is a fusion of the substantive content (religion) and the structural content (instructional practice). The substantive content is religion—a lived experience, not merely a conceptualization. A genuine religious instruction act is a compound of product- and process-content fused together. For Lee, product and process are true contents—as well as true messages. Lee has integrated Marshall McLuhan's basic insight of the process of communication as a true content into his own theory of the nature of religious instruction. Cognitive content, according to Lee, has at least three levels: knowledge, understanding, and wisdom. Affective content refers to feelings, attitudes, values, and love. Verbal content is a symbolic kind of linguistic content; hence verbal content is only an arbitrary pointer to objective reality and not that objective reality itself. Nonverbal content includes all those forms of communication which do not use words, such as body language, facial expression, voice tone, and so on. Unconscious content has a great import on what an individual learns, especially on the affective level. For Lee, the purpose of religious instruction is to develop a lifestyle content. The students need to learn to live in a Christian manner by engaging in Christian behaviors rather than just by talking about these behaviors. Lee notes that theologically based religious education typically attempts to dichotomize religious instructional "content" and religion teaching practice. The social-science approach asserts that these two concepts really constitute *one* reality fused together in the religious instructional act itself. The former view leads to a misplaced emphasis on *either* content *or* method, and the effect is frequently ineffectual religious instruction. Lee prefers to conceptualize religious instruction as a mediation between substantive content and instructional practice. This makes the dichotomy existentially impossible, in Lee's view, and the two fuse into a holistic act of communication that can produce behavioral changes in learners.

For Lee, the *transmitter* (a term he deliberately avoids using) is a teacher who in a religious instructional setting is fundamentally a professional specialist who is able to facilitate religious learning. Lee holds that teaching is basically a facilitational process. Teaching, in Lee's view, is an enabling or helping activity: The teacher needs to identify those behaviors that are desired outcomes and predict those variables that will be efficacious in bringing about those outcomes. The enhancement of the potency of prediction is regarded as one of the most significant of the early benefits to be derived from the social-science approach to religious education.[61]

For Lee, teaching is a cooperative art-science. This cooperative model will contribute to a student-centered religious instructional process in which feedback from the student is "absolutely indispensable" as a component of the overall teaching act.

In Lee's approach the *recipient* (a term he also deliberately avoids using) is a learner. He emphasizes that all learning takes place according to the mode of the learner.[62] Learning for Lee is a construct, an abstract cognitive inference drawing from observing behavioral changes in the individual. The student is considered an integer, a whole self, a holistic person. The student learns everything according to the established laws of human development. Early life is a principal, pervasive, all-enduring variable in human learning, especially in the learning of deeper Christian attitudes and values. Lee holds that religious and moral development take place according to the normal interactive growth patterns of human maturation and learning.[63] Hence, in the social-science approach, religion teaching must become a process in which the teacher continually assesses the developmental state of the learners so that the instructor can skillfully integrate the various contents of the teaching to their present here-and-now state of existence.

The *contact* requires a deliberative attempt to architect the learner's environment so that the desired behavioral outcomes will be achieved. For Lee, the religion lesson can most fruitfully be conceptualized as a deliberately structured environment within which the learner's experience itself is a form of ongoing revelation, a form which is deliberately incorporated into a self-system and behavioral pattern of living. In communication terms, a holistic technological environment is microcosmically reduced to a purposeful program to assist the learner in assimilating a Christian way of life. The goal of this facilitation process is to provide those precise experiences which have been empirically shown to be effective in empowering individuals to acquire behaviors which are truly Christian. For this type of religious education, the evaluation and the measurement of program effectiveness is essential.[64]

Conclusion

Culture commentator Alvin Toffler writes that future shock occurs whenever the familiar psychological cues that help people to function in a society are suddenly withdrawn and replaced by new ones that are strange and seemingly incomprehensible.[65] The Christian church, like the rest of the modern world, is being rapidly altered because of an unprecedented global alteration in the world's information-environment. Since 1950 the principal communication tool for connecting people with their world has radically shifted from the printed text of the literate culture to the kinetic image-amplified sound of the audiovisual culture.

People basically exhibit two distinct psychological responses to sudden, universal change. When mental maps are scrambled beyond recognition, change-resistors strive to preserve familiar traditions and values. They cling to conceptual signposts as perceived anchors against the winds of change. In contrast, change-enthusiasts embrace the new and different as the wave of the future. They float new conceptual signposts to enable them to steer a more or less steady course on the seas of change.

In this information environment, literate people, on the one hand, focus on the *content* of change and evaluate change's worth on the basis of *what* is happening now in relationship to what happened *in the past*. On the other hand, audiovisual people attend to the *speed* or *process* by which change comes about. Audiovisual people evaluate change's worth on the basis of how *relevant* it is to their *present* experience.

Since most religious educators concern themselves with the preservation of the Christian heritage, many of them tend to evaluate this new information environment by passing judgment on the environment's content and by comparing the environment's substance with the moral tradition of the biblical faith. This leads to using the Bible from a totally cognitive perspective. By insisting on this cognitive stance, religious educators tend to lose sight of their obligation to make this Christian heritage alive and relevant to the present media-generation. In pedagogy, a historical/content bias only works with the literate generation. Only a present/process bias works with the audiovisual media-generation. The Bible is not so much a text as a revelation of a lifestyle and religious experience. Hence if the religious educator is to use the Bible in a lifestyle fashion, he or she needs to focus on effecting a kind of synapse between the learner's existential lifestyle and a relevant lifestyle depicted in the Bible.[66]

My own thesis throughout this book is that audiovisual teaching/learning is the best method for facilitating a holistic experience and a Christian lifestyle. Therefore the argument here is that religious educators, to be true to the task, should adapt to the new information environment. Religious educators, to be effective in this electric global village, must understand and accept a new mental map. In this new mental map, religious education is a form of communication. The most effective way to communicate in today's world is by using audiovisual media. Students learn more thoroughly through the kinetic image-amplified sound than through the printed text. For many of today's learners, the printed text represents a past which is often irrelevant and fossilized, while the audiovisual image-sound represents the present and the future.

Change-resistors in religious education may refuse to accept this new mental map. Refusing to adapt, such religious educators may cling to the familiar and traditional signposts of the literate culture. Perceptive religious educators, however, will immediately note that such an attitude satisfies the needs of the teacher but not of the learner. As we have seen in this chapter, religious education is a form of audiovisual communication. Hence to adapt religious education to a pedagogy of the kinetic image-amplified sound is actually to release its full potential. Such a religious education facilitates a true learning/teaching experience for the present media-generation.

This book is intended as a guide for those religious educators who are willing change-enthusiasts. Such religious educators want to adapt pedagogy to the global village of instantaneous electric communication. The information in this book is intended as buoys to facilitate development of a personal cognitive chart for teaching/learning in the audiovisual world that will enable the religious educator to navigate in the new waters of change.

Part I of this book discusses the basic concepts of modern communication theory and how this macrotheory relates to the task of religious education. Part II explicates some media opportunities and how these opportunities can be integrated into the practice of religious education. Part III presents some ideas on media-appreciation and offers religious educators some practical advice on fostering audiovisual learning-skills in their students. Competent media-literacy enables learners to become active participants in the new audiovisual environment instead of remaining passive recipients.

All three parts are intended to provide the practical and theoretical information needed by religious educators to cope with the audiovisual environment of today's learners.

Notes

1. Paul A. Soukup, "Communication and the Media," in *The Context of Our Ministries: Working Papers* (Washington, D.C.: Jesuit Conference, 1981), pp. 65-68.
2. Walter J. Ong, "Transformations of the Word," in *The Presence of the Word: Some Prolegomena for Cultural and Religious History* (New Haven, Conn.: Yale University Press, 1967), pp. 17-110.
3. Walter J. Ong, *Orality and Literacy: The Technologizing of the Word* (London and New York: Methuen, 1982), New Accents Series.
4. Walter J. Ong, "Educationists and the Tradition of Learning," in *The Barbarian Within and Other Fugitive Essays* (New York: Macmillan, 1962), pp. 149-163.
5. John L. McKenzie, "Proclamation and Teaching in the Early Church," *Living Light* 1, no. 2 (Summer, 1964), pp. 118-136.
6. Walter J. Burghardt, "Catechetics in the Early Church: Program and Psychology," *Living Light* 1, no. 3 (Autumn 1964), pp. 110-118.
7. Pierre Babin, "Catechetics in the Audiovisual Civilization," *The Catechist* 8, no. 5 (February 1975), pp. 10-12.
8. John H. Westerhoff III, "A Catechetical Way of Doing Theology," in *Religious Education and Theology*, ed. Norma H. Thompson (Birmingham, Ala.: Religious Education Press, 1982), pp. 218-242.
9. Babin, "Catechetics in the Audiovisual Civilization," pp. 10-12.
10. William Clayton Bower, *Christ and Christian Education* (Nashville, Tenn.: Abingdon, 1943), pp. 72-73.
11. Eric A. Havelock, *Preface to Plato* (Cambridge, Mass.: Belknap Press, 1963).
12. For an example of the critique from black theology, see Olivia Pearl Stokes, "Black Theology: A Challenge to Religious Education," in *Religious Education and Theology*, pp. 71-99.
13. For an example of the critique from feminist theology, see Mary Daly, *Beyond God the Father* (Boston: Beacon, 1973).
14. Norma Thompson, "The Role of Theology in Religious Educa-

tion: An Introduction," in *Religious Education and Theology,* pp. 1-2.

15. Randolph Crump Miller, "Theology in the Background," in *Religious Education and Theology,* pp. 17-41.

16. Gabriel Moran, "From Obstacle to Modest Contributor: Theology in Religious Education," in *Religious Education and Theology,* pp. 42-70.

17. Pierre Babin, *Audiovisual Man: Media in Religious Education* Dayton, Ohio: Pflaum, 1970), pp. 33-54.

18. Horace Bushnell, *Christian Nurture* (New Haven, Conn.: Yale University Press, 1967).

19. Harold William Burgess, *An Invitation to Religious Education* (Birmingham, Alabama: Religious Education Press, 1975), p. 63.

20. Dorothy Jean Furnish, *DRE/DCE: The History of a Profession* (Nashville: Christian Education Fellowship, 1976).

21. Ibid.

22. Maria Harris, *The DRE Book: Questions and Strategies for Parish Personnel* (New York: Paulist Press, 1976). See also Furnish, *DRE/DEC: The History of a Profession,* pp. 217-232.

23. Maria Montessori, *The Montessori Method* (New York: Schocken Books, 1974), pp. 86-106.

24. Luke 16:8. Jerusalem Bible translation.

25. It should be underscored that concentration on behaviors is not tantamount to behaviorism. Indeed, behaviorism is only one way of interpreting and dealing with behaviors. In contrast, behavioralism is a term coined by Lee to denote attention to behaviors without involving or even implying the espousal of any one form of interpretation or dealing with behaviors. On the issue of behaviorism (as opposed to behavioralism), many religious educators accuse behaviorism of being materialistic and antihumanistic. They claim that behaviorism is impersonal, mechanistic, and deals with people as if they were mechanical devices. Proponents of behaviorism counter that they do not have a mechanistic view of human nature, that in many ways science can be personal and caring. See B. F. Skinner, *About Behaviorism* (New York: Alfred A. Knopf, 1974), pp. 237-241.

26. Eric A. Havelock, *Origins of Western Literacy: Four Lectures delivered at the Ontario Institute for Studies in Education, Toronto, March 25, 26, 27, 28, 1974* (Toronto: Monograph Series/14, The Ontario Institute for Studies in Education, 1976), p. 18.

27. Walter J. Ong, *Ramus, Method and the Decay of Dialogue: From the Art of Discourse to the Art of Reason* (Cambridge, Mass.: Harvard University Press, 1958).

28. A summary of the social-science approach can be found in Burgess, *An Invitation to Religious Education.* The complete presentation of Lee's work can be found in his trilogy: *The Shape of Religious Instruction* (Birmingham, Ala.: Religious Education Press, Inc., 1971); *The Flow of Religious Instruction* (Birmingham, Ala.: Religious Educa-

tion Press, 1973); *The Content of Religious Instruction* (Birmingham, Ala.: Religious Education Press, 1985).

29. Avery Dulles, *Models of the Church* (New York: Doubleday, 1974).

30. David Tracy, *Blessed Rage for Order* (New York: Seabury, 1975).

31. William McSweeney, *Roman Catholicism: The Search for Relevance* (New York: St. Martin Press, 1980), pp. 198-224.

32. George Tavard, *The Pilgrim Church* (New York: Herder and Herder, 1967). For a treatment of transcendism and immanentism in religious education, see Ian P. Knox, *Above or Within?* (Birmingham, Ala.: Religious Education Press, 1977).

33. For an explanation of the experiential tradition in medieval Aristotelianism, see Ronald A. Sarno, "The University of Padua in the Middle Ages: The Growth of Aristotelianism From Philosophical Synthesis to Scientific Analysis," in "A Sixteenth Century War of Ideas: Science vs. the Church," *Annals of Science* 25, no. 3 (September, 1969), pp. 210-227.

34. Ong, *The Barbarian Within and Other Fugitive Essays*, p. 88-130.

35. Neil Postman, *Teaching As A Conserving Activity* (New York: Dell, 1979), p. 186.

36. Skinner, *About Behaviorism*, pp. 90-93.

37. James Michael Lee, "The Authentic Source of Religious Instruction," in *Religious Education and Theology*, pp. 184-192.

38. Roman Jakobson, *Essais de linquistique generale* (Paris: Minuit, 1963-1973), Vol 2.

39. Burgess, *An Invitation to Religious Education*, pp. 127-165; see also Enrique Garcia Ahumada, "Theology and Catechetics in Communication Theory," *Living Light* 12, no. 1 (Spring, 1975), pp. 32-39.

40. For an explanation of the traditional theological approach to religious education, see Burgess, *An Invitation to Religious Education*, pp. 21-58.

41. Frank E. Gaebelein, *Christian Education in a Democracy* (New York: Oxford, 1951). Lois E. LeBar, *Education That Is Christian* (Old Tappan, N.J.: Revell, 1958).

42. Johannes Hofinger, *The Art of Teaching Christian Doctrine* (Notre Dame, Ind.: University of Notre Dame Press, 1962).

43. George Albert Coe, *A Social Theory of Religious Education* (New York: Scribner's, 1917), p. 41.

44. Ibid., pp. 13-37.

45. George Albert Coe, *What Is a Christian Education?* (New York: Scribner's, 1929), p. 46.

46. Coe, *A Social Theory of Religious Education*, pp. 74-84; and 97-116.

47. William Clayton Bower, *Religious Education in the Modern Church* (St. Louis: Bethany, 1929), pp. 115-121.

48. Coe, *A Social Theory of Religious Education*, pp. 19, 29, 65.

49. William Clayton Bower, *Moral and Spiritual Values in Education* (Lexington, Ky.: University of Kentucky Press, 1952), pp. 39-47.

50. George Herbert Betts, *How To Teach Religion: Principles and Methods* (New York: Abingdon, 1919), pp. 39-40; 91. A synopsis of the social-cultural approach can be found in Burgess, *An Invitation to Religious Education*, pp. 59-93.

51. Lewis Joseph Sherrill, *The Gift of Power* (New York: Macmillan, 1955), p. 82; pp. 65-91, 105.

52. Gabriel Moran, *Vision and Tactics: Toward an Adult Church* (New York: Herder and Herder, 1968), p. 75.

53. Ibid., p. 18. See also Gabriel Moran, *Catechesis of Revelation* (New York: Herder and Herder, 1966), pp. 100-102.

54. James D. Smart, *The Teaching Ministry of the Church* (Philadelphia: Westminster, 1954), p. 107.

55. Randolph Crump Miller, *The Clue to Christian Education* (New York: Scribner's, 1950), p. 6.

56. D. Campbell Wyckoff, *The Task of Christian Education* (Philadelphia: Westminster, 1955), pp. 52-56.

57. Sherrill, *The Gift of Power*, pp. 79-91; 174-175. Howard Grimes, *The Church Redemptive* (New York: Abingdon, 1958), pp. 104-106.

58. Moran, *Visions and Tactics*, pp. 38-68. See also *Catechesis of Revelation*, pp. 30-40. See also Knox, *Above or Within?*

59. Smart, *The Teaching Ministry of the Church*, p. 158. See also Miller, *The Clue to Christian Education*, pp. 55-70.

60. For a synopsis of the contemporary theological approach to religious education, see Burgess, *An Invitation to Religious Education*, pp. 94-126.

61. Lee, *The Flow of Religious Instruction*, pp. 212-215. See also James Michael Lee, "Prediction in Religious Instruction," *The Living Light* 9 (Summer, 1972), pp. 43-54.

62. James Michael Lee, *Principles and Methods of Secondary Education* (New York: McGraw-Hill, 1963), pp. 111-143. Many religious educationists theoretically accept the principle that all learning is according to the mode of the learner. In practice they often succumb to theological assumptions which hold that the learner is obligated to assimilate the mode of instruction most suitable to the logical subject matter of theological science.

63. Lee, *The Flow of Religious Instruction*, pp. 135-136.

64. Ibid., p. 277.

65. Alvin Toffler, *Future Shock* (New York: Random House, 1970), p. 11.

66. Lee, *The Content of Religious Instruction*, p. 642; see also James Michael Lee, "Religious Education and the Bible: A Religious Educationist's View," in *Biblical Interpretation in Religious Education*, ed. Joseph S. Marino (Birmingham, Ala.: Religious Education Press, 1983), pp. 1-61.

2

Modern Communication Theory: An Overview

Introduction

Communication theorists Lewis Mumford, Norbert Wiener, Jacques Ellul, Harold Adams Innis, Marshall McLuhan, Walter J. Ong, and Neil Postman have made major contributions to the development of modern communication theory. Their religious views are also pertinent, since this book studies how modern communication theory influences contemporary religious education. Although not a religionist, B. F. Skinner provides what some persons regard as a helpful model for viewing language as a form of verbal behavior. He offers a keen insight into how verbal behavior determines response, that is, the act of *heeding, doing* what is asked, is distinct from the act of *hearing, recognizing the sounds* of what is asked but not necessarily doing.

Lewis Mumford writes as a humanist committed to the progressive philosophy that human technology can overcome the evil effects of ignorance and poverty. Mumford holds the progressive faith that human intelligence in control of technology can deliver on the promise of nineteenth-century optimism. However, the reality of the depression of the thirties forced him to reconsider how technological development—especially the new tools for communication—have now warped human values.

During the period 1948-1964 the field of cybernetics began. This exciting new field deals with machines for artificial intelligence. Norbert Wiener has greatly influenced that development. As a humanist, Wiener is committed to the view that progress can enhance the quality of human life. However, as a Jew, he is also mindful of the traditional Hebrew biblical injunction against human pride in magnificent technological developments.[1]

Jacques Ellul is a Protestant French sociologist who is also deeply troubled by what he regards as the deleterious effects of technology. His writings in the 1950s reflect the bitterness of French intellectuals over the destruction wrought on their country by the technical war machines of the Nazis in World War II.

Economic determinism is a special concern for the economist Harold Innis, who did most of his research on the staples of the national economy of Canada. A Canadian, he is able to view the media-environment in the United States as a critical outsider. As an Episcopal, he is in some ways an heir to the British tradition of an established national religion. As a economist, he views the media as economic staples, or sources of wealth. For him, a monopoly control over the staples of the media enables a nation to stabilize itself and thereby avoid the Hegelian swings of change.

Marshall McLuhan is a convert to Catholic Christianity from Protestant Christianity. In his own personal spiritual journey, McLuhan is a believer who left the Protestant tradition, which focuses on the printed word, for the Catholic church, which tends to focus more closely on kinetic imagery and the spoken word, especially in the liturgy. By such a spiritual journey, McLuhan emerges as an exponent of the entire Christian church's contemporary need to move from the print culture of the past to the imagistic media-culture of the present.

Educationist Neil Postman explicates how the audiovisual media have replaced the Christian church and the school in the socialization of the young.

B. F. Skinner, the psychologist, denies the validity of mind, intentionality, and free will. For Skinner, language is conceptualized solely as verbal behavior.

Walter Ong is a Jesuit priest. The Jesuits have long been exponents of intellectual scholarship in the Catholic church. Ong brings to modern communication theory an ability to synthesize the cultural history of the Christian church with the findings of modern scholarship on the media and media-effect.

Lewis Mumford: Initiator of Modern Communication Theory

Lewis Mumford introduces many of the key ideas which reappear in later communication theorists. Mumford's strengths, which are also found in later theorists, include the following: (1) He clusters centuries of historical change into one compelling metaphor or concept; (2) he awakens the reader to the unrecognized effect of technology on the individual and on society; (3) he identifies values that are being enhanced or being lost by modern mass communication; and (4) he introduces a bold sweep of new breakthrough concepts and ideas.

Mumford's weaknesses are also repeated by the post-Mumfordians. These flaws consist of the following: (1) He oversimplifies complicated historical changes; (2) he asserts, without any rigorous proof, that the effects of technology on individuals and on society are self-evident; (3) he employs neologisms which only serve to confuse and alienate even a sympathetic reader; and (4) he places value judgments on what constitutes humane and inhumane behavior without any explicit objective ethical code.[2]

Mumford initiates modern communication theory by introducing the following key ideas: (1) There is a relationship between historical change and the introduction of new inventions; (2) there is a symbiosis between humanity and the machine, which includes the relationship between biology and mechanics and the relationship between psychology and technology; (3) there is a fundamental conflict between humanism and determinism; (4) modern technology has brought humanity a reductionism in the traditional theological meanings of the terms "creation," "resurrection," and "immortality"; (5) modern media are situated in the center of the contemporary conflict between good and evil; and (6) value judgments must be made on the social changes which are being caused by the advancement of technology.

Mumford utilizes traditional Judeo-Christian theological language to critique the exacerbation of the dehumanization process caused by modern technology. Each inventor creates a machine in the image of the self. From this Mumford perceives a new chaos dawning, one that is even more confusing than the disorder envisioned in the ancient myth. This modern chaos arises from sacrificing human values; in the end, technological humanity achieves a sort of mockery of the true divinity. Hence, for Mumford, modern forms of communication have led to a radical reinterpretation of traditional theological concepts.[3] The human "creator" fashions a dehumanized image. This image is one of power, but of a power sundered from the flesh and isolated from humanity. By preserving memory through film images, humanity can achieve a sort of "immortality." Through recordings of sound and image, past leaders and celebrities can be "resurrected."[4]

For Mumford, the media directly fuel a mass consumer society. The machine expands wants, expands markets, expands enterprises, and expands consumers. The machine also works to guarantee the success of these expansions.[5]

Besides stimulating economic greed, the media, in Mumford's view, also encourage immoral behavior. Once people callously witness innumerable fantasy deaths and crimes on the radio and cinema, they become eager for the actual rape, lynching, murder, or war.[6] Mechanized fantasy enhances immoral behavior.[7] Because the mass media have the power to multiply good or evil on such a grand scale, Mumford feels compelled to pose the moral question: What is actually being multiplied?[8] Mumford holds that as long as technology is abstracted from human values, technology will not benefit humanity. However, once technology is imbued with human values, technology will then benefit humanity enormously.[9]

Norbert Wiener: Probability, Technology, and Pride

Following Lewis Mumford's initial modern communication theory, Norbert Wiener's approach applies probability predictions to the field of technology. Wiener is best known for his development of probability mathematics, which contributed to the prediction and the consequent revolutionary development of computers. He also writes popular explanations of the humanistic side of computer technology.

Wiener conceptualizes every machine as a communication tool. Each tool is a device for converting incoming messages (the input) into outgoing messages (the output).[10] An interlocking feedback mechanism assures that both communicate with each other and affect each other when necessary. For Wiener, computers are extensions of human thinking much as earlier machines are extensions of human muscle and movement.[11]

As an optimist, Wiener believes that computers do not destroy jobs but instead enhance human values and preserve jobs. He asserts that machines, since they have the capacity to take over many of the onerous tasks accomplished by people, will therefore free workers for leisure and self-improvement.[12]

Wiener is intrigued at how the invention of artificial intelligence has affected the traditional theological concepts of "creation," "thinking," and "life." Human beings have created the computer which, Wiener claims, is now able to perform intellectual activities. At one time the act of creation was predicated only of God, and thinking was predicated only of spiritual beings. An ancient proof for the spiritual nature of human beings was their ability to think, a fact which supposedly distinguished people from the rest of material creation.

Wiener believes that the very existence of computers challenges these traditional theological assumptions. For him, orthodox theology claims that only a spiritual being can learn. Traditional theology claims that only life can reproduce itself. Traditional theology holds that only God has the power to create a being that possesses the power to live and to think. By creating computers, humans form a new synthesis of humanity and machinery; this synthesis, according to Wiener, tends to destroy all the above-mentioned traditional theological assumptions.[13]

Assuming that all machines are basically input-output devices, Wiener predicts through mathematical probability that humanity is approaching the point—rather has reached the point—at which it possesses the power to input into the machine the ability to reproduce the same device exactly (self-duplicational output). In traditional theology, only life has this capacity.

According to Wiener, it is an intrinsic contradiction to claim that humanity can communicate this God-given perfection to an artificial being. Yet, Wiener warns, soon machines will have many different ways to reproduce themselves and so bear a close resemblance to the self-multiplication phenomena of life.

Just because humanity *can* do this, does not mean that human beings *should* create such machines. Modern people have become technology-worshipers to such an extent that people no longer consider the moral consequences of their exploration into the edge of human potentiality.[14]

Wiener finds it personally difficult to see any compatibility between theology and contemporary science.[15] He demonstrates that the conceptual vocabulary of traditional theology has exhausted its utility in the contemporary world, but he does not know of any other theological approach. Like Lewis Mumford, Wiener has only *univocal* understandings of the terms "thinking," "life," and "creature." He does not realize that he is dealing with *analogous* concepts.

JACQUES ELLUL: TECHNOLOGY, DETERMINISM, AND FREE WILL

Norbert Wiener's probability predictions argue that humanists will soon have to make moral judgments about media development. Interestingly enough, the first theorist to make an explicit moral evaluation on media development was not a humanist, but rather a determinist, namely, Jacques Ellul. This French Protestant sociologist brings the strict moral judgment of the Calvinistic tradition to modern communication theory.

In his seminal work *The Technological Society* (the original French edition was published in 1954; the English translation in 1964), Ellul utilizes the Hegelian dialectic to explain the relationship between technology and society. Using the dialectic, he elucidates the contemporary synthesis and the mutual causality of economics, production-consumption, and advertising. Technology, in Ellul's view, has reduced the qualitative to the quantitative. Hence human beings are now the objects of mathematical calculations.

The second half of the eighteenth century had begun with the myth of the basic goodness of industrial progress. Ellul warns that this myth is a false religion. Technology overwhelms and conquers whatever culture technology is within, even a religious one. Technology does not tolerate moral judgments which might check its progress.

Ellul explicates his view of the role of the sacred in a technological society in the following manner: In the first half of the eighteenth century, the prevailing Christian milieu had opposed the development of technology as sacrilegious. It was believed that through technology humanity would usurp the prerogatives proper to the divinity. For Ellul, humanity is called upon to love the world. Traditionally, this means the human response to the divine presence in the world. However, technology desacralizes the world. Consequently, humanity, because of this spiritual vacuum, sacralizes the very technology which has desacralized everything else. For Ellul, humanity is made to worship, and if humanity does not worship God, then humanity lapses into the ancient biblical temptation to idolize the works of its own hands. At the start of the Reformation, Luther had taught justification by faith alone. However, in the contemporary world, Ellul charges, humanity is creating a new religion. This is the religion of the rational and technical order. In this new religion, humanity justifies its own work, and technology enables humanity to be justified in it.

The first and clearest consequence of this process of desacralization, for Ellul, is in the modern application of psychoanalytical mass technique. This technique consists of the use of propaganda by those in power. Such political propaganda forces the suppression of the critical rational faculty. Propaganda strengthens the formation of a "good" social conscience, which, according to Ellul, is more accurately the fitting of the individual into a mass society. Political propaganda in Ellul's view leads to the creation of a new definition and locus of the sacred.

According to Ellul, the all-pervasive media-effect erases every vestige of free will and moral judgment. Thus modern humanity is becoming a determined automaton. In the West this kind of automaton is a slave to commercial powers; in the East this automaton is a slave to political powers.[16]

HAROLD ADAMS INNIS: THE HEGELIAN DIALECTIC AND MEDIA-BIASES IN GOVERNMENT AND RELIGION

In his pungent moral critique, Jacques Ellul involves the Hegelian dialectic as a component of modern communication theory. For Harold Innis, the Hegelian dialectic is no longer a component, but assumes a more universal role. Hegelianism affects all space and time.

In his media theory, Innis assumes a universal Hegelian dialectic of thesis, antithesis, and synthesis. Innis argues that an empire sustains itself by synthesizing the thesis-antithesis of government and religion. He holds that government is sustained by light and disposable media, which provide rulers with control over large areas of space. Religion, according to Innis, is sustained by heavy and durable media, which give ecclesiastics control over long periods of time. Successful empires monopolize space and time by synthesizing these two opposing forces of government and religion. This synthesis, already fragile because of its tenuous unity, falls apart whenever technological advance introduces any significantly new medium. Innis claims that empires which fail to achieve a new synthesis die. Those empires which succeed in synthesizing the new medium endure.

In Innis's view, oral cultures have a spiritual bias, while visual cultures have a secular bias. He claims that Europe in the Middle Ages was basically an oral culture. Since that era was oral, the people remained predominantly Catholic and spiritual. Renaissance printing brought in a new emphasis on the power of the book, created a visual society, and thereby sparked the Reformation. The printing press destroyed the monopolistic position of the Bible and of learned Latin in the Christian church. There emerged a widespread market for the Bible in the vernacular. The printed Bible then led to a concern for the literal interpretation of the sacred text. Biblical literalism became the source of many competing sects. Consequently, Innis contends, the elite control of the clergy and of the nobility crumbled.

At first the printing press had produced Bibles, but very soon afterward there appeared the scientific tracts which Innis considers the natural consequences of the visual orientation. Innis holds that these tracts challenged the orientation to the sacred which characterized the previous medieval culture. Then science led to the belief in the inevitable progress of humanity through technology. Later the Enlightenment combined this progress with a new interest in the future, and in the technological advance of the human race. This secular faith in technological progress further weakened the older, traditional interest in

Modern Communication Theory: An Overview 49

life beyond the grave. Progressivism, Innis asserts, also worked to dissolve the debilitating effect both of the doctrine of original sin and of the radical corruption of humanity.

For Innis, a parallel reductionism also took place in morality. The question of what was right or wrong was replaced by a social science which was free of moral restraint. This "amoral" social science produced confident predictions of what is possible or not possible. These predictions irritated the clergy, because the methods proved to be irrefutable. Innis sees here the root of the modern clash between liberalism and conservatism.

Innis provides exceptionally clear metaphors on how specific cultures or eras synthesize the various media of space and time at their disposal. For example, he is the first historian of media-effect to indicate the signal importance of papyrus and the alphabet to the ancient Roman empire and subsequently to the spread of primitive Christianity.

Innis provides a coherent explanation of how new media can radically change religion. Print media tended to divide Christendom into Protestantism and modern Catholicism. Both of these branches of Christianity in their own way are wedded to the printed word. This bond (and perhaps bondage) to the printed word is quite distinct from the oral bond of the ancient and medieval Catholic church.

Innis warns that both in the modern world and in the modern church, the mass media are stimulating a new universal conservatism. This conservatism leads to a total passivity before authority. (Innis was writing before the national distribution of television, which most authors hold increases a disrespect for authority.)

By concentrating on the media as *the* source of historical change, Innis neglects to address the crucial role of educational, psychological, sociological, philosophical, military, geographical, and political forces which all contribute significantly to historical change.

Innis explains historical change as a consequence of the Hegelian dialectic, which he portrays as relentless swings from government power-blocs to religious power-blocs. Both blocs are completely dependent on the media-bias of the time. This model of Hegelian dialectic becomes a relentless, monstrous reality.

It is no longer a conceptual metaphor for comprehending large amounts of contradictory data. But it must also be noted that Innis enriches modern communication theory by providing a powerful tool for enabling moderns to recognize that media-orientation is one of the most significant contributory factors in historical change. His overstatements do not denigrate the fundamental value of his basic insight: A change in the means of communication heralds significant changes within a religion.[17]

As a member of a national religion (Episcopal) whose original pre-Revolutionary American roots were controlled by the government, Innis holds that societies that have a government-orientation endure longer than those with a religion-orientation. Adolf Hitler's "German Christianity" constitutes a refutation of this sanguine view. Christians in the United States are more comfortable with perceiving the church and state as equal but separate partners rather than with placing the state over the church. Such a government-oriented society limits the church in the exercise of its prophetic role. However, post-Shah Iran, with its religion-orientation, demonstrates Innis's claim that such cultures are too fragile to maintain a long-term synthesis of religion and government.

Neil Postman: A Summary of the Key Ideas on Modern Communication Theory: How the Mass Media Replace the Socializing Role of the School and the Church

Neil Postman utilizes many basic assumptions of Harold Innis about media-effect. Postman holds that the dominant patterns of information within a culture form a substantial portion of the "genes" of that culture. When the "genes" are changed, the culture also changes.

Innis, as Postman views his theory, argues that the printing press undermined the information monopoly of the Catholic church, not only by making the word of God accessible to large numbers of people, but also by moving it with unprecedented speed throughout Germany and then throughout the rest of Europe. Print was the new medium which changed the religious culture of Europe. Print also relocated the centers of learning from the south to the north.

Innis postulates three types of alterations which a change of media bring to a society: (1) New media of communication alter the structure of interests (the things thought about), (2) they alter the character of the symbols (the things thought with), and (3) they alter the nature of the community (the area in which thoughts develop).[18]

For example, Postman argues, in the manuscript era, the Catholic church had fostered a craft literacy which aided the church in maintaining control over the ideas, the organization, and the loyalties of a large and diverse population. It was in the interest of the church to encourage a more restricted access to literacy by having clerics form a scribal class which alone had access to theological and intellectual secrets.

As Innis notes, this gnostic situation changed when the media of communication changed. Print put the vernacular into a mass medium. Print in the Renaissance placed the word of God on every family's kitchen table, in a language which was understood. With God's word so accessible, some Christians believed they no longer required the papacy or the episcopacy to interpret the faith for them. If there was ever an instance of a medium and a message coinciding in their orientations, Postman asserts, it is in the case of printing and Protestantism. For Postman, Protestantism is a form of nationalistic Christianity, while Catholicism is an international form. Through print, God became an Englishman, or a German, or a Frenchman, depending on what vernacular was used to reveal his words. God no longer was a voice out of the past, but a present experience. Hence religion took on a new vitality, but it also fragmented into many tongues.

At first, Postman contends, Catholics regarded print media as a means of instilling a greater obedience to scripture. By the mid-sixteenth century, however, Catholics began to pull away from social literacy because by this time the print media was perceived as a disintegrating agent. Eventually the Catholic church prohibited the reading of vernacular Bibles, as well as the works of such writers as Erasmus. Reading became equated with heresy, and the Index of Forbidden Books inexorably followed. For the most part, Postman asserts, Catholicism remained a religion of images. Catholicism continued an intensified icon worship and gave extraordinary attention to its elaboration in church buildings and worship services. Protestantism, on the other hand, developed as the religion of the printed book and as a consequence discouraged icon worship. Inevitably, then, Protestantism moved instead toward an austere symbolism. Catholicism appealed to a public still habituated to concrete iconographic symbolism. By way of contrast, Protestantism appealed especially to those people whom book reading had conditioned to think more abstractly.

In the modern era, Postman claims, television prevails in the information environment because effects of television are continually being reinforced by the other media of communication, including records, tapes, radio, photography, and the films.

Television and the school both constitute total learning systems. The school is primarily centered on verbal communication, while television is centered on communication through imagery. Between the school and television lies the conflict between words and images as sources of knowledge. The image is concrete, unique, nonparaphrasable. The word is abstract, conceptual, and translatable.

The audiovisual environment has replaced both the school and the church as the principal agent for socialization in our culture. Postman uses two metaphors to describe the socialization power which television exerts on youth. Television offers youth a media-curriculum and a media-pulpit. A curriculum is not a series of academic subjects with the stated goal of enabling learners to master past knowledge. Instead, Postman conceptualizes a curriculum as a total information environment that enculturates the learners into a specific society. If one accepts this meaning for the term curriculum, then it is quite evident why Postman considers television the most powerful teaching instrument ever invented.

Postman asserts that the television curriculum is value-laden and moralistic. Since television's primary form of communication is the iconic image, television is both aesthetic and quasi-religious. Like religion, television appeals to the heart and mind simultaneously. Hence television is a powerful form of holistic communication appealing to the *total* person and *motivating behavioral changes*. Since television's style of teaching is narration, this medium possesses a power normally associated with religious communication, that is, television preaches "moral" teachings which rest on an affective base. Thus, television has a holistic, technological appeal.

For Postman, the school curriculum rewards persistent, sequential work. The television curriculum, however, is quite different. A viewer's attention to television often constitutes its own reward. Hence, in the media-religion, the "kingdom of God" is of the present world, now, and not of any other world, later.

According to Postman, the television commercial constitutes the most voluminous information source in the education of our youth. This pervasive television curriculum sets out to expound in commercial "parables" the concept that serious human concerns are resolvable through relatively simple means. Therefore the resolution of a problematic reality is never very far away. To the extent that television can be said to put forth a "theology," Postman insists, it is a "theology" without a moral center, without historical precedents, and without a general application.

Since the Renaissance the printed word and its extensions have constituted the hierarchy. Postman contrasts this verbal environment with the television environment, which he sees as fundamentally hostile to the conceptual, segmented, and linear modes of expression associated with the printed word. In the contemporary television environment, oral and written communication necessarily lose some of their power. In a total media environment, where nonlinguistic information is rampant, Postman claims that printed and oral words and all that they stand for must lose prestige, power, and relevance.

Audiovisual media, in Postman's view, cause moderns to search for time-compressed experiences, short-term relationships, present-oriented accomplishments, and simple and immediate solutions. This must lead inevitably to a disbelief in long-term planning, in deferred gratification, in the relevance of tradition, and in the need for confronting complexity.

While insisting that electronic media undermine hierarchies, Postman believes that television amplifies the appeal of personality. In such an environment, totalitarian ideas expressed by a charismatic person and broadcast through an iconic image find a fertile field for growth. This view helps to explain the appeal of television evangelists, which will be studied more closely in a subsequent chapter.

According to Postman, the medium-environment which is

centered on the present debases the past theological language of the print era. In television commercials it is not facts which are offered to viewers, but idols. Both adults and children can attach themselves to these idols with equal devotion, without the burden of logic or of verification.

For Postman, the masters of the media have quite simply usurped the role of religious leaders in formulating the moral imperatives by which we ought to live. Hence God is not dead. The deity of the modern world is very much alive. It is Technique.

In medieval society the fundamental conflict in the human soul was the choice between good and evil. In modern society this cosmic conflict is reduced to the choice a consumer has between purchasing the nationally advertised brand or the "no-frills" product.[19] The most basic conflict in contemporary society is between the *haves* who can afford the lifestyle depicted in the media and the *have-nots* who are unable to do so.[20]

Media theoreticians Marshall McLuhan and Walter Ong contend that audiovisual media have stimulated a new era of genuine dialogic communication. Postman challenges this assumption. For Postman, the television curriculum is authoritarian, since television's information moves in only one direction. It is therefore more precise to state that the modern media have atrophied dialogic communication.

Hence the proper role for educators in the media-age is to foster a media-literacy, because such literacy enables learners to be aware of the effects which audiovisual forms of communication have on their psyches and to their value-systems. More than ever, modern society needs that kind of education which enables us to maintain those values associated with the printed and spoken word, that is, rational thought, critical judgment, sequential logic, and a social order which recognizes that adult teachers have something of value to communicate to young learners.[21]

B. F. Skinner: Language As Verbal Behavior

B. F. Skinner is the leading exponent of modern behaviorism. Behaviorism is a major theoretical school within the academic discipline of psychology. Skinnerian behaviorism is properly called operant conditioning. Principal tenets of behaviorism include the following: (1) All human behavior is a one-to-one relationship between a particular stimulus and a response; (2) learning is the result of conditioned responses; (3) data drawn from "inner" experience or from introspection are worthless; (4) there is no reference or connection between behavior and the mind, or consciousness. Behaviorism is compatible with a philosophy of materialism which is a monistic, atomistic, and mechanistic view of human activity.

Both modern communication theory and social-science religious instruction are accused by certain religious educators of being a form of technological determinism, or behaviorism. Such accusations are clearly erroneous, and reflect an abject lack of understanding by those who level these charges. Both modern communication theory and the social-science approach to religious instruction do indeed place great stress on human behavior in all its forms. But behavior and behaviorism are quite different, and indeed are different modes of reality. Behavior is a fact, while behaviorism is a theory. Behavior is an activity of an organism, while behaviorism is one among many competing explanations of behavior. It is proper to give the term behavioralism to any science, discipline, or field which concentrates on the analysis and practice of human behavior. Thus, for example, James Michael Lee's form of social-science religious instruction is decidedly nonbehavioristic in that it opposes many central tenets of behaviorism. But Lee's social-science approach is behavioralistic in that it seeks to render religious instruction optimally effective by concentrating and then empowering human behavior in all domains, notably cognitive, affective, and lifestyle.[22]

Although many of the philosophical tenets of Skinnerian behaviorism are unacceptable to most religionists, still his research and insights on verbal language constitute a key contribution to modern communication theory. Skinner has shown how verbal language determines much of our behavior. Too often contemporary religious educators fail to utilize insights which have their source in nonbelievers. By contrast, the finest ancient, medieval, and modern Christian thinkers borrowed liberally from pagan sources.

Christian humanists, like Walter Ong, conceptualize vocalized sounds as intentional language, that is, a mental tool used to express meanings, thoughts, and ideas. For Skinner, or for any deterministic psychologist, vocalized sounds are the equivalent of verbal behavior.

Verbal behavior is reinforced by its effect on other people, and eventually, on the speaker as well. A speaker's utterances depend on the practices of the verbal community of which one is a member. Different verbal communities shape and maintain different languages within the same speaker. The speaker then possesses different verbal repertoires that have similar effects on different listeners.

Verbal behavior does not require any environmental support. Hence verbal behavior can occur on any occasion. One can vocalize a concept without being present to the concept. A consequence of this is that a speaker also becomes a listener, and the speaker-listener can richly reinforce his or her own behavior.

For Skinner, "meaning" should not be properly regarded as a property either of a response or of a situation. Rather, "meaning" is basically a property of the contingencies responsible for both the topography of behavior and the control exerted by stimuli. Therefore the meaning of verbal behavior is not intentional language, as the humanists claim. For Skinner, a speaker is in contact with a situation to which a listener is disposed to respond but with which he or she is not yet in contact. A verbal response on the part of the speaker makes it possible for the listener to respond appropriately. For example, in making an appointment with another person to meet at a specified time and at a specified place, there are three terms which appear in the contingencies of reinforcement. These three contingencies generate an operant between the two people involved: (1) The speaker responds to the setting, (2) the listener engages in the behavior, and (3) the listener is affected by the consequences. This occurs only if the behaviors of the speaker and of the listener are supported by additional contingencies arranged by the verbal community (See Figure 1).

According to Skinner, one of the unfortunate implications of humanistic communication theory is that meanings are perceived as the same for the speaker and the listener. Supposedly a speaker's mental possession through language becomes the mental possession of the listener. By contrast, in Skinner's view, there are *no* meanings that are the same for the speaker and the listener.

According to Skinner, a stimulus which is present when a response is reinforced acquires some control over the probability that the response will occur. This effect generalizes that stimuli sharing some of the original stimulus's properties also acquire some of the original's control. Hence, when considered as verbal behavior, metaphor constitutes a response generated because of a *similar* (not *identical*) stimulus.

Skinner holds that concepts are the contingencies which bring behavior under the control of properties or of classes of objects defined by their properties. Accordingly, in expression and in communication a speaker and listener respond to the conditions in one's body which one has learned to call "feelings." But for Skinner, so-called "feelings" are actually behavior, due to the contingencies of which the felt conditions may be by-products. Verbal behavior does not communicate feelings, though verbal behavior may result in conditions *similarly* felt.

The child responds in sentences to events in the child's environment. The child's environment consists of events involving more than one property or thing, or relations among things, or relations of acted and acted upon, and so forth. The child's responses contain elements which the child never has any occasion to emit alone.

With the invention of the alphabet, it became possible to record verbal behavior in more or less permanent form. Since they are free of any supporting environment, these written words *seem* to have an independent existence. Skinner holds that true verbal behavior takes place only when a speaker-listener can enact a stimulus-response.

In Skinner's view, verbal behavior has a *kind of* independent status when verbal behavior is transmitted from speaker to listener. Such a situation occurs, for example, when verbal behavior as "information" passes over a telephone wire or when it takes the form of a text between writer and reader. Hence, in Skinnerian behaviorism, the only authentic meaning of literary criticism is what such criticism means *for the reader*. Skinner

FIGURE ONE: SKINNERIAN MODEL FOR VERBAL BEHAVIOR

STIMULUS ⟶ RESPONSE
VERBAL COMMUNITY

1. Verbal Setting	2. Activity at Setting RAILROAD STATION
Speaker stimulus: "I will meet you at 2:00 P.M. under the clock at the railroad station." Listener verbal response. I will be there."	Listener response: meets speaker at setting (time and place). Both reinforce *behavioral* activity associated with *verbal* setting
S = stimulus R = response	R = response RN = reinforcement

ESTABLISHES CONDITIONS WHICH ENABLE THESE BEHAVIORS TO OCCUR

Three terms required for an operant (activity) to occur:
1) Speaker responds to setting
2) Listener engages in requested behavior
3) Listener is affected by the consequences

The large box represents the verbal community which establishes the conditions that enable the appropriate behavior to occur (stimulus-response) on the part of both the speaker and listener. Box 1 represents the verbal setting. Neither speaker nor listener are in contact with the setting where the activity will take place. Verbal behavior does *not* require being in the setting (time and place). Box 2 represents the actual setting (time and place) where the operant or activity occurs.

insists that the original circumstances which obtained when the writer first produced the text have long since been forgotten.

Much as the human species evolved through evolution under the contingencies of survival, so also the child's verbal behavior evolves under the selective action of the contingencies of reinforcement. According to Skinner, the origin of this behavior is not unlike Charles Darwin's concept of the origin of species. New combinations of stimuli appear in new settings. The responses which describe these may never have been made by the speaker before or heard or read in the speech of others.[23]

Christian communication theorists Marshall McLuhan and Walter Ong require a more detailed synopsis. These two theoreticians are major contributors to the humanistic interpretation of modern communication theory. Their influence on religionists is also significant. More pertinent still, both of these theorists address the issue of modern communication and its relationship to religious education. The remainder of this second chapter will review their theories concerning modern communication, the church, and religious education.

Both authors owe a significant debt to the evolutionary immanentist philosophy of Pierre Teilhard de Chardin.

Marshall McLuhan: An Introduction

In 1955, a book written by Teilhard de Chardin, a Catholic paleontologist, *The Phenomenon of Man,* was published posthumously.[24] This seminal study profoundly affected both Marshall McLuhan and Walter Ong, as well as many other educated Christians. In direct contrast to the refusal of fundamentalist and even some evangelical Christians to accept the challenge of biological evolution, Teilhard attempts to demonstrate the compatibility of the Christian view of creation with the scientific notion of Darwinian evolution. His macrotheory, which emerged in a series of posthumous books, is an original synthesis of St. Paul's concept of universal redemption, Scholastic philosophy's idea of final causality or teleology, and Darwin's theory of the evolution of the human species. For Teilhard, the crowning achievement of evolution is the emergence of self-consciousness. The final goal of evolution in Teilhard's view is universal self-consciousness.[25] This universal self-consciousness, the "noosphere," is a world of the mind, which he sees evolving toward an inevitable union of awareness with the risen Christ.[26] Modern science does not impede this progress toward the divine, but instead aids this progress.

McLuhan was profoundly inspired by this Teilhardian vision. McLuhan's term "implosion" which describes the new consciousness within the person that is caused by audiovisual media has a conceptual parallel with Teilhard's term "noosphere," which describes the new consciousness within the entire human race that is caused by the fusion of many minds and their machines around the world.[27]

Although Teilhard's evolutionary immanentism is a contributory factor to McLuhan's positive macrotheory about technology, yet McLuhan's approach to human consciousness is quite distinct from Teilhard's, and actually is not as bold. Teilhard suggests the eventual emergence of a collective consciousness of the human race, of which global electrical communication is the first harbinger. McLuhan, on the other hand, notes that a global consciousness is already emerging within each human psyche, which is dependent on audiovisual communication. McLuhan does not see the human race losing its dependence on instantaneous electrical communication devices. Teilhard views the evolution of consciousness as a perfection of the Darwinian biological thrust. McLuhan instead sees the evolution of consciousness as a direct consequence of the communication tools which are invented by human ingenuity.

For Teilhard, certain biological dead-ends are the failures in the course of the inevitable drive of matter toward life and then of life toward consciousness. For McLuhan, certain inventions, especially those associated with visuality, frustrate the drive of species toward holistic consciousness. These viually oriented inventions limit rather than enhance consciousness.

In Teilhard's view, the inevitable evoltionary biological thrust succeeds with each brilliant adaptation of life toward greater awareness (or complexity). Greater complexity implies greater awareness. Since this biological thrust is placed within life and matter by God, human consciousness will eventually merge with divine awareness, which is both its origin and its destiny. For McLuhan, humanity's inventive genius succeeds with each brilliant new communicative device toward greater communicability and awareness. In McLuhan's argument greater communicability implies greater awareness. Hence he asserts that audiovisual media facilitate global consciousness. With such a consciousness humanity can become God-like in its omniscience.

Teilhard predicts a time when humanity will no longer need communication devices because humanity will achieve a universal consciousness with all knowing beings and with God. McLuhan does not attempt to predict any further than the present, except to warn that the future will bring more sophisticated communication devices, greater awareness, and that consequently humanity will continue to become more God-like through technology.

Marshall McLuhan: General Theory of Modern Communication. In his two seminal texts, *The Gutenberg Galaxy* and *Understanding Media*, McLuhan grounds his theory of communication on the following premises: (1) Change in the media of communication determines change in both the individual and corporate psyche. Both the Freudian and the Jungian unconsciousness are affected by media change. (2) Technological advances automatically improve the quality of human life. (3) When all of the senses are involved in awareness, the individual psyche is in harmony with the Self and with the external world. However, whenever one of the media forces an individual to overuse one sense, then the ratio of all of the other senses is disturbed. This causes conflict within the Self and with the external world. (4) Humans anesthetize themselves against this discord by becoming deliberately unaware of the media-effect on the Self and the external world. (5) Conservatism is basically a vain attempt to maintain societal structures which have become obsolete because of media-effect. Hence backward-looking traditionalism in Christianity is the obstinate refusal to leave the moribund print culture.

McLuhan's principal theses are: (1) There are four basic media-cultures both for the individual psyche and for the whole group: (a) oral-aural; (b) visual (alphabetic); (c) intensely visual (typographic); and (d) tactile (audiovisual/global). (2) "Hot" media are intense in detail, require a low degree of participation on the part of the person, and cause explosive expansion (awareness driven outward as if by a centrifugal force). (3) "Cool" media are low in detail, require a high degree of participation on the part of the person, and cause "implosion" (McLuhan's neologism for awareness assaulted by centripetal information). (4) Visual media destroy humanity's sense ratio. (5) Audiovisual media are restoring humanity's sense ratio and reconstituting an integrity not experienced since the oral-aural period.

For McLuhan, language extends and amplifies a human being, yet language also fragments the human faculties. The collective consciousness of the race is diminished by the technical extension of consciousness through speech. Speech is the outering or utterance of all of our senses at once. Since the experience of communication (the speaking/listening act) is whole and simultaneous, the psychic awareness of the milieu in an oral culture is also whole and simultaneous. Accordingly, oral language constitutes an ecological harmony.

McLuhan holds that script writing constitutes an abstraction from speech. Since the script experience of communication is fragmented (the writing-reading act is totally different than the immediacy of the speaking-listening act) and sequential, therefore psychic awareness of the milieu is also fragmented and sequential. McLuhan asserts that script enables humans to *see* the vernacular. Language, once made visible, becomes open to the idea of a "point of view." Visual language exists in a unified and homogenous space, which is alien to the plurality and diversity of spoken words. Accordingly, visual language constitutes an ecological discord.

McLuhan states that with each form of communication the human psyche beholds an extension of the Self and is free to become that extension. For example, alphabetic letters are lined, fragmented analyses of speech, which lead inevitably to homogenization, that is, the blending of disparate units. With the introduction of the audiovisual media, humans quickly discover causal connections and patterns in language which are not so easily observable at the slower pace of mechanical change. Accordingly, audiovisual media constitute a restored ecological harmony.[28]

Marshall McLuhan: Media-Effect on the Church. For McLuhan, the church changes according to the communication milieu in which it finds itself. As the world moves from an oral to a scribal to a typographical and now to an audiovisual culture, the church experiences substantial changes in its own structure and in its educational mission.

In the Renaissance, for example, according to McLuhan, the church provided a concrete example of how a shift in media can cause a shift in spiritual perspective. With print, medieval spirituality turned from a concentration on objective piety to a concentration on subjective piety. Renaissance print produced visually homogenous cultures which consisted of psyches which were experiencing a new subjective sense of the Self. Hence the ancient communitarian ecclesial identity in the believer's psyche became instead modern and individualistic. Consequently, there was a shift in the Renaissance from emphasizing the union of the whole church with God to emphasizing the union of the individual soul with him.

The audiovisual media of the present world bring simultaneity, instantaneousness, inclusiveness, and a concentration on the present. The print psyche of the Renaissance had been poised between the medieval corporate experience of Catholicism, and the modern individualism associated with Protestantism. The contemporary psyche is affected by a new technology which is rendering individualism obsolete, and makes corporate interdependence mandatory.

Marshall McLuhan: Media-Effect on Education. Today's students, McLuhan asserts, live mythically and in-depth. School, however, remains a print product which is organized around classified information. McLuhan insists that such school subjects are unrelated and are usually conceived of as if they are items in a blueprint. The learner's psyche can find no means for self-involvement in this type of school. Such a school, McLuhan complains, cannot discover how the present educational scene relates to the mythical world of electrically processed data which the television generation of learners takes for granted.

In the new world economy, mass entertainment and mass advertising are truly becoming the primary educational enterprises. He asserts that these media-events are more effective in processing and dispensing information than the schools.

When a learner cannot comprehend the hidden power of media advertisement, that person's psyche is easy prey to the commercial determinism fostered by such hucksterism. Knowledge, however, does have the power to mitigate this determinism. The true goal of education, therefore, is emancipation from the trap of technological determinism.

Marshall McLuhan: Media-Effect on Religious Education. For McLuhan, the shift from a visual culture to a restored oral culture also implies a shift from secularism to a restored interest in the sacred. Audiovisual media constitute iconic imagery and hence appeal to religious sensitivity. Therefore present communication conditions are ripe for a dramatic improvement in religious education.

McLuhan adds, however, that religious education must be ready to cope with the new role that religion has in the contemporary world. In-depth biblical knowledge constitutes only one aspect of this mentality. Like all other education, religious education has been shaken to its very roots by the speed of the new information environment. Speed accentuates the problems of form and structure. The older educational arrangements had not been made with a view toward coping with those speeds. McLuhan asserts that therefore people can see a draining away of their life-values as they desperately try to make these older physical forms adjust to new and speedier movements.

For McLuhan, the church is a living part of the context of history and hence is radically affected by changes in the media of communication. McLuhan does not accept the traditionalists' position that the church is so stable and so divine that it cannot be fundamentally affected by the flux of human history. Religious education will *always* be in a state of crisis as long as its practitioners remain wedded to the outdated printed word of the past. Once religious education totally adapts to the audiovisual culture, McLuhan concludes, religious education will thrive in the present world.[29]

Probably the only Christian religious educationist who has taken McLuhan seriously is James Michael Lee. Virtually alone of all religious education scholars, Lee insists that the form and mode of communication in religion teaching is a content. Lee underscores this thesis by calling the communicative act of teaching "structural content." The teaching act, the flow of communication, is thus a crucial content in its own right. Method or practice is content. Religion changes in the act of teaching it. Lee adduces considerable empirical research evidence to support his thesis. For Lee, as for McLuhan, the medium is the message.

WALTER ONG: AN INTRODUCTION

Walter Ong's insight that in the development of the modern mind there was a shift from an auditory to a visual axis did not come from the works of any modern communication theorist. Rather, in reading the great German biblical exegete Rudolph Bultmann, he came across a discussion about the difference between the Greek word *gignoskein* and the Hebrew world *yadha'*, both of which are translated into English as the verb "to know." The Greek word, according to Bultmann, means to be able to analyze, to explain abstractly, to take apart, while the Hebrew word means to know what's what, to know what end is up, to know one's way around, to be "savvy." (One has here in capsule form one crucial element in the distinction between theological language and religious language.) Bultmann notes that the Greek word associates knowledge with visual activity, while the Hebrew word associates knowledge with auditory activity.[30]

With this insight, all of Ong's previous research on the form and structure of communication fell into place. He was now in a position to realize that Renaissance sensibility shifted from an auditory base to a visual one and that print contributed significantly to this shift.

Ong's theory assumes that the media of communication in any age or culture are *in a relational mode* with mental attitudes. The media are significant indicators of change in the history of human attitudes. Rather than proposing a total technological determinism in which the media *cause* attitudinal change, the religious humanist Ong contends that the human mind *first* changes its own attitudinal approach to experience and knowledge and *then* selects or invents those media most appropriate to this change in attitude.[31] Once invented, these media have an exceptionally strong influence in reinforcing the prevailing mental attitudes.

Walter Ong: General Macrotheory on Communication. Ong

synthesizes key ideas from immanentist theology, existential philosophy, traditional epistemology, language studies, linguistics, literary criticism, Freudian psychology, a modified Skinnerian behaviorism, and modern communication theory. In his immanentist theology, he affirms the basic Christian doctrine that God communicates to humanity through Christian revelation. Humanity must strive—however ineffectually—to communicate back to the divinity. In his existential philosophy, Ong asserts that person-to-person communication is superior to person-to-object communication; he holds the latter is less human, and hence intrinsically frustrating and demeaning. From traditional epistemology, Ong assumes that knowledge is an identification of the knower with the known in the mind (either subject-with-subject or subject-with-object). Without accepting Skinner's mechanistic philosophy, Ong utilizes the Skinnerian principle that communication between speaker and listener, especially in an oral setting, is a powerful motivation for behavioral change.

For Ong, unlike Skinner, language represents the intention of the subject to share the Self's consciousness with the Other. Since this identification can never be a complete union, no form of language can ever fully satisfy the user's intent. From linguistics, Ong takes the position that the study of language shifted during the print era from the study of the synthesis of vocalized sounds for response to the study of analyzing visual words for meaning. This shift brought a concomitant loss of the realization that the spoken word has the power to make personal demands on the listener. (Note here the similar distinction between theological language, which is concerned with communicating cognitive meaning, and religious language, which is concerned with stimulating a personal lived response.)

Metaphor can analogously explain insights into theology, philosophy, history, and so forth. Writing out of the Catholic tradition, Ong adopts a sanguine approach to the use of metaphor in religious language. Malcolm Muggeridge, on the other hand, writing out of the Evangelical Protestant tradition before his own conversion to Catholicism, holds that metaphorical usage in religious language detracts from the gospel responsibility to communicate the true New Testament message. Ong is representative of that tradition in Catholicism that is accustomed to

FIGURE TWO:

SCHEMATIC SYNOPSIS OF McLUHAN'S THEORY ON COMMUNICATION AND MEDIA-EFFECT:

When communication is . . .	then . . . the information environment is	then . . . the human psychic response is	then . . . the cultural values are . . .	then . . . the state and the church are	then . . . the teaching/learning act is
ORAL	AURAL	EMOTIONAL	PERSONAL	TRIBAL	TUTORIAL
WRITTEN	VISUAL	FRAGMENTED	IMPERSONAL	NATIONAL	SCHOOL
AUDIOVISUAL	TACTILE	HOLISTIC	TECHNOLO-GICAL	GLOBAL	THE TOTAL ENVIRONMENT

FIGURE THREE:

WALTER ONG: A SCHEMATIC SYNOPSIS OF HIS THEORY ON THE HISTORICAL TRANSFORMATIONS OF THE WORD

When the human word is . . .	then . . . the race's psychosexual stage is	then . . . information is stored and retrieved by	then . . . the teaching/learning act requires	then . . . the opposite view is treated with	then . . .* faith education relies on	AVERY DULLES'S HISTORICAL ECCLESIOLOGY then . . . the Word of God comes to the Church through
VOCALIZED SOUND	ORAL	MEMORY	RECITATION	Vigorous polemic against other viewpoint	APOLOGETICS	SPOKEN WITNESS
WRITTEN TEXT	ORAL/ANAL	A LIMITED NUMBER OF SCROLLS	DEBATE ON THE MEANING OF TEXT		THEOLOGY	WRITTEN DOCUMENTS OF CHURCH OFFICIALS
PRINT	ANAL	INDICES TO MANY BOOKS AND LIBRARIES	SILENT READING	Tolerant acceptance of the other viewpoint	CATECHISMS	PRINTED TEXTS AS MAGISTERIAL DOCUMENTS FOR CATHOLICS; THE BIBLE FOR PROTESTANTS
AUDIOVISUAL	GENITAL OR HOLISTIC	INSTANT AND OMNIPRESENT	PARTICIPATION		RELIGIOUS EDUCATION	ALL HUMAN EXPERIENCE

* This column is a suggestion of the present writer from a synthesis of church history and modern communication theory based on the works of Walter Ong and educationist Pierre Babin.

iconographic symbolism. This symbolism is found in the Catholic church's sacramental system and in the medieval use of allegory in biblical interpretation. Muggeridge is representative, at least before his own conversion to Catholicism, of the tradition in Evangelical Protestantism that distrusts nonverbal symbolism or metaphorical approaches to the facts of Christianity. This Evangelical Protestant tradition is found in the Reformation's insistence on the literal or plain-meaning interpretation of biblical texts.[32]

For Ong, language unifies cognition and communication. People think as they talk—to others and to themselves. The human voice, in giving utterance to the human word, looks inward and outward simultaneously. Accordingly, speech unifies the subjective-objective polarity between Self and Other, mind and reality. The subjective-objective polarity is only fully dichotomized when there is an unreflective visualist approach to reality. Too frequently, for example, science and philosophy are represented as dichotomous and even alien from one another, whereas both are visualist constructs of reality.

For Ong, modern children and youth become lonely and alienated because of the barrier created by the press-radio-television. Teachers must strive to penetrate this barrier, Ong insists, and unless they do, learners cannot react intelligently to verbal language at all. Contemporary youth possess an indiscriminatory hypnotic response to these media, a response acquired from years of exposure to these media. Teachers need to replace this indiscriminatory response with a discriminatory response. If teachers do not succeed in this endeavor, learners will remain impervious to any intellectual communication other than the crudest sort.

The developing global consciousness of the human race also places a new accent on communication, on verbal language as a function, on verbal language as living rather than as frozen in grammatical analysis, and thus, ultimately, on that mysterious entity called sound. *Sound, for Ong, is the crucial element in all verbal communication.* He holds that communication is truly rooted in persons, not in things—so communication resists being "structured." A true study of communication concentrates on the interaction of sounds with persons and not on the structure of verbal language.[33]

Ong's principal ideas may be summarized as follows: In the ancient world, knowledge was communicated through the spoken word. Sound required a speaker and a hearer who was personally summoned to respond. In the medieval world, knowledge was written on manuscripts. Knowledge was communicated through scribal specialists who controlled access to the chirographic manuscripts. Oral communication continued through vigorous debates on the meanings of the texts.

Renaissance typography shifted the method for all learning. Renaissance print reinforced the notion that knowledge could be contained in a visual space; there was no longer a need, as there had been for medieval scholars, for a prodigious memory. The ability to locate the proper place for topics (subjects of knowledge) was now essential.

In the modern era, the mass media are replacing the printed book as the principal source of communicable knowledge. Ong believes humanity is coming to the end of the visile's person-to-object approach to knowledge. It is returning to the audile's world of sound and a person-to-person approach to learning.

For Pierre Teilhard de Chardin, humanity is the perfection of matter. Humanity in Teilhard's view is the pinnacle of complexity. As a direct consequence of its material complexity humanity thus achieves consciousness, which makes humanity God-like. The ultimate goal of humanity's shared consciousness, according to Teilhard, is to merge with the divine awareness.

Ong's notion of the relationship of humanity and communication in some ways parallels Teilhard's view of the relationship of humanity and consciousness. For Ong, humanity is the perfection of communicability. Humanity is the pinnacle of interiority. As a consequence of the intensity of humanity's interiority, humanity is thus capable of external communication, which makes it God-like. The ultimate goal of humanity's person-to-person communication is full communion with the divine communicator.

Ong will not accept the traditional term "the beatific vision" as the best metaphor for explaining this ultimate union with the divine. Some term like "divine sound," or "beatific harmony" is a much more appropriate metaphor. Such a term more accurately recognizes that the optimal form of communication is the

Modern Communication Theory: An Overview 71

enunciation of intelligible sound coupled with the hearing and comprehension of that intelligible sound as the most authentic expression of the interior of another.

Walter Ong: Media-Effect on the Church. Ong holds that the Christian community is fundamentally those who have heard and heeded the voice of God speaking through revelation and history. The church, for Ong, is radically affected by the transmutation of this divine word. As the word passes from speech to script to print to electronic amplification, the word also brings about parallel changes in the Church. Thus, as James Michael Lee contends in his book *The Content of Religious Instruction,* verbal content is not simply the bearer of some other substantive content but is a genuine substantive content in its own right. Avery Dulles, a Catholic theologian, utilizes Ong's model of the transformations of the word to develop a historical ecclesiology based on distinct communication forms.[34] For the relationship of Dulles's ecclesiology to Ong's modern communication theory, see Figure Three.

Ong believes that the mysteries specific to Christianity, that is, the incarnation, the Trinity, and redemption through Jesus Christ, are only knowable through a special revelation. Hence the human intellect, relying solely upon reason, would be justified in rejecting them, except that these mysteries are known and accepted upon the revealed word of God. Since these revealed truths are fundamentally beyond human comprehension, any theological language used to describe such revealed truths is inherently in a state of tension. This tension exists because there is not a complete identity between verbalization and conceptualization. The human mind can only assent to the content of these truths of mystery with the aid of divine grace. This assent cannot be done without divine grace, since these truths surpass the natural reasoning activity of the human intellect. (Such a view of theological language in effect undermines any claim theological imperialism may have on the religious language of religious education and gives additional support to James Michael Lee's contention that there is a difference between theological language and religious language.)

The gift of faith, according to Ong, is what sets the mind to the task of comprehending what is fundamentally beyond the human mind. This task causes a certain psychic stress for the Christian mind. Ong maintains that belief is only an imperfect and in some ways a feeble contact with the truth. Certitude comes not from the weak human intellect but from faith in the source of this knowledge, which is God himself. In the center of Christianity, Ong reminds us, there exists a maximum of certitude coupled with a minimum of cognitive understanding. Hence there is something in Christianity which is not rational, but transrational. The whole of Christian theology may be termed a superparadox. This gives immanentist theology a natural affinity with wit poetry, since that poetry is a natural expression of this inherent psychic tension.[35]

Ong believes that immanentist theology requires that the human mind must reach its objective through a flank movement. In poetry the mind is in contact with a reality too fragile for it to comprehend. In immanentist theology the mind is in contact with a reality too massive for it to rationally comprehend. Hence both theology and poetry work on the periphery of human comprehension. Accordingly, verbalization and cognitive concepts are never quite adequate either for theology or for poetry. Traditionalist theology ignores the gross inadequacy of verbalization to capture the full meaning of the concept of God.

In human communication, Ong holds, one always means more implicitly than one says explicitly. Hence myth exists, not by nature of what myth says explicitly, but by nature of what one means symbolically. Ong believes that *mythos* complements *logos;* imagination complements reason. Myth is playing a game with language. It is word-play, or wit. Such symbolic language is more suitable for both poetry and religious language.

Ong regards the movements of church history as analogues to the movements in a dialogue. Ong prefers this dialogic view to the Hegelian dialectic, which Harold Innis employs. Ong finds the dialectical interpretation of history too little concerned with the vocal. The Hegelian nonvocal dialectic deflects attention from words as sounds and fosters a visualist analogue of the word: the idea. This idealistic approach in turn produces an equally visualist reduction of personal dialogue itself. For

Ong, any such idealism regarding history constitutes an avoidance of the real problem. The history of philosophy itself is largely the search for increasingly visualist or spatialist analogues by which to represent and deal with the real universe and the universe of the mind. Ong claims that this visualist-spatialist system must inevitably fail because philosophy actually requires an auditory approach to succeed in its task. History must study the world of sound, since sound is the actual constitutive of reality.

Ong claims that classical theology is excessively rooted in the visualist approach. Transcendists concentrate on *logos;* these transcendists avoid *mythos* as too vague. Transcendists wind up idealizing theological language by asserting it is capable of communicating much more about divine truth than it can. In the Catholic church, until Vatican II, the Latin language represented a chirographically controlled language isolated from the give-and-take of everyday speech. Hence the ancient Latin language reinforced the transcendist approach to the Catholic church's theology, ritual, and government. Latin was the tool used by Catholic traditionalists to keep the church isolated from the dynamism of historical change.

Walter Ong: Media-Effect on Education. For Ong, teaching is communication par excellence. Education is intimately connected with the study of the word, because education is essentially a communication process. Indeed, education is that form of communication which is the most basic and most central to the community. Formal education begins normally with the study of the community's media of thought and communication. Education has always been in the hands of the professional educationists, whom Ong defines as teachers who are preoccupied with the techniques of communication and also with the techniques of communicating those techniques.

Ong notes that all school learners were originally apprentice teachers. Medieval logic was basically a course in educational methodology meant for the training of future teachers. When the Renaissance humanists critiqued Scholastic logic, they were basically attacking Scholasticism's elitist educational methodology. Renaissance humanists protested that this Scholastic logic was unrelated to realism and to here-and-now existence.

Renaissance educationist Peter Ramus set out to produce a "real" logic. This logic was a kind of rhetorical logic or visualist epistemology which corresponded to what Ramus took to be reality. According to Ong, Renaissance humanists like Ramus had an agenda to liberate education from the professional educators of the day.

Renaissance printing was the liberators' promotional tool. Ong contends that with the advent of typography, education shifted away from a quasi-mathematical model which was the language of Scholastic logic. The educational process moved over toward an explication of literary texts, and then to an analysis of verbal language, and finally to the production of new literary works modeled on the Greek and Roman texts. Ong claims that the schools run by Renaissance humanists sought to prepare learners for the whole life, and not solely for teaching.

In the modern world, with the restored environment of sound, the communal aspect of communication and of thought itself has now assumed much greater importance than in former times. Ong claims that contemporary educationists should acquire a more sophisticated knowledge of the history of education so that they will be better able to become attuned to the distinct requirements of the auditory world.[36]

Ong believes that Peter Ramus developed a new system of learning based on the visual use of textbooks which were produced in massive numbers by the Renaissance printing presses. Ramism can be properly called an educational methodology based on a spatial module. Indeed, Ramism directly concerns the mental and communicational processes. Ong claims that Ramism indirectly implies a visual construct to the extramental world. In Ramism, the teacher is the dominant figure in the Renaissance passage from early discourse-knowledge to observation-knowledge.

It is Ong's contention that Ramism deliberately impels the teacher toward the visualist bias of the oral-visual dialectic. This Ramist bias includes the topical ideas of "clarity," "precision," and the like. Ramus persists in regarding the order of teaching, and through this all cognitive activity, as reducible to some kind of simple spatial arrangement or rearrangement of intellectual atoms.

Walter Ong: Media-Effect on Religious Education. Ramism, according to Ong, also alters the educational methodology employed in Christian religious education. In the medieval church, the basic tenets of the Christian faith were learned through recitation, the liturgy, and iconographical art. The medieval learner came to know the tenets of the Christian faith through dialogic communication of the holistic, existential sort. The most powerful teaching method in the medieval church was the actual experience of living within a believing, worshiping community.

Ramus and the other Renaissance humanists changed all this. Ramus exemplified the "topical logic" approach to Christian religious education. For Ramus, the faith is no longer to be transmitted through communal existential encounter, through the liturgy, through holistic community living, or even in formal educational settings through spoken communication between teacher and learner such as university disputations. Rather, in the new era of the Renaissance, Ramism tilts religious education in such a way that it becomes *faith taught through the use of printed textbooks.* These texts, called catechisms, explicitly deal with or "situate" the theological loci or topics. Ong states that Ramus is setting out to schematize the truths of the Christian religion into four distinct loci or topics.

Ramus begins his own text, *The Commentary on the Christian Religion*, by stating that the task of his book is to illustrate the theological loci. He schematizes the Christian religion into four general topics: (1) faith, (2) law, (3) prayer, and (4) the sacraments. For Ramus, this is all that is needed to contain all of the truths of Christianity. Ong complains that Ramus's method fails to engage either cognitive dogma or existential practice in any effective manner. Also, Ramus's personal conversion from Catholicism to Protestantism weakened his credibility among Renaissance French Catholics since he wrote in the heat of a very polemical era.

However, in the long run Ramus made an enormous impact on the educational methodology of the Renaissance and post-Renaissance world. His view of religious education, however, never came to exert the same powerful impact. Nonetheless, semi-Ramist followers still exercised a great influence on Christian religious education, especially within the Protestant tradition. Ong lists the following as the Protestant heirs of Ramus's visualist religious education: John Calvin (1509-1564), Elizabeth I of England (1533-1603), James I of England (1566-1625), Philip Melanchton (1497-1560), John Milton (1608-1674), and John Wesley (1703-1791).[37]

For a schematic synopsis of Ong's theory on communication and media-effect and how it correlates with Avery Dulles's historical ecclesiology, see Figure Three. One column in this chart represents my own view on the history of religious education.

Summary: Modern Communication Theory and Its Significance for Religious Education

As audiovisual media continue to grow in power and influence, certain scholars are rightfully engaged in formulating theories about media-effect. Such scholars conceptualize all human enterprise as forms of communication; within this broad framework, communication scholars examine the nature of media as well as the ways in which media influence both the individual psyche and the whole society. The authors treated in this chapter approach media from three distinct positions: pure determinism, a determinism modified by a certain humanism, and a humanism modified by a certain determinism. Most of these authors have managed a personal synthesis of technological determinism and Christian humanism. The last-mentioned orientation is crucial, because it illustrates that modern communication theory can be approached as a behavioralist study of how contemporary media effect people.

B. F. Skinner is a true determinist who emphatically rejects the negative labels that humanists attach to that viewpoint. Media determinists who are on a continuum ranging from strong determinism to a weak humanism are Jacques Ellul, Harold Innis, Norbert Wiener, Lewis Mumford, the early Neil Postman, and the early Marshall McLuhan. In this continuum Ellul is the closest to the determinist pole and the early McLuhan is the closest to the humanist pole. Media humanists who are on a continuum ranging from strong humanism to weak determinism are Walter Ong, the later Marshall McLuhan, and the later

Neil Postman. In this scheme, the later Postman is closest to the determinist pole and Ong is closest to the humanist pole.

For the most part, theorists closest to the determinist bias remain pessimistic about media-development. Determinists believe the audiovisual media are detrimental to any attempt to sustain humanistic values in the contemporary world. For their part, humanists counter that the audiovisual media are relational to any social change and therefore people still have the power to control media-effect. Unfortunately, many people are opting not to exercise such control. Humanists remain optimistic about technological development despite the present failure to exercise proper control. For humanists, the audiovisual media do not only sustain humanistic values but, far more importantly, the audiovisual media have the inherent power to enhance these values and disseminate them more widely.

Lewis Mumford, Norbert Wiener, Jacques Ellul, Harold Innis, Marshall McLuhan, Neil Postman, and Walter Ong all articulate theories that attempt to explain contemporary change as a consequence of the media-revolution. Viewed as a whole, these scholars form a cogent argument on the necessity of all the Christian churches to incorporate the media revolution in the very heart of their educational mission.

The concepts from modern communication theory summarized in this chapter are central to the task of updating religious education. The following ideas from modern communication theory are of special relevance to the task of religious education: (1) Theological language is relative and cannot be considered an absolute in its attempt to articulate truths about God; (2) the church is a living part of the dynamism of human history; (3) history can be conceptualized as consisting of distinct periods which are understood in terms of the principal tools used to communicate; (4) education is always intimately connected with the contemporaneous media of communication; and (5) religious education needs to meet the challenge posed by the present worldwide development of audiovisual communication.

Religious education is always a part of the education common to a particular age. In the Renaissance the printed book became a focal point for the Christian church. Certain values associated with print technology become operative in all denominations. The Catholic church, for example, became more hierarchical, more centralized, more authoritarian, and more monolithic. Even as Christianity fragmented, each branch maintained its own particular uniformity by the use of printed missals, sacramentaries, theological manuals, and catechisms. It was an irony of the Renaissance age that each branch of the Christian church became obsessed with its own coherence, yet became even less concerned about maintaining the whole.

From the Renaissance to the middle of the twentieth century, the printed Bible or catechism was the symbolic center of the life of the Christian church. Holy writ was the source of the Christian church's dogmatic statements. Scripture was considered a compendium of all a learner needed to know in order to be a true Christian. Theology ruled the printed texts of the Christian church. Consequently theological imperialism reigned unchallenged.

Today the new information environment created by the audiovisual media is undermining virtually all of the past structures which were formed by the print technology. There is an urgent need for all the Christian churches to break with the characteristics associated with the past print age, and to assimilate the forms and structures of the contemporary audiovisual media. Incorporation of the forms and structures of the media revolution will lead the churches to become less hierarchical and more participatory, less centralized and more local, less authoritarian and more democratic, and less monolithic and more pluralistic.

Religious education needs to wholeheartedly participate in the media revolution with all its realities and benefits. Print media can no longer serve as the symbolic center of the Christian church. Print media tend to make dogmatic statements into absolutes; but the Christian church requires a language which is more flexible and more suited to religious dynamisms. Catholic teachers and learners must come to recognize that the verbal language of the catechisms is *not* the universal experience of the faith community. Protestant teachers and learners must come to recognize that the theological language of critical interpretation is *not* the original religious language of the ancient biblical authors. Hence the entire Christian church's religious education activity needs to move away from its excessive reliance on printed texts to other media of communication. The Christian church today requires a creative use of audiovisual language, that is, teaching the life of faith through the use of media which are more directly linked to both life and faith, namely images and sounds. Teachers and learners need to undergo significant role changes in order to meet this enormous challenge posed by the audiovisual media. Teachers should cultivate a new type of literacy, one that is more a skill in comprehending contemporary media-effect and less a concentration on reading and writing. It should be obvious that I am not advocating illiteracy. What I am advocating is a special emphasis on media-literacy as an essential tool for enabling learners to understand the contemporary world in which they live and to participate effectively in this world. Teachers are well advised to abandon their traditional authoritarian roles and be more willing to become fellow-participants in a mutual learning process.[38]

The crucial task of becoming media-competent is not only for teachers. Learners in turn need to move away from their passivity both toward their teachers and toward the audiovisual media as the sole providers of information about their world. Learners will have to take a more active and more participatory role in their own education. They need to develop that kind of media-literacy which enables them to recognize the total effect which audiovisual communication now has over their lives. Once they possess this skill, they should be able to enjoy a new freedom that enables them to overcome the all-pervasive media-determinism. This is an enormously difficult task, since most learners remain oblivious to media-effect.

In order to foster such a media-literacy—which in today's world is actually the gospel call to enable learners to make free personal moral choices—religious education needs to change its basic agenda. The contemporary task is no longer teaching the church's verbal doctrinal statements. Verbal doctrinal statements are a lifeless skeleton, isolated from the flesh and blood of life. The task in the modern world is an education that prepares learners to live as believers in the contemporary culture. A religious lifestyle is the flesh and blood of a mature faith, and such a lifestyle is more effectively communicated by audiovisual media than by print media.

Too often religious educators complain that they do not know what to do in a teaching/learning situation. They often appeal for the latest gimmick or fad to stimulate interest on the part of the learners. Both traditionalist print-oriented teachers and progressive media-oriented teachers lament that today's learners are not interested in religious education. The argument of this book is that learners are not interested in being prepared for a church and a world which no longer exists. *Once religious educators recognize that their primary task is not verbal communication about a past message but a holistic communication about today's church, they should find eager learners at their doorstep.*

The next chapter will summarize what modern communication theory has to say about the art-science of teaching religious education. That chapter will provide a theoretical foundation for the teaching/learning of holistic communication.

Notes

1. Genesis 11:1-9, Jerusalem Bible Translation. Note that according to the ancient biblical account, magnificent human technical achievement depended on the universality of language. Global communication has restored universal communication, and consequently technology has taken quantum leaps forward.

2. For an overview of the strengths and weaknesses of modern communication theory see the positive evaluation by John Culkin, "The New World of Marshall McLuhan," in *McLuhan: Hot and Cool: A Critical Symposium*, ed. Gerald Emmanuel Sterne (New York: Dial, 1967), pp. 35-44. For a negative critique, see George P. Elliot, "The New World of Marshall McLuhan," in *McLuhan: Hot and Cool*, pp. 65-73.

3. In classical Thomism these linguistic terms or concepts would be considered analogous predications, that is, the terms would be both like and unlike the theological meanings. Mumford implies a reductionism, i.e., the traditional and more supernatural meaning of the word is replaced by a modern meaning which connotes much less than the original term. For an explanation of analogy, see Bernard J.F. Lonergan, *Insight: A Study of Human Understanding*, 2nd ed. (New York: Philosophical Library, 1958), pp. 361-362.

4. Lewis Mumford, *Technics and Civilization* (New York: Harcourt, Brace 1934), pp. 51, 243, 245. I recall attending a concert at the Hollywood Bowl in 1970 which began with a player piano automatically moving the piano keys from a roller tape that had been cut by George Gershwin five decades earlier. In a sense, the audience heard the dead man's performance.

5. Mumford, *Technics and Civilization*, p. 104. This theme of technology dehumanizing humanity by fueling a selfish consumptive society is repeated by John Paul II, "Redemptor hominis," in *Origins*, 8, no. 40 (Washington, D.C.: National Catholic News Service, 1979), p. 634.

6. Mumford, *Technics and Civilization*, p. 241.

7. Mumford presents no hard evidence for this charge. Muggeridge claims that it is self-evident that the depiction of immoral behavior stimulates depravity. See Malcolm Muggeridge, *Christ and the Media* (Grand Rapids, Mich.: Eerdmans, 1978), p. 28.

8. Mumford, *Technics and Civilization*, p. 241.

9. Ibid., p. 254.

10. Norbert Wiener, *God and Golem, Inc.: A Comment on Certain Points Where Cybernetics Impinges on Religion* (Cambridge, Mass.: M.I.T. Press, 1964), p. 32.

11. Norbert Wiener, *Cybernetics* (Cambridge, Mass.: M.I.T. Press, 1961).

12. Norbert Wiener, *The Human Use of Human Beings* (Boston: Houghton Mifflin, 1950).

13. Wiener, *God and Golem, Inc.*, p. 11.

14. Ibid., pp. 46, 54-55.

15. Like Mumford, Wiener is using technical theological terms and univocally applying them to human situations; however the cogency of his argument is germane. Too often the proponents of classical theology cause the problem by asserting that certain perfections can only be predicated of God. Once human beings start producing these so-called exclusively divine perfections, the dilemma presented by Wiener emerges. For a more nuanced position paper on the conflict between science and theology, see Ian C. Barbour, *Issues in Science and Religion* (New York: Harper Torchbooks, 1971). Theological imperialism unfortunately continues to create these moral dilemmas for contemporary believers. Pierre Teilhard de Chardin argues that one cause of the dilemma is the absolute refusal of the traditionalists to see a spiritual power intrinsic to *material* being.

16. For a synopsis on Ellul's views on technological determinism, see John Wilkinson, "Introduction," in Jacques Ellul, *The Technological Society*, trans. John Wilkinson (New York: Vantage, 1964), pp. ix-xi; xvi. See also Ellul, *The Technological Society*, pp. 47, 49 (cf. Wiener, *God and Golem, Inc.*, pp. 54-55), 79, 97, 142-143, 221, 234, 324, and 370.

17. For a synopsis of Innis's interpretation of the influence of media in religion see Harold Adams Innis, *Empire and Communication* (Toronto: University of Toronto Press, 2nd ed., 1972; original edition, 1950), p. 7. Harold Adams Innis, *The Bias of Communication* (Toronto: University of Toronto Press, 1951), pp. 54-55, 75-76, 80, 82, and 87. Cf. Wiener, *God and Golem, Inc.*, pp. 54-55; Mumford, *Technics and Civilization*, pp. 241, 315-316. Ellul, *The Technological Society*, pp. 138 and 378-379.

18. Neil Postman, *The Disappearance of Childhood* (New York: Delacorte, 1982), p. 23.

19. Len Badia and Ronald A. Sarno, "The Mass Media As the Modern Bible," in *Morality: How To Live it Today* (Staten Island, N.Y.: Alba, 1979), pp. 208-209.

20. Jim Wallis, *Agenda for Biblical People* (New York: Harper & Row, 1976), p. 84.

21. For a synopsis of Postman's view on audiovisual media replacing the socializing role of the school and the church, see Neil Postman, *Teaching As A Conserving Activity* (New York: Dell, 1979), pp. 31, 42-43, 45, 48-49, 54-55, 57-69. 74-78, 81, 97-101, 113, 175-176, 180, 184, 186-194, 202, and 209-213. See also Postman, *The Disappearance of Childhood*, pp. 12, 23, 32-36, 38-49, 107-117, and 149-153.

22. James Michael Lee, *The Flow of Religious Instruction* (Birmingham, Ala.: Religious Education Press, 1973), pp. 289-290.

23. A synopsis of behaviorism's view of language as verbal behavior can be found in B. F. Skinner, *About Behaviorism* (New York: Alfred A. Knopf, 1974), pp. 88-101.

24. Pierre Teilhard de Chardin, *The Phenomenon of Man* (New York: Harper & Row, 1959). The original French edition appeared in 1955.

25. Ibid., pp. 300-310.

26. Pierre Teilhard de Chardin, *The Divine Milieu* (New York: Harper & Row, 1960), pp. 56-62. The original French edition appeared in 1957. For a theological and metaphysical analysis of Teilhard's position, see Christopher Mooney, *Teilhard de Chardin and the Mystery of Christ* (New York: Image Books, 1968), pp. 70-71.

27. For a further explication of the mutual ideas of McLuhan and Teilhard, see Richard Basil McCafferty, "The Influence of Teilhard de Chardin and Marshall McLuhan," *Dissertation Abstracts* 30 (1969), 3126 A (Northwestern University).

28. Marshall McLuhan, *The Gutenberg Galaxy: The Making of Typographical Man* (Toronto: University of Toronto Press, 1962), pp. 43, 136, 265-266. Marshall McLuhan, *Understanding Media: The Extensions of Man* (New York: Signet Books, 1964), pp. 83 and 305.

29. For McLuhan's position on media-effect on church history, see McLuhan, *Gutenberg Galaxy,* pp. 1, 56, 98-99, 111, 120, 123, 127, 135, 138, 139, 140, 143-144, 185, 186 (Cf. Innis, *The Bias of Communica-*

tion, p. 14, 191, 226) See also McLuhan, *Understanding Media,* pp. 67, 183, 203, 222. For an elaboration of media advertising as a modern form of the communal liturgy, see Postman, *The Disappearance of Childhood,* pp. 109-112. For McLuhan's views that the visual culture is secular and the oral culture is sacred, see McLuhan, *Gutenberg Galaxy,* pp. 70-71, 74. Cf. Mircea Eliade, *The Sacred and the Profane: The Nature of Religion,* trans. Willard R. Trask (New York: Harcourt, Brace, 1959), p. 178; and Ellul, *Technics and Civilization,* pp. 142-143. For his views on the relationship between communication and education, especially religious education, see McLuhan, *Gutenberg Galaxy,* pp. 242 and 247; McLuhan, *Understanding Media,* pp. viii, 39, 64, 95, 159, 268-269, and 280.

30. Rudolph Bultmann, *Gnosis,* trans. J.R. Coates (London: A. and C. Black, 1952), pp. 1-6 and 15-18. Letter from Walter J. Ong to author, 1 June 1978.

31. Ong assumes that humans select their communication tools which subsequently have an almost determinist power on the human psyche. Jacques Ellul terms his own theory "voluntary determinism," but it is a much more fatalistic view than Ong's. Cf. John Wilkerson, "Introduction," in Ellul, *Technics and Civilization,* p. xviii.

32. For the argument against metaphorical language in religious education, see Muggeridge, *Christ and Media,* pp. 45-49. Cf. Postman, *The Disappearance of Childhood,* pp. 38-39.

33. For Ong's views on language in communication, see Walter J. Ong, *The Barbarian Within and Other Fugitive Essays* (New York: Macmillan, 1962), pp. 30-34, 38, 154, 162, 174-175, 251-252, and 284.

34. Carl J. Pfeiffer, "The Church as Multi-Media," *Religion Teacher's Journal* 11, no. 3 (April, 1977), pp. 20-22.

35. For a fuller explanation of conceit in poetry, see T.S. Eliot, "The Metaphysical Poets," in *Major British Writers II,* ed. G.B. Harrison et al. (New York: Harcourt, Brace and World, 1959), pp. 847-851.

36. For a synopsis of Walter Ong's views of media-effect on education, see Ong, *The Barbarian Within,* pp. 9-10, 152, 155-163, and 220-221.

37. Ong's analysis of Ramism and its influence on education is summarized in Ong, *Ramus, Method and Decay of Dialogue,* pp. 197-198, 275, and 315. For Ong on Ramus's application of topical logic or visual epistemology to Christian religious education, see Ong, *Ramus and the Talon Inventory* (Cambridge, Mass.: Harvard University Press, 1958), p. 391. For Ong's list of the Protestant educators who are semi-Ramist, see *Ramus and Talon Inventory,* pp. 515, 517, 521, 524, and 533.

38. It is of interest that Neil Postman now denies the validity of this assertion. He urges a return to the traditional literacy of the print culture as the only effective method for combatting media determinism. See Postman, *Teaching as a Conserving Activity.*

3

Communication and the Teaching Act

Most teachers do not seem to be able to conceptually divorce the teaching act from book-learning. This concept is even more difficult for religious educators since in Western culture the Book represents an archetypal symbol for the life of faith. Ernst Robert Curtiss once noted that Jesus is the *only* ancient deity portrayed holding a book scroll.[1] For Christians, the Bible is the core communication about their faith. In the Bible, their faith in God and his deeds can be summed up as if in book form. Creation represents the opening chapter. The chapters in between narrate the salvation history of the ancient People of God. The final chapter foretells the end of the world, when all believers will be united with the Father. This same symbolism can be seen in the story of Jesus. The New Testament opens with a written account of his birth and initial public ministry. The middle of the New Testament relates his passion, death, and resurrection. Subsequent chapters tell of the early history of the church as it was being formed through the power of Jesus's Spirit. The final chapter foretells of the last things, namely, Jesus's Second Coming, the Final Judgment, and the union of all of the saved with the glorified Christ. Hence the Book archetype symbolized a concise summary of most of the essential teachings of Christian doctrine. The kinetic image and other forms of audiovisual communication are much too recent to have assimilated that strong an association with the written account of the life of faith.

Many religious educators (not only traditional ones, but even contemporary ones) strive to maintain religious education in its classical book form. The book-connection has a long and venerable history. As a result, many Christians remain reluctant to disavow anything so definitely associated with the heroic past of the church. People simply do not want to discard cherished traditions, even those that have exhausted their usefulness. Written material such as the Bible and the catechism creates clear and distinct ideas. Most Christians are much more at ease with precise cognitive formulations and become uneasy with less cognitive, "direct" language.

A further cause of the great adherence to print on the part of religious educators working in formal settings is that print has proven to be a highly effective medium for maintaining control over the masses. It should not be forgotten that religious education activities which are conducted in formal settings are under the watchful control of ecclesiastical authorities. These authorities view the prime purpose of religious education as socialization, namely to obey the mandates and suggestions of these selfsame ecclesiastical authorities. Church officials are obviously enamored of print-structures that shore up the hierarchy and manage also to maintain an external uniformity among the faithful. For all of these reasons, it is very hard for religious educators to understand that the act of teaching is distinct from book-learning.

It is the theme of this present volume, however, that the above-mentioned distinction must be made. The task today is to teach learners as they are, not as teachers wish them to be. Modern learners are simply not book-oriented. Therefore, to approach learners as if they were primarily print-oriented is to guarantee failure. Moreover, such an approach brings even more frustration to a field already characterized by burn-out and crisis.

Ian Knox, in his book *Above or Within?* lists three metaperspectives that form and shape religious education today. They are: (1) the transcendist position, which serves as a basis for traditional religious education, (2) the immanentist position, which serves as a basis for contemporary religious education, (3) the integralist position, which strives to unify the other two. Knox wryly notes that some religious educators are unaware of which metaperspective constitutes the philosophical ground for a specific form of religious education. Consequently, these religious educators frequently select practices which are not actually in conformity with their own metaperspective of what they should be doing.[2]

Knox's three categories enable us to analyze how certain religious educators use modern communication theory as a conceptual tool for structuring the teaching act.

The transcendists (Harold Burgess calls them the exponents of traditional theology) hold that modern communication theory is not an adequate reason for changing the church's historical reliance on verbal communication. Other transcendists, however, do admit that modern communication theory provides the church with a coherent explanation of why today's religious education is in a crisis. All transcendists insist that traditional theology must remain the sole judge both of religious education and of its use of modern communication. Malcolm Muggeridge (when he wrote as an Evangelical Protestant before his conversion to Catholicism) and two Catholic writers, James Hitchcock and George Kelly, represent those traditionalists who are challenging the value of modern communication theory.[3] They see no need to modernize religious education. Though William Fritts, a Baptist minister, sees much value in McLuhan's theory, nonetheless he steadfastly clings to the view that it is necessary for religious education to be subject to traditional biblical theology.[4]

There are two basic varieties of immanentist religious educators. Some wish to have a theological control over religious education. Others hope to free religious education from theological control. The second group prefers to view religious education as a form of education that is subject to the norms of the actual teaching-learning dynamic. (Harold Burgess describes the first group as exponents of the contemporary theological approach. He describes the second group as exponents of the religious education approach, especially of the social-science form of this approach.)

Representative authors of the contemporary theological approach to religious education include: (1) Allen Maruyama, a Presbyterian minister; (2) John XXIII, who inspired the modernization of the Catholic church; (3) the Catholic bishops who published the Vatican II document "The Church in the Modern World"; (4) the Catholic officials who published the postconciliar document "Pastoral Instruction on the Means of Social Communication"; (5) Walter Ong, a Catholic theorist; (6) Avery Dulles, a Catholic theologian; and (7) the early Gabriel Moran, a Catholic religious educationist.[5]

Representative authors of the religious education approach include: (1) George Coe, one of the Protestant founders of the Religious Education Association; (2) Bruce O'Donnell, a minor author; (3) the later Gabriel Moran; (4) Charles Cook; (5) Marshall McLuhan and Pierre Babin; (6) James Michael Lee, who is the founder of the social-science approach to religious instruction; and (7) Thomas Groome, a Catholic priest, who presents an immanentist position with a strong neo-Marxist political bias.[6] Each of these immanentist authors to some extent apply the tenets of modern communication theory to the modernization of religious education. Their opinions vary as to how much credence is to be given to modern communication theory, with Allen Murayama being the least receptive and James Michael Lee being the most enthusiastic.

Ian Knox cites few authors as representatives of the integralist position. He lists Randolph Crump Miller, a Protestant, and Marcel van Caster, a Catholic from the periodical *Lumen Vitae*, as integralists. He also recognizes a basic transcendist bias in their efforts and indeed seriously questions the validity of the existence of a separate integralist category.[7]

These specific authors are selected for further scrutiny because they are all in some way concerned with the relationship between modern communication and the act of teaching religion. In general, immanentist authors possess a more rich and complex understanding of what constitutes the actual communication process. Hence these writers are more likely to discuss how modern communication can enhance the effectiveness of the religion teaching act itself.

The Transcendist Critique of Modern Communication

Transcendist Christians, especially Evangelical Protestants, witness to the historical unity between the Christian faith and the doctrinal verbalization of that faith as it is found in the printed Bible. Hence it is no surprise that such Christians severely criticize the modern communication theorists who are attempting to separate Christian teaching from its traditional anchor, the printed text.

Malcolm Muggeridge for the Prosecution

Imagine a trial similar to the famous one which tried John Thomas Scopes for teaching Darwinian evolution.[8] In this new version of *Inherit the Wind,* the conflict is not between creationists and Darwinian evolutionists. Instead, the new antagonists are the critics and the proponents of modern communication theory. In this new version, Marshall McLuhan represents the defense for modern communication theory. McLuhan's position is that audiovisual communication is significantly contributing to preevangelization. He believes modern communication theory certainly facilitates the successful teaching of a Christian lifestyle. Malcolm Muggeridge, when he wrote as an Evangelical Protestant before his conversion to Catholicism, represents the prosecution. Muggeridge counter-charges that the audiovisual media on a global scale are actually destroying the morality and the spirituality of the Christian lifestyle. For Muggeridge, the audiovisual media facilitate Satan's work, not Christ's. Hence in Muggeridge's view, the task of religious education is to shield and to protect learners—especially the young—from such a vast assault on sacred tradition.

For Muggeridge, technology, especially the camera, enormously interferes with any genuine communication between people; it distorts and deflects communication. Muggeridge admits that technology can be *advantageous to communication,* but only in the sense that technology in the audiovisual media facilitates deception. His basic charge is that technology fundamentally makes it more difficult for people to communicate what is true and real.

William Blake once noted about poetry that people look *with* not *through,* their eyes.[9] Muggeridge claims the same is true for television. People see what they expect, or have been induced to expect, to see. For Muggeridge, therefore, the audiovisual media are not a form of objective communication. Instead, the media represent a vast, powerful, global network of subjective communication and self-deception. Muggeridge charges the audiovisual media with three principal sins: (1) The audiovisual media present the Big Lie by replacing reality with fantasy; (2) the audiovisual media reflect demonic, self-destructive images of human nature; and (3) the audiovisual media on a global scale are destructive of traditional Judeo-Christian values and morality because the media glorify and encourage sinful behavior.[10]

Muggeridge sharply contrasts the fantasy-world of the audiovisual media with the reality of Christ's kingdom as it is proclaimed in the New Testament. Modern communication theorists such as Marshall McLuhan attribute a powerful effect to the audiovisual media. Muggeridge attempts to refute this claim. The audiovisual media really possess no intrinsic power. Like nuclear weapons, audiovisual media have only as much power over people as such technical devices can obtain by exploiting human beings. Audiovisual media excite human carnality and thereby make people vulnerable to the pornographer. The audiovisual media stimulate human greed and thereby make people willing to be gullible to the claims of the advertiser. The audiovisual media satisfy human credulity and thereby make people susceptible to the fraudulent prospectuses of both fanatical ideologues and deceptive politicians. Above all, Muggeridge argues, the audiovisual media reinforce human arrogance and thereby induce people to be deceived by any revolutionary agitator who can bring to their nostrils the heady scent of raw power.

Simone Weil once noted that nothing is so sweet and pleasing as actual good, while no desert can be as boring and as dreary as actual evil.[11] Muggeridge holds that with fantasy it is the other way around. He claims that fictional good is boring and flat; while fictional evil is varied, intriguing, attractive, and full of charm. Television is the greatest fabricator of fantasy ever invented. Television attracts huge audiences all over the world. In television, *eros*, which Muggeridge perceives as selfish sexual excitement, provides all of the interest, but not *agapē*, which he perceives as self-sacrificing love.

So on television, Muggeridge asserts, celebrity and success are eminently desirable. A broken and contrite heart goes unheeded. In the audiovisual world, Jesus enthralling the masses as a broadway rock star is shown on prime time. Rarely is Jesus portrayed as dying in loneliness on the cross. The transposition of good and evil in audiovisual fantasy leaves people with no sense of the objective moral order. Without this moral sense, Muggeridge charges, no order, whether social, political, economic, or any other, is ever attainable.[12]

Muggeridge reminds us of the traditional biblical injunction against graven images. Although an image on the screen may not be a graven one, yet it is still an image and so carries with it a strong association with narcissism. By making *oneself* (instead of some ancient deity) into a "graven" image, there results a doubling of the offense against the law of the second commandment. Performers and television personalities live continuously with these false images of themselves. Those involved with this surreal existence of striving with a fantasy-duplicate often suffer unbearable psychological trauma.

In dealing with the mentally afflicted (for whom he always showed a particular concern), Jesus restored them to sanity by exorcising their demonic alter ego. By so doing he made each of them a whole person again and delivered them from their own false images. Jesus, the supreme antidote to fantasy and the master of reality, can be considered as extricating these suffering people from their personal television screen and restoring them back to real life.[13]

If modern communication theorists can assert that edifying scenes on television are able to uplift the values of the viewers, then according to Muggeridge, these same thinkers should also admit that unedifying scenes can significantly degrade the values of the viewers. Every actor knows that a television appearance can have a powerful impact on a career for good or ill. Accordingly, Muggeridge cannot understand how any Christian, knowing this, can deny that the spectacles of carnality and violence frequently portrayed on the audiovisual media have a profoundly detrimental effect on the viewer. If a person spends a total of eight years of his or her life watching television, then such a large investment of personal time, must have a profound effect on the mores of the viewer. For Muggeridge television is not an instrument of truth. Even when supposedly reporting the news, television never presents objective reality. There is an inherent subjective bias in all reporting. Not only can the camera lie; the camera always lies. Muggeridge gives as an example an incident which took place in Africa. An execution was delayed so that the camera crew could recharge and reload their equipment. Muggeridge berates the barbarity of the executioners, the camera staff, and the home viewers—all thirsty for human blood.

Muggeridge laments that in Britain audiovisual media are undermining traditional sexual mores. The audiovisual media ridicule the values of Christians who strive to maintain that chastity is a desirable virtue. Christians are vainly trying to keep eroticism and lasting love conceptually and factually united, while the audiovisual media strive to keep them apart. Muggeridge holds that Christians believe that the divine purpose of eroticism is procreation, while the audiovisual media concentrate solely on the personal pleasure involved.[14]

In the stories frequently portrayed in films and on videos moral misbehavior is almost inevitably shown as if it were the result of extrinsic forces. Never are moral misdeeds portrayed as due to deliberate wrongdoing. Hence the concept of sin is largely disappearing. The concept of virtue, Muggeridge laments, is now solely associated with social acts and social attitudes.

Muggeridge lists three apocalyptic portents in the modern age: nuclear weaponry; the birth control pill; and the camera. In his view, nuclear weaponry signifies power in terms of destruction. The birth control pill signifies human sex in terms of sterility. The camera signifies here-and-now reality solely in terms of fantasy.

The audiovisual media for Muggeridge vividly demonstrate the fatuousness of the false gods of the modern age. Modern humans worship money; inflation reveals money's inherent absurdity. Modern humans are obsessed with eroticism; the audiovisual media gives them pornography, which reduces sexual love to the absurd. Modern humans, especially radical politicians, plan for the kingdom of heaven here on earth (not in the future in heaven). All such social efforts lead inevitably to the Gulag Archipelago. Modern humans worship facts; and so they idolize computers. Modern humans are avid for the news; the audiovisual media assail them with meaningless newspeak.

In summary, Muggeridge expounds the traditional, Evangelical, transcendist distrust of the works of human hands. As a journalist for the British Broadcasting Corporation (BBC), he frequently experienced first-hand how facts could be manipulated and twisted by the audiovisual media for base purposes. (The eagerness for higher viewer ratings often led to such distortions.) So modern communication theory has nothing of value to offer the contemporary religious educator. In the final analysis, Muggeridge charges that audiovisual media only make the task of teaching the traditional Christian message considerably more difficult.[15]

James Hitchcock: A Catholic Critique

In some ways conservative Catholics share the same metaperspective as Evangelical Protestants. James Hitchcock, a Catholic layman, vigorously objects to the idea that modern communication can facilitate the incubation of Judeo-Christian values. Like Muggeridge, Hitchcock charges that the audiovisual media greatly empower the principal antagonists of religion, those modern enemies of truth. This prevents religious educators from inculcating traditional Judeo-Christian values in learners of all ages. The media expound and disseminate the humanitarian values associated with the secular Enlightenment but not the theistic values of the Catholic church.

According to Hitchcock, contemporary audiovisual media assert that there is now a struggle in progress within each church between enlightened, progressive, ecumenical, nondogmatic, and modern Christians, on the one hand, and rigid, backward, and authoritarian Christians, on the other. Religion will secure its future, according to this pervasive media-thesis, only by the victory of the progressive group. The audiovisual media supposedly demonstrate the current direction of human history so as to persuade as many people as possible to go along with the progressive, liberal agenda.

Hitchcock denies that any culturally conditioned movement, even one which expounds ethical values, can ever adequately express the total and true meaning of Christianity. He believes that audiovisual media create a "universal moral consensus." This media-biased behavioral code tries to discourage the media-congregation from having any private moral views distinct from the consensus. In this context, moral issues are viewed as valid only when they have been "discovered" by media-attention. In the media, these values are properly defined, then publicized, and thus attract a national constituency. Only then is the media-congregation granted "permission" from the media-hierarchy to hold such views. Hitchcock ruefully admits that in some ways, this media-biased consensus can actually be an improvement over the past, traditional morality.

According to Hitchcock, the church's religious educators must counter this prevailing media-bias. By so doing, religious educators can preserve the very concept of a distinctively Christian ethics. At times, traditional Christian ethics may coincide in some points with the global ethical code that is expounded in the audiovisual media. Hitchcock insists, however, that religious educators must continue to assert that Christian ethics cannot be totally identified with this media-consensus.

Hitchcock claims that Christianity needs to maintain a stubborn resistance to this pervasive media-bias, especially in the area of specific religious values. Christianity must always and everywhere witness to the transcendent dimension of reality. Without this transcendist dimension even a radical ethical code is quickly assimilated into the global culture. Then the radical code loses its Christian distinctiveness and inevitably lapses into humanitarianism.

For Hitchcock, the basic problem for the Catholic church today is that an audiovisual-media generation is growing up severely alienated from the Judeo-Christian religious tradition. Media youth and young adults do not comprehend the language of traditional theology. Media youth and young adults are unresponsive to traditional iconographic symbols. Today's youth depend far too much for their religious knowledge on the agencies of the Enlightenment culture, especially on the audiovisual media and on the non-church universities. The crucial task facing today's religious educators, therefore, is to acquaint learners with traditional religion. In this way religious educators can make these learners aware that historical Christianity is not the civil religion of the secular Enlightenment.[16]

In summary, Hitchcock insists that only a firm loyalty to the traditional verbal communication forms of transcendist theology and of prescriptive morality will preserve the genuine spiritual heritage of the Catholic church. Modern communication is in the hands of liberal, irreligious people who undermine traditional Christianity. These powerful, irreligious people encourage a nondenominational, fuzzy civil religion.

According to Hitchcock, the so-called "religion of progress" has replaced the religion of Jesus Christ largely because of the efforts of liberal Christians. These immanentist reformers (Hitchcock includes the proponents of modern communication theory in this group), hold the erroneous view that humanity is currently undergoing a profound transformation. This transformation will supposedly eliminate the need for law, tradition, authority, and duty. Supposedly, future humans will live totally spontaneous lives. They will be guided only by their own inner promptings and their concern for others. Such idealistic reformers believe that they are creating a brave new world which will be enormously superior to any yet seen.

For Hitchcock, this naive progressivism is based on the Teilhardian assumption that humanity stands on the threshold of a new and higher state of consciousness. At this higher level, supposedly, traditions and institutions and the social fabrics which have been necessary in the past will no longer be needed. This progressive faith reflects an insensitivity concerning transcendist values. Hitchcock charges that certain radical (or immanentist) Christians are deliberately attempting to eliminate transcendist values altogether.[17]

On the one hand, Hitchcock can be perceived as defending the values of the past culture in a world which no longer needs or wants those values. On the other hand, he can also be considered a prophetic voice crying out in today's media wasteland that such traditional values cannot be shunted off; they are very much needed by any culture that wishes to maintain even a tenuous union with the divine presence in the world.

George A. Kelly: The Catholic Magisterium Objects

George A. Kelly, a Catholic clergyman, argues that modern communication theory is hostile to the proper role of the magisterium. (In the Catholic church, the magisterium consists of the papacy, the episcopacy, and certain other hierarchically approved persons who teach in a formally approbated and official fashion.) These authorities are responsible for assuring the orthodoxy of the Catholic tradition.[18] Evangelical Protestants will find most of Kelly's transcendist argument congenial to their view, even though they naturally deny the validity of the Catholic hierarchy as an arbiter of authentic biblical tradition. While Kelly champions the cause of the Catholic bishops, in a similar way, Evangelical Protestants vigorously support the cause of church leaders who are grounded in the conservative biblical tradition.

For Kelly, the Catholic church has erred in substituting the term religious education for catechetics. (Catechetics is that kind of religious education under the direct political control of the Catholic hierarchy.[19] Religious education, on the other hand, is education in religion, and one which is not controlled per se by any political force.) Kelly charges that traditional catechetical pedagogy has lost its original aim. The original aim was to instruct learners in the truths of the Christian faith and to form a good moral character. Kelly laments that search and inquiry now replace the direct and authoritative transmission of knowledge. This vague groping, Kelly charges, is now the dominant methodology for religious education. Kelly complains that the former stress in catechetics on authority and on the magisterially approved tradition of the church has been very diminished.

In Kelly's view, the term religious education connotes that subjective interpretations are now more important than objective reality. (Note the print mentality which esteems objective and impersonal values.) Kelly is one of the very few Catholic educationists to lament that no single printed catechism emerged out of the Second Vatican Council. The rich plurality of catechisms and methodologies in the present church has unhappily fostered varied and contradictory teachings on the purpose and workings of the Catholic church. Kelly argues that a single, uniform, printed catechism will prevent this plurality. (The print mentality also esteems uniformity.)

Kelly holds that the new professional religious educators will keep challenging tradition unless the Catholic church's magisterium begins to forcefully exercise its apostolic authority in a forthright manner. (Kelly avoids discussing the universal religious life of the laity as a source of magisterial authority, despite the fact that this aspect is rooted in patristic theology.[20])

Kelly does not believe there is any value at all in dialogic communication in religious education activity. The official magisterium decides; therefore, in his view, there are no issues for discussion. Dialogic communication only leads to indecisiveness about what is authentic doctrine and then to further confusion on the part of the laity.

Kelly believes that the immanentist reformers, emboldened by certain liberal excesses following the Second Vatican Council, are adroitly using audiovisual media to further their progressive agenda. Intellectuals make good "revolutionaries" in the Catholic church because they are smart, and so are clever at manipulating audiovisual media. Kelly avers that the bishops are prevented from exercising their proper authority because of the sheer volume of opposing voices. These voices tend to intimidate the bishop. The exercise of the authoritative, magisterial role of the hierarchy is made considerably more difficult because the forces opposing the exercise of the bishops' authoritative stance are amplified by the audiovisual media.

As an example of the point made in the foregoing paragraph, Kelly adduces the controversy over the use of artificial contraception by married couples in the Catholic church immediately after the publication of Paul VI's *Humanae Vitae* (1968).[21] The American bishops who strove to support the papal position lost the public relations battle to their critics. This happened because the bishops were content to issue verbal press statements and pronunciamentos while their opponents appeared on national television.

The media newscasters also aided and abetted the dissenters too, since these commentators brought to the issue their own preconceived notion that the traditional Catholic church must change and indeed will change. Kelly states that the representatives of the traditional viewpoint simply did not recognize the important role that the audiovisual media played in the controversy.

Kelly urges Catholic church leaders to be much more willing to use the audiovisual media if they wish to regain their former unchallenged control of the church. Catholic church authorities must recognize that some problems will not be as significant as they first appear. The problems are simply blown out of proportion by the media coverage. Catholic church authorities should realize that they too can utilize the audiovisual media to safeguard tradition in the same way that the immanentists use the media to challenge tradition.

Kelly argues that a small band of changemakers, purportedly representing the spirit of the Second Vatican Council are cleverly succeeding in imposing their will on the governing circles of the Catholic church. They do not hesitate to ridicule Catholic church officials, or "to go over the heads" by eliciting public support through the media. Kelly believes that the Catholic church officials must regain total control of the church. Church authorities can use their pulpits *and* the audiovisual media in a much more personal way. With that combination, the Catholic church authorities can regain their supervisory power over their own agencies and schools, thereby competing with their rivals for public influence.

Kelly warns, however, that unless Catholic church officials are able to project a posture compatible with the television image (which favors bland personalities), authoritarian leaders can be made to appear as undemocratic types. Because of this, Kelly asserts that there is no strong religious leader in the Catholic church today who enjoys a good press. (Kelly avoids stating that any of these leaders might actually be governing in an undemocratic manner). Yet Kelly believes that Catholic church officials can turn this negative image around by combining their traditionalist mentality with an astute skill in using the audiovisual media. With this combination, transcendist Catholic church officials will be able to beat back the assault from the nontraditionalists.[22] (*Combat* metaphors are frequent with the print mentality.)

Kelly clearly indicates how the audiovisual media contribute to the decline in the power and authority of Catholic church authorities. He believes that a clever use of the audiovisual media will reverse this trend. He fails to understand the basic tenet of modern communication theory, namely that it is impossible to shore up print structures with audiovisual means. As Vatican II demonstrated, the audiovisual media are not the only reason that Catholic church authorities have lost much of their credibility with the laity. High-ranking Catholic functionaries have shamefully neglected the true needs of the laity for the last 450 years. It is no wonder that the audiovisual media can clobber the self-complacency of the Catholic church's officials. In the Catholic church, the immanentist agenda for reform finds a huge sympathetic public, not only because of the audiovisual media, but because of a global hunger in the church for a lifestyle that truly addresses the needs of the people.[23] Audiovisual media are generally more congenial to effectively addressing these needs than are print media.

William J. Fritts: An Evangelical Pastor Objects
William J. Fritts, a Baptist pastor, represents an Evangelical Protestant critique of McLuhanism. Fritts wrote a doctoral dissertation on the topic: "The McLuhan Thesis and its Relationship to Contemporary Christian Apologetics."[24] Fritts is relatively unknown in national church circles or among the wider religious education community. His significance, for the present volume at least, lies in the fact that he amply represents an intelligent, well-thought-out American Evangelical Protestant reflection on audiovisual media culture, influence, and practice. In his dissertation, Fritts evaluates Marshall McLuhan's modern communication theory. He analyzes the implications of modern communication for the areas of Christian communication, environmental Christianity, the liturgical revival, and religious education. Fritts's study is a critique of the suitability of modern communication theory for updating religious education.

According to Fritts, Marshall McLuhan relies far too heavily on the ideas of Harold Innis and Walter Ong. Fritts also charges that McLuhan ignores the important contributions made by other significant communication theorists. Fritts contends that McLuhan's approach is much too nonrational for the subject of media determinism and that he fails to take an orderly academic approach to modern communication theory. In Fritts' view, McLuhan fails to make a critical evaluation of his theory's source materials, especially in the presentations of his theory's conclusions. Fritts compares McLuhan's writings to college "bull sessions," where various ideas are thrown out willy-nilly for discussion. The basic intent is to spark creative thinking, rather than a rational argument. This frustrates any scholar struggling to grapple with McLuhan's version of modern communication theory. Because if the scholar refuses to evaluate McLuhan on a nonrational basis, then the scholar has entirely missed the point which McLuhan is making. The scholar is then not recognizing the basic difference between learning through oral dialogue and learning through the silent reading of sequential print.

Fritts contends the Christian church is radically affected by changes in the secular culture. He has studied media determinism and has also reviewed Christian history. Calling on his experience in the ministry for over twenty years, Fritts observes that in certain respects the Christian church does indeed transcend cultural changes in society but is still affected by those changes. The Christian church is essentially a conservative influence in the culture. But the Christian church does not stand outside of the culture, nor is it immune to the culture's influence.[25]

In his dissertation, Fritts examines McLuhan's epistemology, his conversion to Catholicism in 1937, his theories of perception, and his basic view that the communication media constitute fundamental change-elements in human life. For McLuhan, humanity avoids being deterministically manipulated by the audiovisual media by its conscious awareness of the global media environment. With this awareness humans can consciously create anti-environments. The school or the church may serve as such anti-environments. These anti-environments possess the inherent potential to counter or even at times supplant those audiovisual media environments which become falsely manipulative.

Although Fritts values these insights of McLuhan into the modern age, still he charges McLuhan with several failings: (1) His modern communication theory offers more mystical musings than factual knowledge; (2) he has resurrected Jean-Jacques Rousseau's concept of the noble savage, with the now discredited notion that civilization is to be equated with biblical original sin; (3) his view of the media is mythical; modern communication theory, according to Fritts, is not confirmed by the psychological data; (4) few scholars of behaviorism, according to Fritts, will credit the audiovisual media with possessing the total, manipulative power over people that McLuhan unhesitantly attributes to these media.

Fritts holds that traditional theology has the right, the power, and the duty to judge modern communication theory. In Fritts' transcendist view, McLuhan's modern communication theory has the following theological inadequacies: (1) McLuhan emphasizes sensory flux and the relativity of human thought. For Fritts, the Christian expects that stability which flows from authority and epistemology; (2) McLuhan's perceptual models are grounded on a behavioristic concept of the nature of humanity. Fritts contends that behaviorism is unacceptable from a biblically based Christian perspective. (Parenthetically, I should note that McLuhan is not a behaviorist; rather he is a behavioralist.) Fritts believes that McLuhan's "behavioristic" model for human perception is irreconcilable with the biblical concept of the human person as a self-actualizing agent; (3) For Fritts, McLuhan's disregard for content conflicts with the Christian's experience of a "content-filled" gospel.[26]

Both Evangelical Protestants and conservative Catholics accuse McLuhan of denying substantive content. McLuhan's actual assertion is that the process by which humans communicate with one another constitutes a true substantive content. Indeed, McLuhan's contention that process is in fact an authentic substantive content in its own right (the medium is the message) is one of the most seminal and breakthrough theses advanced by McLuhan. This thesis that process is an authentic substantive content in its own right dovetails with James Michael Lee's position on process as a genuine and highly important substantive context in the religious instruction act.

Summary: The Transcendists and Modern Communication Theory

Transcendist Christians are not satisfied that modern communication theory justifies any major change in religious education. They make this assertion for the following reasons: (1) Modern communication theory is not subject to the control of traditional theology; (2) modern communication theory minimizes the importance of printed texts, such as the Bible or documents issued by the magisterium, both of which traditional Christians believe constitute the supreme and paramount core of the faith; (3) modern communication theory is excessively optimistic about the potential for good in the audiovisual media, and conversely, too naive about their potential for evil; and (4) modern communication theory conceives of human beings as determined automatons rather than as free agents responsible for their moral behavior.

Despite their criticism and reserves, transcendist Christians also acknowledge significant contributions made by modern communication theory to the task of religious education. These contributions include: (1) Modern communication theory provides a rationale that explains why the audiovisual media have more influence on moderns than the church; (2) modern communication theory explains the failures that religion teachers have in striving to achieve their objectives with contemporary learners; (3) modern communication theory serves as a warning to transcendist Christians that they must concentrate more on the audiovisual media if they wish to exert a stronger influence on the lifestyle of contemporary learners; and (4) modern communication theory emphasizes the need for transcendist Christians to become more influential in audiovisual programs.

For transcendist Christians, the "message" remains sacrosanct. The "message" for the transcendists tends to be cognitive, printed, and product. Even when the Christian message is being transposed from verbal forms to audiovisual forms, transcendists still think it is absolutely crucial for religious educators to retain absolute fidelity to the original form. In practice, this means that audiovisual forms constitute for transcendist Christians at best derivative and therefore ancillary modes for encapsulating and teaching the authentic Christian message.

THE IMMANENTIST CHRISTIANS AND MODERN COMMUNICATION THEORY

Immanentist Christians who adhere to what Harold Burgess terms the contemporary theological view are for the most part quite willing to accept modern communication theory as a key tool for the improvement of education in general and of religious education in particular. The contemporary theological approach to education and to religious education recognizes the need to update religious education by utilizing the findings of modern communication theory. This group, however, also contends that contemporary theology must be retained as the primary controlling agent over religious education.

Vatican II gave this contemporary theological viewpoint a strong impetus within the Catholic communion. Conciliar and postconciliar episcopal documents reveal a willingness both to accept modern communication theory and to use it as an argument for the need to modernize religious education, but under the aegis of theology. Since Vatican II, Catholic authors are also arguing for the validity of adapting religious education to the prevailing audiovisual culture.

Some Protestants, such as the Presbyterian minister Allen Maruyama, accept the challenge of modern communication theory. Although such authors see theology as still controlling religious education, in an interesting twist they nevertheless accept modern communication theory as a valid argument for the need to modernize traditional theology.

Allen Maruyama: A Protestant Minister Compares Christian Humanism and Modern Communication Theory

Allen Maruyama, a Presbyterian minister, wrote a dissertation on modern communication theory entitled "A Theological Critique of Marshall McLuhan's New Man of the Electric Age." In it, he analyzed Christian humanism and how it has been affected by McLuhan's modern communication theory. The particular significance of this study lies in its lucid interfacing of the contemporary theological approach with McLuhanism.

As a pastor confronting the daily problems of a parish, Maruyama sensed that there is an attitudinal revolution taking place in the people of his congregation. McLuhanism enables Maruyama to understand how audiovisual technology is substantially influencing people and their society. McLuhanism claims that the audiovisual technology is significantly responsible for this attitudinal revolution. Even though McLuhan's insights into how the audiovisual media influence people remain primarily a contribution to cultural anthropology, nevertheless, in Maruyama's view McLuhan's analysis of contemporary humanity is vitally important for contemporary theology. (It is unusual for a Protestant to acknowledge that biblical theology can be dependent on outside disciplines.) McLuhan's probes and precepts are like X-ray views into humanity's environment. McLuhan argues that unless people take control of their technology they will inevitably become servants of this very technology.

Maruyama believes that fundamental concepts of the Christian faith are being challenged in the modern world. Consequently theologians of the open sort are searching for a critical focus for theology in contemporary ideas of humanity. In this milieu, modern communication theory introduces a discussion about the mass-media concepts of humanity which has considerable significance for theology. Contemporary theologians are struggling with new ideas about what it means to be human. For example, in *Projections: Shaping an American Theology for the Future,* Thomas O'Meara and Donald Weisser, both Catholic authors, express their theological concern for the human as well as for the natural environment. O'Meara and Weisser contend that today's crisis in the church is due partially at least to a confused idea about human nature.[27] William Kuhns, another Catholic author, also studies humanity's new technological environment by approaching the "interface" or bonds between humans and their environment.[28] Kuhns traces the general influence of technological environment upon people. However, he does not go into any depth to probe the anthropologies of thinkers such as Marshall McLuhan, Buckminster Fuller, C.W. Mills, George Braziller, Lewis Mumford, and Jacques Ellul. What Kuhns does is to make a broad survey of the technological environment. He subsequently traces the interfaces of people and their environment. This media-study served as a stimulus to Maruyama's dissertation about humanity's relationship to its environment and of the influence of that environment on human nature.

In studying this interfacing of humanity with its technological environment, Maruyama uses Marshall McLuhan as a particular proponent of the new environment. The study raises these general questions: (1) What is humanity's basic nature? (2) What does a technological environment do to this nature? (3) Is there significant adaptability in human beings that justifies the claim that humanity improves itself through technological advancement? McLuhan holds that the audiovisual age, with its audile-tactile environment, is producing a new type of human being.

Maruyama explores precisely how McLuhan's "New-Being of

the Media Age" relates to the traditional concepts of human nature. Both Christian humanism and Christian eschatology have articulated set concepts about the meaning of human life. McLuhanism is challenging this traditional viewpoint. Christian humanism describes *who* a person is, while Christian eschatology foretells *whither* each person is going. By way of contrast, McLuhanism argues that global audiovisual communication changes the nature of each person. It also states that the divine destiny—thought to exist only in the distant future—is actually arriving now.

Maruyama insists that these challenges to the traditional theological viewpoint cannot be ignored by Christian theologians. Some examples will suffice to briefly illustrate this point. McLuhan perceives that his own work is closely allied with other academic disciplines which study human nature. He believes that out of such interdisciplinary studies will emerge a new religious understanding of human nature. This new understanding will offer a greater integration of human knowledge and can lead to a more meaningful existence. McLuhan perceives his own theory as a coming together of psychology, general anthropology, biology, sociology, the arts, and other fields.[29]

McLuhan regards his own integration, which he believes is contributing to a meaningful existence for people, as a direct consequence of humanity's return to a more primitive, global environment. For Maruyama, however, McLuhanism does not present a thoroughly Christian perspective on human nature. Maruyama notes that McLuhan is not a theologian. McLuhan, in Maruyama's view, needs to outline his own theory's anthropology more specifically.

McLuhan recognizes that his own theory is moving in the direction of the total involvement of people with people, and of democracy with Christianity. Accordingly, he acknowledges that he is dealing with a profoundly religious issue. McLuhan believes that the ancient Christian concept of the mystical body, that is, of all people as members of the body of Christ, is rapidly becoming *technologically* a fact today because of global audiovisual media. However, he shrinks from theologizing further on this issue. He uses his understanding of contemporary technology to advance this claim. As a Catholic thinker, McLuhan readily admits that he lacks training in traditional Scholastic theological thought. He wryly acknowledges that his Catholic confreres often berate him for his lack of Scholastic theological terminology and concepts. He attributes this to not having been educated in a Catholic institution.[30]

Maruyama compares McLuhan to the prophet Amos. Amos did not belong to the guild of Hebrew prophets. Nevertheless, he strongly criticized the political and economic problems of Israel.[31] So too, McLuhan, although not a professional theologian, has issued a vigorous criticism of the complacency of traditional theologians in the Christian church. In Maruyama's view, McLuhan, the prophet, is making a greater contribution to theological thought than if he were a professional theologian. Maruyama points out that prophetic insights from outside a system of thought can often help that system to renew itself by challenging its outmoded assumptions and methods. Maruyama maintains that the theological dimensions of McLuhanism now determine the concept of contemporary humanity and thereby offer a valid and pressing challenge to traditional theology.

Maruyama states that it is necessary first to understand McLuhanism's metaperspective on the media and the environment in order to comprehend adequately how McLuhan sees humanity as being fundamentally changed by the technological environment. McLuhan perceives humanity as being profoundly changed by two major environmental influences, print and electricity. (This was synopsized in chapter 2.) Maruyama then proceeds to describe McLuhan's view that a new human being is now being formed by the electrical audiovisual media. He evaluates what McLuhan views as authentic human nature, i.e., a holistic, technological human being. He follows this with a discussion on the future of humanity. Maruyama, even as he admits McLuhan's significant contribution to the modernization of contemporary theology, still considers it pertinent to point out the theological inadequacies in McLuhan's argument.[32]

Arguing from McLuhan's metaperspective, Maruyama notes that religious educators can contribute to the modernization of their discipline by integrating art into their teaching. He urges religious educators to strive to produce those anti-environments which aid in freeing human beings from media-determinism. For McLuhan, art represents a significant anti-environment to the prevailing media-assault. McLuhan believes that art requires individual creativity and an acute awareness of the present technological environment.[33]

John XXIII: McLuhanism and the Papacy
Since the reign of John XXIII (1958-1963), the Catholic church has been engaged in a brave new direction. Until his papacy, the Catholic church's official policy was to make the church the absolute and timeless standard by which the world was judged. In a similar way, Evangelical Protestants consider the Bible as the absolute and unchanging standard by which the world is judged.

During the previous papal policy, the Catholic church maintained an immutable tradition wedded to a print-based cognitive verbal content. In this milieu, Catholic officials were willing to sacrifice communicability in order to retain stability.

John XXIII reversed this trend. He permitted the world, in a sense, to set the standard for the Catholic church. John XXIII acknowledged that the Catholic church's theological language could now be considered mutable, and thereby contemporary. John XXIII was willing to sacrifice the Catholic church's stability in order to achieve communicability. In today's church communicability has achieved a higher value than stability.[34]

John XXIII convened Vatican II precisely to modernize the manner in which the Catholic church communicates with contemporary humanity (*aggiornamento*). In his opening address to the Council bishops, John XXIII distinguished between the unchanging *content* of the Catholic faith, and the *manner,* or theological language, by which it is presented to others. In Aristotelian terms, John XXIII distinguished between form and content; in language reminiscent of McLuhan's modern communication theory, John XXIII made a distinction between the message and the medium.

It is important to comprehend to what extent John XXIII actually utilized McLuhan's distinction between medium and content and to what extent he avoided the full consequence of McLuhan's basic insight.[35]

John XXIII asserted that, when speaking of the doctrinal content of the Catholic church, there exists an unchanging doctrine (or essence), which is different than the theological verbal language (or medium) used to communicate the doctrine. John retained the church's reliance on philosophical Hellenism as the rational superstructure of theology. Hence the pope declared that while theological language is definitely a mutable medium, theological doctrine is an immutable product content. John agrees with McLuhan in acknowledging that there is a way in which the message is distinct from the message. John is also congenial to McLuhan's position that the medium constitutes a changing expression for any given content. However—and this is critical—John did not agree when McLuhan insisted that the medium is a true content in itself. John maintained a conceptual distinction between medium and content while McLuhan claimed a real distinction. Further, McLuhan held that there is an inherent power within a medium (because it is an equivalent substantive process-content) to transform the substantive product-content of its message. Hence a change in any media always signals an eventual radical change in its content.[36]

Despite John XXIII's reluctance to bring McLuhan's argument about substantive process content to its logical conclusion as was feared by the conservatives of Vatican II, his views are being increasingly applied to formulations about Christian doctrine. Once doctrine is severed from the anchor of a stable theological language, doctrine can no longer be immune to the winds of change.

There is a certain naivete in John XXIII's original assertion. Although he recognizes that theological language is inadequate and relativistic, he struggled to retain the notion that doctrine—which can only be learned through theological language—somehow manages to remain unaffected when its medium of communication changes. Like most Catholics, John XXIII did not distinguish carefully between theological language and religious language. Theological language is cognitive and verbal and hence print-oriented. It is stubbornly resistant to change. Religious language is existential and assumes many forms; hence it is free of print control. It is open to change.[37]

In both the Protestant and Catholic communions, theological language is striving to synthesize both traditional faith and modern idioms of expression. Transcendist Christians charge that such an enterprise is doomed to failure, since, in their view, the Christian faith is solidly rooted in its original verbal content as enshrined in print media.

John XXIII's views and *aggiornamento* gave considerable indirect impetus to the modernization of religious education in the contemporary Catholic church. His revolution also exerted some impact on the Protestant communions. One important fallout of John's position is that Christian religious educators are more effective if they demonstrate the validity of the church's teaching in modern idiom and avoid concentrating on condemning past errors.

The Council Bishops: "The Church in the Modern World"

John XXIII's plea for a contemporary theological language for Catholics was taken up by the Council bishops, particularly in their official document "The Church in the Modern World." In its ecclesiology, this Vatican II document teaches that the Christian church cannot be understood except in the here-and-now context of the world.[38] "The Church in the Modern World" is a benchmark for all Christians. The text calls upon the entire church (which is understood to be all who accept Jesus as their Lord and Savior) to shift its perspective. The church is to move from introversion (which McLuhan claims is a consequence of print-technology) to an outward vision of its responsibilities to the world (which McLuhan claims is a consequence of electrical audiovisual technology).[39] The bishops noted that there is an ambivalence in the non-church world. This world is fallen into the bondage of sin and yet is emancipated by Christ.

The "Church in the Modern World" also recognizes that in today's environment there is a great increase in knowledge, power, and unification. Yet the bishops point out that there still persists a sharp division between the educated few who are wealthy and the illiterate many who are poor. The Council bishops say that a Christian's response to the world is not to be regarded as "fleeing from evil." Rather, the response is to become an apostle with something to say *and* to do. Hence, as portrayed by Catholic theologian Karl Rahner, the church is God's sacrament in Christ for enlightening and reforming the world.⁴⁰ For the Council bishops, the church is the continuation of the incarnation of the Son throughout time. The Son had and continues to have a redemptive mission to the world. In terms of McLuhan's modern communication theory, the Council bishops teach that the church is the medium by which the message of Christ continues in time.

The "Church in the Modern World" sees the church as constituting a unique communication-medium in which God speaks to humanity and humanity in turn speaks to God. Using this metaphor, the Council bishops stated that the very nature of the church is to be at the focus of dialogic communication.

For the bishops, the supreme paradigm of all human intercommunication is the complete communion that exists in eternity between the Three Divine Persons of the Blessed Trinity. The bishops teach that each human soul is destined to enjoy full communion with God.⁴¹ (American theologians seem to be more comfortable with the term *communication,* which connotes a mutual sharing while retaining an individual identity. European theologians seem to be more accustomed to the term *communion,* which emphasizes a group's rapport.)

The "Church in the Modern World" also addresses humanity's relationship to technical progress. The bishops teach that it is evident that technology is progressing. They ask if it is also evident that human wisdom is growing as a consequence of this technology. The present problem is that humanity may lack sufficient wisdom. In lacking this wisdom, modern humanity may well fall victim to those very instruments which people create to serve their needs.⁴²

For the Council bishops, it is more accurate to assert that in today's world each person belongs more to an international society than to a single national state.⁴³ However, they warn against any total subordination of the individual to a monolithic society. In fact, the more they stress the need for social change, the more they also emphasize the dignity and the freedom of each individual. The Christian lifestyle is not merely a private perfection; it is a sharing in communitarian responsibilities.

The bishops remind Christians that the development of increasingly sophisticated technologies constitutes a primary way in which people fulfill the divine mandate to subject the world to humanity's needs.⁴⁴ The more humanity progresses, the bishops add, the more does technology have the power to reveal human ingenuity as the image of God the creator. Yet technical progress has no intrinsic value. All such progress must be judged according to the degree to which it fulfills the needs of the human community and of its individual members. The central aim of human society is the communion of all people, not just additional technical progress in and of itself.⁴⁵

For the Council bishops, technical advancement creates the new electrical audiovisual media. These media produce both a revolutionary anger and a universal philanthrophism in the modern world. Most of the youth in Third World countries hunger for the affluence of the American and European middle class. Yet only a fortunate few in these underdeveloped lands can achieve such wealth. The bishops warn that the gap between the rich and the poor grows wider each day. The bishops remind us that the audiovisual media foster a greater consciousness of this gap and so augment increasingly higher levels of revolutionary bitterness.⁴⁶

The bishops insist that technology ought to be at the service of humanity. Too often innovations are brought in solely because technology has become its own master.⁴⁷ At other times innovations develop because the introduction of a new invention brings more profit to a select few. The bishops, however, also note that there now exists, thanks to the audiovisual media, a worldwide solidarity of people who want to aid all people who are in need. Global philanthrophism is a consequence of global communication.

The bishops state that the affluent in today's world are those with technological know-how. Without their theoretical science or practical cooperation, neither the rich nor the poor will fare well. New structures are needed to overcome the inherent tendency of this small group of technocrats to arrogate all power to themselves. The Council urges that all of the people must be involved in the decision making.⁴⁸

Since the Second Vatican Council, certain Catholic laypersons are lamenting that the bishops publish lofty and high-sounding theoretical statements about mutual cooperation but in practice often return to the monarchical form of governance rooted in past outmoded structures.[49] For religious educators, the "Church in the Modern World" offers a solid theological resource for the task of modernizing the teaching/learning act. Protestant Christians are also inspired by its ecumenical tone as expressed in its willingness to accept all Christians as engaged in the mission of continuing Christ's work in the world.

The Postconciliar Commission on Social Communications: The "Pastoral Instruction"

At the conclusion of the Second Vatican Council, many Catholic bishops did not believe that they had adequately addressed the issue of modern communication. They asked the pope to establish a postconciliar commission on social communications to complete the task they had begun at the Council. The "Pastoral Instruction" issued by this postconciliar commission represents the official Catholic church's teaching on mass media. The text uses contemporary theology to integrate modern communication theory with the educational mission of the church. Both Catholic and Protestant religious educators have found and continue to find this document quite illuminative for their work with audiovisual learners.

According to the "Pastoral Instruction," audiovisual media now provide opportunities for great good or for great evil. The commission warns that brewing within the audiovisual media is considerable potential for evil. According to the bishops, the audiovisual media exert a powerful influence for evil by (1) seeking wider audiences by appeals to the baser instincts; (2) eliminating dialogue by concentrating real communication-power in the hands of a few select leaders; (3) weakening human communication by substituting mechanical transmissions for personal sharing; (4) letting fantasy replace reason; (5) allowing passivity to replace alertness and activity; and finally, (6) letting emotionalism totally replace reason. It is obvious from this that the document represents a cognitive print culture warning of the dangers of the emotional audiovisual world.

The commission notes that there are three prevalent opinions about media-effect: (1) Society imposes its values on the audiovisual media (i.e., social determinism); 2) the audiovisual media enhance and support the values of the society (i.e., socio-media codeterminism); and (3) the audiovisual media actually cause contemporary values (i.e., media-determinism).

The document does not approve or disapprove of any of these theories of communication. As a text inspired by Christian humanism, however, the document cannot condone a purely mechanistic determinism and expresses a pastoral concern for whenever base values dominate society.

The text reminds religious educators that when children are to be educated to make mature moral decisions, persuasion is more effective than prohibition. Adult teachers and parents need to realize that the psychology of children is different than that of adults. Youth, for their part, are far more media-literate than most of their adult teachers. The commission states that youth today are capable of asking embarrassing, frank questions. These questions arise when the audiovisual media reveal the inadequacies of both civil government officials and of ecclesiastical leadership. To cope with this new inquisitiveness, religious educators must become much more educated about the nature, structure, and effects of media.

The document suggests that educated persons today join together into large cartels in order to possess the massive political power required to dialogue back to the audiovisual media. In this way, people can avoid becoming completely passive to the global, commercial media-effect. Christian youth are encouraged to become future media-communicators.

To accomplish all of these stated objectives, the "Pastoral Instruction" urges religion teachers to include in their curricula a solid education in audiovisual media and their principal implications. The document further urges Christian theologians to enrich the commission's initial ideas with their own research and insight.

During the very early stages of Vatican II, certain Catholic curial officials were very suspicious of journalists working for newspapers, radio stations, and television networks not controlled by the hierarchy or by its surrogates. These officials were very uncooperative with reporters.[50] Such ecclesiastical stonewalling tended to further erode whatever credibility the old transcendist viewpoint enjoyed among educated Christian laypeople.

In marked contrast to this negative attitude the commission strongly recommends that Catholic church officials maintain an ongoing dialogue with the modern world. This means that Catholic church officials should give accurate information to the news agencies. The commission also reminds church leaders of their obligation to communicate with the press during "critical times," that is, those crises that are embarrassing to the hierarchy. Stonewalling is not a Christian response to a public crisis.

The commission also states that the audiovisual media can support the everyday task of the religious educator. Such media offer a "marvelous opportunity" for Christians to consider the implications of their religious convictions.

In the past, Catholic religious educators often condemned movies that portrayed immoral stories. In contrast, the "Pastoral Instruction" encourages today's religious educators to emphasize and to promote good films. Teacher are encouraged to stimulate their learners to watch films which promote authentic religious themes. This is offered as a much better tactic than condemning those films whose story lines contradict Christian values.

The "Pastoral Instruction" states that the religious programing provided by television and radio can aid the task of religious education. The Catholic clergy, religious, and prominent laity are reminded that they symbolically represent the Catholic Church when they appear in public broadcasts. The text acknowledges that all Christians have an inherent right to freedom of expression. Still, the bishops express their concern that such representatives heed their duty to present the teachings of the magisterium in a loyal fashion.

The "Pastoral Instruction" acknowledges that theaters and playwrights also provide excellent opportunities for the public to become familiar with new ideas. Playwrights have the ability to display humanity's religious preoccupations on the stage.

The document concludes by noting that there is still a need for much more study about media-effect. Universities need to help the Christian church to learn more about media-effect. The commission also admits that the church has yet to learn how it can be more effective through the audiovisual media.[51]

The text represents a refreshing change from previous official documents about the media from Catholic ecclesiastical authorities. Most of the early documents show a preoccupation with sex and censorship.

Walter Ong: Immanentist Theology and Modern Communication Theory

After the Council, Walter Ong, a Catholic scholar of cultural history, enriched his modern communication theory. Emboldened by the freedom of Vatican II, Ong clearly and specifically links modern communication theory to contemporary theology. Ong specifically encourages the application of his enriched modern communication theory to the task of religious education.

Ong's theory about modern communication draws from the psychoanalysis of Sigmund Freud and the evolutionary philosophy of Pierre Teilhard de Chardin. Freud holds that each adult is the end result of the psychosexual stages of the oral, anal, phallic, and genital periods.[52] Chardin believes that the human race is the end result of a material and biological evolution that has led inexorably to a greater complexity, or interiority.[53] For Ong, the human race is in an analogous communication-evolution. Humanity is passing through the psychosexual stages of oral talk (speech), anal retention (script and then print), to a contemporary, genital, audiovisual environment (electric holism).[54] This evolution leads by stages to greater communicability.

Ong considers oral dialogue as the supreme paradigm for all communication. Dialogue is a two-way transaction rooted in the world of sound. Vision, by contrast, is a one-way operation. Human knowledge, interpersonal relationships, and the faith community are all nurtured by dialogue. Lack of dialogue atrophies human values.

Ong explicitly relates his modern communication theory to immanentist theology. Christ's incarnation is an event not only in the objective world, but also in the "mystery" of sound. Ong prefers auditory analogues for discussing the incarnation, instead of resorting to the traditional visual metaphors associated with the print culture. An understanding of modern communication considerably enriches theology, just as an understanding of immanentist theology can yield richer theological implications of communication theory.

Ong prefers the auditory analogues because he holds that sound-symbols convey much more impact than visual metaphors. Sight-objects do not put the learner in touch with reality in the same forceful manner as sound-experiences do. A sight-object puts the learner in touch with the surface, but a sound-experience puts a learner in touch with the interior of another reality or person. Since divine communication consists of one interior sharing with another interior, sound is the most apt symbol for this religious experience.

So, according to Ong's understanding of the incarnation, Christ comes to humanity as the Word of God. As the incarnate Word, Christ subjects himself to the historical evolution of humanity's verbal communication system. Traditional explanations of the incarnation in transcendist theology state that God *manifested* himself to humanity. Ong prefers to employ an alternate expression: The Son *communicated* himself, and Christ's communication peaks in sound, or, more precisely in the spoken word. The divine Word is not so much seen as heard. For believers, the incarnate Son represents a divine intrusion into the world of human sound. The divine Word became immanent to humanity in Jesus Christ. Christ constitutes in the mystery of his being *both* God's communication to humanity and humanity's response to God. Christ is at the center of the dialogue between God and humanity.

Ong believes that Christ's incarnation occurred precisely at that time in history when humanity had the technology—the alphabet—to provide the Christian message with endurance and stability. The alphabet provided the early Christians with a vast imperial communicative structure with a huge audience of potential believers. Ong, who normally values oral communication as greatly superior to written communication, uncharacteristically admits that the permanence of Jesus's message depends very much on the consequent written forms of Jesus's original spoken words.

Ong's ecclesiology centers on the Christian church. The Christian church is the focus in the present for the word of God given to humanity in the past. In the Christian church the divine word is currently spoken, alive, and vividly present to contemporary people. The Christian church constitutes the continuity of the divine revelation. It possesses an oral continuity of hearing and speaking the divine word. The meaning of anything written in the past can only be ascertained through the present spoken word. Hence the Christian church is sacred history, for within its communion is the presence of the divine word. For Ong, the Christian church is driven by the divine word to maximum communication through personal contact by means of the spoken word.

According to Ong, in the Hebrew and Christian religions there are set times when God has entered into humanity's time and space. The doctrine of the incarnation is crucial to this theological perspective of realized immanentism. There is a relationship between time and space and human consciousness. Although consciousness transcends time and space, all three meet in the utterance of the human word. Accordingly, the expressed word is the means by which God can communicate his conscious concerns to humanity.

For Ong, this divine word takes on a greater reality when it is spoken instead of read. The modern electrical audiovisual media, with their restored oral word, facilitate the wholeness and the power of God's communication with humanity. The restored oral word also enables the Christian church to improve its communicability. The restored oral church is more self-conscious, reaches out to more people, and dialogues more effectively with the very faith communities it avoided during the print era.

As noted earlier in chapters 1 and 2, Ong distinguishes different cultures according to their predominant form of communication. An oral culture fosters auditory harmony, a visual culture fosters visual synthesis, and an electrical audiovisual media-culture fosters holistic and global awareness. *Of prime importance for pedagogy is that each culture forms distinct personalities which learn in different ways.*

Ong holds that transmutations in the word affect knowledge, communication, and community. Dialogue continually enriches these transmutations. Learning through dialogue keeps options open. There is always an opportunity for new insights and ideas. In stark contrast, writing and print effect closure. Written communication is actually arrested dialogue: The words are locked in place and become immutable idols. New ideas or insights have no way in. Consequently, transcendist Christians tend to be print-oriented personalities who are unwilling, even unable, to enter into a meaningful dialogue. Such an open dialogue tends to cause unwanted change in their cherished assumptions.

Ong holds that pedagogy depends entirely upon the transmutation of the word. As noted in chapter 2, Ong shows that oral formulas are used in oral cultures for education. Even in the script era, the oral disputation constituted the predominant method for learning. Renaissance print introduced the silent, visual approach to education. Today, audiovisual media are restoring oral dialogue as the normative means for attaining knowledge.

Ong contends that the Christian catechism is an example of how learning became wedded to the printed book. In the modern era there is now a return of interactive teacher-learner dialogue in the learning process. Dialogue is once again emerging as a technique for the teaching/learning of religious truths.[55]

Ong's personal blending of modern communication theory and immanentist theology offers religious educationists a theoretical foundation for moving away from traditional print-forms. These print-forms are dependent on published texts and are often formal or popularly informal summaries of dogmatic theology. Ong does not provide an explicit method for utilizing new forms of audiovisual communication in religious education. Nevertheless, Ong formulates a substantial argument that this contemporary approach is rooted truly in the Christian tradition.

Ong considers contemporary theology, when attuned to the history of the transmutations in verbal communication, as a suitable control for both modern communication theory and for religious education.

Avery Dulles: Immanentist Ecclesiology and Modern Communication Theory

Avery Dulles, a Catholic theologian, employed communication analogues when discussing the history of the Christian church in 1971 at a meeting of Catholic bishops. For Avery Dulles, the church is itself a medium of communication. Dulles uses Walter Ong's three stages of communication-eras to distinguish three ecclesial models for the church. (See Figure 3 in chapter 2.)

Dulles considers the Christian church as the incarnate Word extended through the world of time and space. The Christian church shares in the communication of God's life and love. The church is essentially a medium, or more precisely, a multimedia. As an extension of the word, the Christian church not only uses the media in communication but *the church is itself a unique medium of communication*. Hence the church is subject to the transmutations of the word in history. As the word changes, so too does the church.

Dulles states that the oral church is characterized by a biblical-kergymatic ecclesiology. The oral church emphasizes the spoken witness of individuals. These individuals testify to God's personal involvement in their lives, and in the lives of those cited in the Bible. Authority and credibility come, not from holding an office, but from having enjoyed a personal experience of the Spirit. (This ecclesial model survives today in the charismatic and pentecostal communities.)

Dulles sees the print-based church as characterized by a hierarchical-institutional ecclesiology. In the Catholic communion, the hierarchy authoritatively proclaims ecclesiastical teachings often couched in abstract propositional theology which is more often than not rooted in Scholastic philosophy. In the Protestant communion, ecclesiastical officials also couch their authoritative statements in abstract propositional theology, often with specific allusions to biblical texts. (Written and printed words thus dominate ecclesiastical communication and represent a transcendist approach. An immanentist perspective leads much more to a nonverbal and to a nonprint kind of communication.)

Dulles believes that today the church is experiencing an incipient secular-dialogic ecclesiology. The immediacy and the impact of the audiovisual media demand new forms for both authority and witness. Dulles reminds the bishops that the audiovisual media invite participation and that they encourage dialogue. The divine word might now take shape, Dulles argues, in images. The divine word may even now be found in the broad secular world of human experience as well as in the narrow confines of the church community. (This ecclesial model is the contemporary agenda for immanentist Christians.)[56]

Therefore, contemporary religious educationists argue that teachers can use *all* of the present environment in the teaching/learning act. Transcendist Christians, such as Malcolm Muggeridge and James Hitchcock, counter that if everything is a pedagogical tool for religious education then Christian religious education has been reduced to mere secular humanism. Such a religious education has no need to discern what are spiritual realities. Dulles's ecclesiology offers a strong dissent to this transcendist argument. He insists that religious educators ought to discover the "signs of the divine presence" in the contemporary audiovisual environment. Since everyone and everything is now part of the whole, Dulles contends, then God and the church can no longer be confined to those specific places (and those particular books) where transcendist Christians insist they remain.

As an immanentist theologian, Dulles contends that contemporary theology, if it is sensitive to the historical transmutations that the communication system has made on ecclesial models, is a valid control over religious education.

The Early Gabriel Moran: Theology and Religious Education As Forms for The Communication of Divine Revelation

Among those educationists who espouse contemporary theology, Gabriel Moran, a Catholic writer, represents a bridge. He is a link between those theorists who hold that theology should control religious education and those other theorists who contend instead that religious education should be free of theological control. In his books *Theology of Revelation* (1966)[57] and *The Catechesis of Revelation* (1966),[58] Moran argues that religious education is a subordinate messenger for contemporary theology. By 1970, Moran, however, definitely moved over to the opposite view that religious education is subject to the norms of education. Moran now holds that religious education is simply not subject to the requirements of theological control.[59]

Moran is among the first of the post-World War II religious educationists to clearly understand that religious education is a form of communication. In *The Catechesis of Revelation,* Moran synthesizes the Vatican II document "The Dogmatic Constitution on Revelation" with the theories of Walter Ong and Marshall McLuhan. Moran, however, does not accept any superficial application of McLuhanism to the task of religious education. Such an approach is inadequate since it too neatly separates content (theological doctrine) from the medium of method (religious education). For Moran both theology and religious education (or both content and method) are united in that both center on the revelation of God in Jesus Christ. Moran also rejects the transcendist bias that religious education must remain wedded to the past prescriptive forms associated with the print culture. Such a reactionary attempt to escape from history denies Christianity's dynamic existential development. The transcendist approach does not succeed, as its proponents think, in choosing God over humanity. According to Moran, such traditionalism merely idolizes certain selective elements from a dying culture.

Moran holds that whenever words which are expressive of God's revelation are spoken by believers their verbal function mediates the very intersubjective communication that is revelation. Whenever these same words are written down in books, however, people too readily reduce the meaning of revelation to a collection of objects extrinsic to humanity. When a learner is confronted with a written text rather than with a person there is more likelihood that he or she will remain a disinterested spectator. Such a spectator considers the significance of the communication from a neutral point of view, rather than as a direct appeal for a personal commitment.

Moran considers revelation to be the communication of God's love to humanity. He holds that theology and religious education are true to their purpose when they enable people to accept this communication and respond in love to it.

Moran claims that Christianity has always honored the oral preacher and teacher because through them the biblical word emerges as a personal and communal experience. In this oral mode, the written Bible can become God's invitation to the hearer to believe. In the Protestant communions, fidelity to the written word is normatively coupled with the oral preaching about the text.

For Moran, however, the total identification of revelation with any written doctrine is disastrous. Despite its historical significance for Protestant Christians, Moran contends that it is not the best use of terms to claim that "all revelation is contained in scripture." Moran draws from Walter Ong's basic insight about the power of the spoken word and asserts that the divine word simply cannot be "contained" in scripture in any of the usual meanings of that term.

Moran believes that no religious educator can claim to speak the revelatory word. Such a power is simply beyond the innate or cultivated ability of the teacher, because the conditions of the revelatory word are beyond human control.[60] What the religious educator actually does is to prepare the ground for allowing the learners to hear God in the events of the learner's life. The traditional prescriptive approach associated with the print mentality can abuse its authority by claiming to "contain the truths of revelation." Moran also warns that the contemporary approach associated with oral/audiovisual communication can abuse its credibility by asserting that personal charm is a comprehensive communication of revelation. (See the chapter on television Evangelists). In each case, the religious educator fails to recognize that he or she is the messenger and not the message.[61]

Ironically, Moran's writings never break free of the very print culture that he is critically analyzing. Moran does not focus on the communication process *per se*. He does denounce technology as an oppressive effect on attitudes. He distinctly treats religious education as if it all takes place in the verbal mode. He specifically speaks of the lectern as *the* teaching place. Furthermore, he does not break from his cognitive approach to religious education. (Cognition and the verbal mode of communication are inseparable.) Despite his rhetoric about heeding the emotional side of religious education, there is very little in his work about affectivity, attitude, lifestyle behaviors, and so forth. The early theological discipline associated with the print mentality is still very much a part of Moran's views on religious education.

In Moran's view, however, the transcendist bias is *too* locked into the print mentality. The transcendists insist on maintaining a system of abstractly defined truths which sustain no supportable relationship to the real world. This represents a useless cause. Moran contends that religious educators should be more concerned with helping their learners *to know God* and less involved in transmitting *information about God*. Consequently, Moran considers the contemporary debate among religious educationists about content and method to be, for all practical purposes, meaningless. The significant theoretical questions that religious educators need to address relate to those precise circumstances whereby any human being (whether a religious educator or not) can help another person to know and to love God. A person's present existential experience is the pivotal point needed for any religious educational practices to have any hope of achieving a revelationally vivified knowledge of God.[62]

For the early Moran, modern communication theory provides a conceptual tool for unifying the task of religious education and theology. Both are concerned with the communication of God's revelation. Revelation itself is a communication from God to humanity. Religious educators need to concentrate less on printed theological facts and pay more attention to those precise personal experiences which are revelatory of God's presence and love for the learners.

The early Moran represents an articulate exposition of the view that contemporary theology controls religious education. Although he states that religious education is a form of communication that needs to be open to the powerful affectivity of audiovisual media, he still perceives divine revelation as primarily a verbal, cognitive experience. Therefore, theology and religious education remain focused on reasoning and verbalization. Moran discusses the need for emotions and a Christian lifestyle of loving others, but unfortunately he never quite manages to integrate this viewpoint into his position. The later Moran is one of the leading exponents of the need to free religious education from theological control, as will be shown in the next few pages.

Summary: The Approach of Contemporary Theology and Modern Communication Theory

For the most part, Catholic and Protestant exponents of the approach of contemporary theology to religious education are ordained clergy and ecclesiastical officials. For these theorists, modern communication theory is a new science which is contributing to the updating of Christian theology. Once theology has been updated, it can still exercise its hegemony over religious education with full legitimacy. The proponents freely use Marshall McLuhan's idea that the medium and the message are truly distinct. Yet, for the most part, they balk at the corollary in Marshall McLuhan's argument that the medium is a true content in its own right. Thereby they fail to comprehend the true radicalness of modern communication theory and its contemporary effect on religious education. Modern communication theory does not shore up old forms. It does not call for a new window-dressing. Modern communication theory calls for an entirely new approach to the task of religious education.

The religious education approach which is described below is the most sensitive to this need for an entirely new form.

THE RELIGIOUS EDUCATION APPROACH

A religious education approach to the task of religious education seems to be at first glance a redundancy. Most religious educators are confused about the denotations of several terms used in the work of faith education. A glossary of these terms and their precise meanings for this present volume will help the reader to understand the following section on the religious education approach more clearly.

The following words are used to describe the major aspects of experience of faith education: theology, religion, catechetics, religious education, and religious instruction. Each term also connotes certain distinct aspects which root the term in a specific communication culture (See chapter 1.)

Theology is an intellectual reflection on the life of faith. It is almost always verbal and hence found primarily in books of verbal transactions. Verbalization is an expression of cognitive reflection. The print culture is ideal for this form of faith education.

Religion represents a lifestyle, a concrete way of living based on a specific faith tradition. Existential human experience is most apt for this form of faith life.

Catechetics has classically meant the authoritative transmission of cognitive doctrine. The term catechetics is usually used exclusively in the Catholic church. It refers to that type of cognitive-oriented religious education under the direct political control of the Roman Catholic hierarchy. Historically, catechetics began as a form of oral instruction, and in the Renaissance it became completely associated with printed books called catechisms. These printed catechisms are normally summaries of theological doctrine. Traditional catechetics is grounded in transcendist dogmatic theology. A great deal of contemporary catechetics is grounded in immanentist pastoral theology. *Catechetics is always subject to theological control.* Almost all ecumenically oriented authors, including the present one, avoid using the term "catechetical" since for many non-Catholic readers it is unfamiliar. Also, it implies magisterial control, and true religious education is free of such political control.

Religious education in the most authentic sense refers to a faith education free of theological control and governed by the rules of the teaching/learning dynamic. For religious education, theology constitutes one resource and one aid, a resource and aid which are external to religious education activity itself. Theology, consequently, is a help to religious education and not an area which dictates to religious education.

James Michael Lee, the initiator of the social-science approach, makes a careful distinction between "religious education" and "religious instruction." Lee regards religious education as a wider term than religious instruction. In Lee's view, religious education includes counseling, administration of religious education activities, and teaching. (The terms instruction and teaching are synomynous for Lee as they are for virtually everyone throughout the educational community.) Lee states that when most religious education writers use the term religious education, they actually mean religious instruction, since they typically do not write about counseling processes or administrative endeavors. Lee's own version of the social-science approach emphasizes holism, which for him means that Christian lifestyle is both the stuff and goal of religious instruction activity.

Audiovisual communication represents an especially apt form of communication for religious education and/or religious instruction since it is particularly suitable for effecting a change in lifestyle behaviors.

Consequently a "religious education" approach tends to make use of immanentist theology as a resource and an aid for what is basically understood as a pedagogical enterprise. Major exponents of the religious education approach include George Coe (a Protestant religious educationist), the later Gabriel Moran (the Catholic counterpart of Coe), Marshall McLuhan (a prominent Catholic communication theorist), Pierre Babin (a French Catholic priest who is renowned for his work in adolescent pedagogy), Thomas Groome, a former Catholic priest with a neo-Marxist political bias, and James Michael Lee, a Catholic layman. Charles Cook (a Catholic writer) and Bruce O'Donnell (a Christian commentator) represent two lesser-known writers who adapt the theory of the religious education approach to the practice of daily teaching.

George Albert Coe: A Founding Father of the Religious Education Association

George Albert Coe, a liberal Protestant, is a seminal representative among immanentist theorists of the contemporary approach which holds that religious education is free of theological control. In the first half of the twentieth century Coe exerted a pervasive influence within liberal Protestant religious education. Commentator Fred L. Brownlee calls Coe "the father of religious education in America."[63] Coe influenced future religious educators from his teaching position at Northwestern University in Chicago, at Union Theological Seminary in New

York, and toward the end of his career, at Teachers College, Columbia University. Coe was one of the founders of the Religious Education Association of America. He remained active in the Association until his death in 1951. In the Association's journal, *Religious Education,* Coe's liberal-immanentist metaperspective pervades the pre-World War II religious education scene. Most of Coe's 260 articles on religious education were published in *Religious Education.*

Coe does not regard himself as a theologian, and his approach to religious education does not utilize many theological concepts. In most of Coe's writing the dominant theological concept coming through is the divine-human democracy of God. Coe perceives God as immanent in all social process, particularly in the democratic republic of the United States. For Coe, God is a co-worker with humanity. Coe weaves this basic theological metaperspective of immanentism into his three foundational concepts of religious education theory, namely, the scientific process, personality development, and the social process. Coe places God at the heart of all scientific progress. As a human being enters into the scientific process, he or she participates with God in the ongoing evolution of the moral order. Social democracy constitutes the basic objective moral order. Proper scientific inquiry contributes to the growth of each human personality. Coe holds that this personality growth is the clearest manifestation of God's dwelling within (*immanens,* in Latin) the entire human enterprise. Coe perceives the human personality as sacred. Since the coming-to-be of each person is sacred, social process and social reconstruction are therefore the final goals for all true education. Consequently, Coe believes that all true education is actually religious education, because the coming-to-be of persons (which is the central concern of all education) is the essence of religion. It is not evident whether Coe conceives of God as a personal deity or simply as a type of social personality. Coe emphasizes God as active (1) within the social process and social interaction, (2) within evolution and an ever-changing world, and (3) within personality growth. As Ian Knox states in *Above or Within,* Coe simply does not deal with person-to-person relationships of a human being with God in a mystical sense apart from social interaction.[64] Coe, like the Catholic theorist Pierre Teilhard de

Chardin, does not admit to any fundamental distinction between the natural and the supernatural. William Clayton Bower describes Coe's contribution to the development of liberal religious education in America in this way: Coe's theory enables religious educators "to close the gap that has historically risen between the natural and the supernatural, between the religious and the secular, and between the temporal and the eternal."[65]

Coe does not explicitly refer to modern communication theory. Yet in many ways his ideas are compatible with the immanentist metaperspective of McLuhanism. Both Coe and McLuhan accept the presence and the power of God as active within the evolutionary process. Coe inserts this evolutionary immanentism within social progress, while McLuhan inserts it within technical progress. Both theorists consider it obligatory for all education to address the issue that technology is changing the nature of humanity. Both authors decry any traditional theory of education that remains convinced—despite all evidence to the contrary—that human nature is immutable. A corollary of this erroneous belief, both authors remind us, is that supposedly the same methods which worked in the past with learners will be successful now. Both authors hold, on the one hand, that mutual social interaction among human beings contributes to persons coming closer to God. On the other hand, both authors contend that God is present and active within the social progress of humanity. Both consider religious education to be an enterprise free of theological control. For both, religious education is essentially concerned with the social and personal development of learners. Coe, however, views social integration as essential for all personality development. By way of contrast, McLuhan holds that true personality development requires media-literacy that enables each person to become free of total social control.

The Later Gabriel Moran: The Shift from Catechetics to Religious Education

The earlier Gabriel Moran applied the insights of contemporary theology to catechetics (catechetics, it will be recalled, is that political form of religious education which views religion teaching as being subject in almost all details to the norms, directives, and guidelines set down by the Roman Catholic hierarchy). By 1970, however, Moran began to radically switch his position. He gradually abandoned catechetics for full-blooded adherence to religious education. So total was Moran's change of fundamental position that Ian Knox in his book *Above or Within?* was able to depict the later (postcatechetical) Moran as the Catholic counterpart of George Albert Coe.

By 1970 Moran had become severely skeptical of the aim of catechetics, which he perceived as the socialization (domestication) of learners directly into a specific form of belief and practice. Moran contended that the catechetical form of religious education is, at bottom, indoctrination. Consequently catechetics does not accord sufficient respect for the learners' freedom to make their own faith decision. Such an indoctrination effort is ultimately anti-educational. Moran holds that the principal aim of all authentic education is to empower learners to achieve personal freedom. By virtue of its political and denominational nature, catechetics consists in the unswerving and precise handing down of the corpus of revelation as the Catholic magisterium both defines that revelation and approves the methods by which this revelation is handed down. Moran, in contrast, believes that revelation is a gradually unfolding encounter with the divine through experienced relationships. Moran contends that the true reason for studying religion "is to understand it so when one chooses to live by it, the choice will be an intelligent one."[66]

The "later" or post-1970 Gabriel Moran perceives religious education as free of theological control. Thus there is no way in which catechetics can be equated with religious education properly speaking. Like Coe, Moran considers the aim of religious education as the humanization and social empowerment of the learner. Thus the later Moran holds that the ultimate aim of religious education is an openness to the wider community of humanity and a re-creation of a more humane society. Moran specifically associates this aim with an immanentist theological concept of revelation viewed as the totality of human experience. It should be noted that Moran's juxtaposition of religious education and immanentist theology does not suggest, for him at least, that religious education is under theological control. Associating—and even sourcing—does not mean control, at least for Moran.) Hence the principal aim of religious education is the awakening within the learner of a conscious awareness of experience. This process of awakening is *social,* since it provides a person with a religious outlook. From such a religious perspective, a person can then relate to other persons who share in the same experience. In addition, this awakening awareness expands a person's scope of freedom and intelligence. Such an awakening empowers a person to join in the re-creation of the world. This re-creation is specifically a Christian endeavor. Therefore immanentism is not so much about God's presence in the world as it is about God's activity.[67]

In terms of modern communication theory, Moran urges religious education to abandon traditional print-culture which fosters the catechetical (and hence narrow) bias. For Moran, revelation is really a holistic experience of God's communication to humanity, but a catechetical bias reduces revelation to a visible object outside of humanity. Such reductionism is a consequence of the print-culture's theological insistence that revelation is "only contained in texts."

Moran prefers a religious education that is devoted to nurturing human freedom. Marshall McLuhan holds that media-literacy, that is, the talent to create an anti-environment in response to the pervasive media-environment, enables a learner to achieve a personal growth. This growth, according to McLuhan, is characterized by a more humane freedom from a total social control. Similarly, Moran urges religious education to nurture an awareness of all contemporary experience within the present environment, including global media-effect. Both Moran and McLuhan agree that the more that learners are conscious of the world around them, the more human and the more God-like they can become. McLuhan, however, does warn that total social consciousness through media-effect can inhibit authentic personal growth. By way of contrast, both Coe and Moran perceive such global social consciousness as a preparation for a solid personal freedom.

Charles Cook: A Popular Explanation of Modern Communication Theory in the Practice of Religious Education

Gabriel Moran's theory of religious education and modern communication theory is scholarly and speculative. Charles

Cook, a Catholic writer, offers a more popular explanation of the use of modern communication theory in religious education. Cook's text, *Media in Catechesis,* demonstrates that some nonscholarly religious educators are listening to the serious advice of the communication theorists. Cook presents a personal synthesis of modern communication theory and of its application to contemporary religious education.

Cook grounds his synthesis on the documents of Vatican II, and on the works of William Kuhns, Avery Dulles, Gabriel Moran, Marshall McLuhan, Pierre Babin, and the artist Corinne Hart. His popular explanation is also grounded in immanentist theology, in general, and in process theology specifically. Modern communication theory, according to Cook, is making religious educators aware of the emergence of "the New Person of the Electric Age."

For Cook, revelation cannot be considered as a summons to repeat memorized doctrine. In such an outdated view, the verbal language of traditional theology suffices for religious education. Citing Moran, Cook states that religious education is fundamentally an invitation to live more humanly. Revelation achieves its goal when a dual interactive communication occurs between God and humanity. By communicating, humans are brought into a spiritual communion both with God and with one another. The church is a communication from God to humanity and from humanity back to God, as both Avery Dulles and Walter Ong state.

Cook's ecclesiology is based on the works of Avery Dulles. In this view, communication in the church requires the sustaining of a balance between both (1) fidelity to the word of God, and (2) respect for the receiver of the message. Cook contends that the ancient Hebrew prophets brought these dual elements into union.

Cook asserts that a static faith uses a static teaching, that is, the repetition and the memorization of past deeds in set verbal formulas. A dynamic faith requires a dynamic teaching/learning, that is, an education that recognizes the inability of the language of traditional theology to communicate completely the mystery of God's revelation to humanity.

True faith is to be found in the process of believers hearing and responding to the divine presence. Hence the church now needs a new pedagogy, that is, a new religious education. (Cook terms this new religious education a "contemporary catechesis," even though he perceives it as an enterprise free of theological control.) This new religious education teaches faith as an event happening within the network of human, interpersonal relationships.

Cook claims that too often the church's religious educators assert that revelation is solely the telling of what happened in the past. Such educators regard the language of traditional theology, which relies on printed catechisms, as being totally adequate for religion teaching. Cook argues that whenever the church's religious educators are willing to acknowledge that revelation is actually an ever-renewing process, then the inadequacy of the print-language of traditional theology becomes painfully evident. Both faith and audiovisual media share an innate ability to go beyond words, that is, to transcend verbalization as communication. Both speak to humans through powerful symbols. Hence audiovisual communication possesses the power of "co-expression." Co-expression is the ability to overcome the limitations of verbalization and cognitive thinking. Co-expression relies on nonverbal preconceptual symbols that awake in learners the deeper mysteries of life. Despite the reluctance of some transcendists to acknowledge the power of imagistic communication, co-expression does point to a beyond, to a transcendist reality. As noted in chapter 2 of this book, Walter Ong claimed this power existed within wit poetry. For Cook, the audiovisual media can suggest mystery precisely because the media do not possess the logical precision of the language of traditional theology. Therefore there is a genuine value in the lesser substantive precision of audiovisual communication.

Cook holds that the audiovisual media promote an inner personal search and a dynamic creativity that leads to discovery, an essential component of true learning. Sharing the experience of the audiovisual media with others ideally promotes dialogue between learners and their teachers and can have a facilitating role in the healthy development of interpersonal relationships. Media assist in the building of a community of persons who are open and trusting of one another.

Cook also admits some negative effects of the media. Audiovisual media can promote passivity so that learners uncritically accept the thoughts and concerns of others as their own. The audiovisual media can be erroneously regarded as superb vehicles for entertainment but poor vehicles for education of the deeper sort.

At their best, Cook holds that audiovisual media move learners, unsettle learner's passively held views, encourage learners to question, and lead learners to be open to further developments as persons. Audiovisual media provide a concrete experience instead of abstract speculation, therefore media can be more effective in deepening the learner's personal commitment to religious values.[68]

Cook's writing indicates that some religious educators are finding an immanentist interpretation of modern communication theory effective in the classroom, particularly among adolescent learners.

Marshall McLuhan and Pierre Babin: The Use of Modern Communication Theory in the Religious Education of Adolescents

Charles Cook acknowledges his debt to Marshall McLuhan and Pierre Babin. These two major Catholic theorists collaborated on a key French volume entitled *Autre Homme, Autre Cretien, a L'age Electronique* (1977).[69] This book applies McLuhanism to the religious education of adolescents.

Pierre Babin is a former leading exponent of the contemporary theological approach. In this 1977 book, however, he shifted dramatically to the religious education approach. Babin perceives Vatican II as a summons to *all* Christians to use both dialogic communication and personal affectivity in teaching. He claims both are exactly what is needed by the contemporary adolescent.[70] He laments that too often traditional religious educators cut themselves off emotionally from any genuine personal communication with their learners. Such religious educators falsely assume that what *they* understand about the Christian faith is being understood in the same way by their younger learners.[71] Babin asserts that there is a need today for religious educators to communicate and to share their subjective selves as well as their objective religious truths. One of the most effective ways of achieving this communicating and sharing is through interpersonal dialogue between learners and teachers about mutual media experiences.[72]

In their book (which can be translated as *Electric People, Electric Christians*), McLuhan and Babin argue that modern youth are profoundly affected by the audiovisual media. Positively, a new sense of the sacred is awakened.[73] A new type of religious sentiment is emerging, one characterized by an interest in worldly values, in a personal attachment to Jesus, and in Eastern mysticism. Negatively, there is a malady which permeates today's youth. Youth fear that nothing in their experience will remain permanent. Inverting tradition, youth today are the cultural leaders, while adults are the followers. This inversion is evident in both fashion and social mores. Youth are no longer given moral guidance by their elders. The very elders who should be guiding them are mimicking them.[74]

McLuhan and Babin state that the Christian churches need to present authentic moral guidance to youth. To do this effectively, the churches must be willing not only to lead, but also to adapt and to change. For McLuhan and Babin, Christianity is basically a dynamic reality, since it is a continuation of Christ's incarnation. This incarnation means that the Christian churches are subject to time and to change. As Walter Ong states, transcendists confuse a stable church with a static church.[75] Psychodynamically, transcendists, in McLuhan and Babin's view, are visile psyches, that is, they are those who cannot hear the voice of change in the modern world.

McLuhan and Babin argue that any contemporary religious education enterprise which is fundamentally print-based is doomed to fail if its target is modern media-influenced youth. To reach such media-saturated youth teaching must present the Christian faith as contemporary, imaginative, and as distinct from the official communication of ordained church leaders.

Despite their enthusiasm for this new approach, both authors are still afraid that the audiovisual media will possibly not produce active, adult Christians, but instead passive, technological slaves. To avoid this problem, the authors advocate a new form of religious education. In the ancient church, there had been a religious education by *initiation,* that is, learning from the example of an elite group of believers who were to be imitated. In the Middle Ages there had been a religious education by *immersion,* that is, learning through a social osmosis of belonging to the total environment of Christendom, a culture through which religious values were communicated to all. In the post-Renaissance period, religious education is by *indoctrination,* that is, learning by the memorizing of printed documents in a question-and-answer format.

Since 1977, McLuhan and Babin have been urging the creation of a new religious education. This new form employs kinetic imagery and amplified sound rather than silent, printed words. Babin argues that there is a need to abandon print communication for audiovisual communication, that is, to shuck the language of the printed text, for the language of sound-and-imagery. Religious education now is more concerned about the emotional impact of its pedagogy, and concomitantly less concerned about the precise cognitive formulations of its verbal statements. *Implicit in the positions of McLuhan and Babin is the notion that religious education should free itself from the bondage of theological imperialism and seek its own identity as a communicative process.*

McLuhan and Babin admit that a change from print culture to media culture is having a profound effect on the morality of this generation. They further believe that there is a contemporary need to integrate both the liturgy and the media. Such an integration can bring about a more modern, symbolic pedagogy. This symbiotic pedagogy has the power to affect both the mind and the heart of the learner.[76] Audiovisual media facilitate a *total* learning experience. Hence teaching/learning through the mass media is ideally suitable for contemporary religious education, which requires holistic communication if it is to succeed.

Bruce O'Donnell: The Use of Audiovisual Communication as a New Religious Language

Although certainly a minor author, Bruce O'Donnell nevertheless represents many religious educators who are aware that audiovisual communication is a new form of religious language.

For O'Donnell, most of the language of traditional theology is very stilted. It is too abstract to be appreciated by today's youth. Hence religious educators should substitute audiovisual media for printed texts whenever possible. According to O'Donnell, "co-expression" is the language of the new audiovisual media. The new electrical audiovisual media have a synergistic power. This power allows the media to take two forms of thought and coalesce them into a third form. This third form possesses a greater impact of meaning than either of its constituent parts by themselves. Synergistic co-expression is the unusual case of 2 + 2 = 5, or even more. Accordingly, media co-expression is inherently a religious language. Like religious language, media-co-expression has the power to convey a greater meaning than any of its constituent parts by themselves. When discussing religion, modern teachers must be able to translate the experience of Christianity into an audiovisual language. In the current media-environment, the faith becomes meaningful, or at least comprehensible, to modern learners only if it is communicated in audiovisual forms.[77]

Thomas Groome: Political Language and a Cognitive-Verbal Social Science Approach

Thomas Groome, a Catholic priest, employs an immanentist approach with a strong political bias in *Christian Religious Education*.[78] Groome claims his approach will successfully end the impasse between the immanentists and the transcendists about the modernization of current religious education. Groome utilizes a neo-Marxian variant of Hegelian synthesis which he asserts is able to join together modern education and the church's theological tradition. For Groome, both are vital constituents of an effective contemporary religious education. However, in the present writer's view, Groome seems excessively sanguine about uniting transcendists and immanentists. For example, Groome never quite succeeds in overcoming his own strong immanentistly flavored political bias. Like many other neo-Marxists, Groome perceives the audiovisual media as a powerful shaping force in society for keeping oppressive control in the hands of the elite. On the one hand, Groome's neo-Marxist political bias tends to prevent transcendists from accepting his view. On the other hand, his total reliance on verbalization and cognition as the primary constituents of religious education weakens his argument for other immanentists who view communication in a broader perspective.

Groome credits his own verbal dialogue with his learners for converting him from a proclamation-lecturer into a verbal dialogic communicator. For Groome, dialogic communication cannot be a mere "gab" session. Teachers and learners need a dialectic that sustains in the present both the past and the future, the individual and the community, aspiration and tradition.

In Groome's view, religious education stimulates "orthopraxis" (the doing of Christian deeds) and not simply orthodoxy (the correct knowledge of Christian doctrine).

Groome contends that if it is to be faithful to its own history, contemporary religious education must re-echo and retell the story of faith. The kerygma for Groome is not just a "message" about Christ and his kingdom. The kerygma is the making present of these truths in a contemporary educational experience. Here Groome links religious education with Karl Rahner's sacramental theology, where the church "makes present" the redeeming work of Christ.[79]

Groome asserts that in traditional religious education faith becomes synonymous with belief and then belief is reduced to intellectual assent to the officially stated doctrine. Consequently, in the Catholic tradition, faith is reduced to those statements which come down from the magisterium. (In a similar way, in the transcendist wing of the Protestant tradition, faith is reduced to those theological statements which can be directly biblically grounded.) Consequently, Groome argues, faith becomes an affair of the head, while the affective and the conduct dimensions of Christian belief are either overlooked or are made secondary in importance. Such a rationalistic faith increases the split between faith and daily life. Groome asserts that true religious education requires attention to the affective and to the behavioral. Groome's version of a social-science approach, however, despite this rhetoric, never frees itself from almost total dependence on verbal and cognitive contents. To be sure, Groome's position is extremely rationalistic and nonholistic and is quite different than James Michael Lee who integrates emotional and nonverbal contents into his version of a social-science approach.

Groome utilizes the Hegelian dialectic as his philosophical ground for the task of religious education. Christian *agape* must sustain a dialectical relationship between what is believed and what is done. Such a Hegelian synthesis between these two poles of human activity heals the dichotomy between either traditional faith (the transcendist agenda) or relevancy to the world (the immanentist agenda). Groome claims this dichotomy is the bane of modern religious education.

Groome claims that faith is both rational and passional. Hence the task of religious education is to unite what moderns believe with how they engage themselves in the world. Despite this statement, however, he never departs from his ultra-cognitive position. This is especially true in Groome's concrete enfleshment of his theory in his "shared-praxis" teaching method, a method which is extremely rationalistic.

Groome utilizes the primacy of political language more than modern communication theory in his argument. For Groome, a culture is embodied and expressed in a system of symbols, of which the most basic and most persuasive is verbal language. This view is similar to Neil Postman's about the socializing effect of human language.[80] Both argue that by appropriating these language-symbols, people come to know their world and to engage in it with the patterned behavior of their culture. By appropriating linguistic symbols, people become socialized into the group's ideology. This interaction between self and society does permit, in Groome's view, the possibility of still maintaining an individual identity.

The whole thrust of Groome's pedagogy is basically a political one, namely, to liberate persons by political means from the oppression under which they labor. Groome tends to be opposed to the audiovisual media, which he perceives as an instrument of oppression.

Placing himself in the humanist tradition, Groome (unlike the media-determinists) claims that the social/cultural context never completely conquers the individual. In fact, Groome asserts that an individual's self-identity possesses the power to alter the social/cultural context. Not only are moderns shaped by history, but moderns also possess the innate dynamism to shape history. However, he does accept McLuhan's view that the present media-matrix is a massive world environment for exerting social control on each individual.[81]

Groome cautions against too readily identifying Christian religious education with a socializing process. Socialization, after all, is domestication. A learner should be free to challenge the social/cultural determinants within the group, especially since historically Christianity has too often been used to legitimate sinful social structures. The major task of genuine religious education is to raise moderns' consciousness about the pervasive media-effect, especially when this media-effect denigrates Christian values and apotheosizes consumerism. Here Groome's thesis agrees with many modern communication theorists, especially the humanist ones.

In discussing religious education, Groome prefers the term "approach" because he thinks this term connotes a dialectic synthesis of *theoria* and *praxis*. These two Greek words mean, respectively, cognitive reflection and political activity. (It should be noted that Groome uses the term politics in its original Aristotelian sense, and not in the modern sense. Yet often in his book he uses the term politics in the contemporary sense. This confounding of terms leads to considerable confusion.) Groome's use of the key term "approach" thus differs markedly from the way in which this term is used by James Michael Lee, the person who originally used the word approach in treating of a global yet directed orientation to religion teaching.

Groome makes a vital distinction between a content approach to religious education and an experiential approach. The content approach is associated with traditional movements such as the kerygmatic approach to religious education. The experiential approach is exemplified by Pierre Babin and Marcel van Caster, two Europeans. Groome emphasizes that both the content approach and the experiential approach rest on solid biblical foundations. Consequently, the proponents of each approach ought not accuse the other side of abandoning the Christian tradition. For his part, Groome urges a dialectic synthesis of content and experience. (It should be noted that Gabriel Moran and James Michael Lee—especially Lee—reject the very distinction between content and experience which Groome takes for granted in erecting his Hegelian-based synthesis. Lee, for example, views experience as a content in and of itself.) Hegel provides Groome with the philosophical structure of the dialectic for the purported reconciliation of *theoria* and *praxis*. The Hegelian dialectic does not polarize *theoria* and *praxis* as Aristotle did.

In the view of the present writer, Thomas Groome does not even so much as address an especially potent difficulty in his religious education theory, namely, how his totally cognitive and wholly verbal teaching methodology can directly forge experiential religious education. (After all, experience is largely noncognitive and largely nonverbal.) Appeals to Hegel or to neo-Marxian Hegelians are not sufficient; concrete demonstration on Groome's part is required.

Groome places heavy reliance for the validity of his theory on the work of Jürgen Habermas, a brilliant German neo-Marxist social scientist and active political Communist. Groome especially utilizes Habermas's theory of hermeneutic, an approach to interpretation which is geared toward maintaining in one synthesized reality both communal consciousness and intersubjective communication.[82] Groome's heavy reliance on Habermas is also shown by his adoption of Habermas's position on "communicative competence." In Groome's view, "communicative competence" is essential in religious education because it connotes a working understanding of both past tradition and present circumstances.

Groome examines the modern equivalent of the Greek term *technē*. Through the political lenses which form his theoretical orientation, Groome sees *technē* as the manipulative power to critique and unmask all forms of social control which dictate communication. This manipulative control is exercised primarily by repressing genuine dialogue. Groome's interpretation of *technē* is somewhat related to, though by no means identical with, Walter Ong's view that dialogue has the power to weaken absolute social control. Groome asserts that the modern Christian must be able to critique and unmask the entire oppressive symbol-system of present reality and not merely the economic system as Karl Marx urged.

Groome develops a teaching methodology which he calls

"shared praxis" to place the entire instructional process on a critique-and-unmask basis. He believes that his "shared praxis" methodology is a new and unique form of teaching. Actually, however, his "shared praxis" is a variation of the general action-reflection method which has been in widespread use in general education for years. Indeed, when viewed from the perspective of the lesson itself, "shared praxis" is actually a reflection-reflection mode of the action-reflection procedure, thus underscoring the total cognitive base and thrust of Groome's "shared praxis" way of teaching.

"Shared praxis" methodology includes the following steps in pedagogical enactment: (1) present action; (2) critical reflection; (3) actual verbal dialogue; (4) linkage of the present with the Christian story (i.e., shared past traditions); (5) linkage of the present with the Christian vision (shared future aspirations).

Groome takes pains to emphasize that true dialogue cannot consist in simply discussing abstract ideas. True dialogue demands a revelation, at least to some extent, of each participant's own personal faith-story. Such a deep sharing demands faith, humility, hope, and critical thinking. Such a dialogical sharing will lead the participants to a deeper dialogue with (or prayer to) God. Prayer is the dialogic dimension in humanity's relationship with God and with Jesus. Without dialogue, Groome adds, citing Ong, no relationship can survive.[83]

It should be underscored that there is no valid or reliable empirical evidence which supports the efficacy of Groome's "shared praxis" teaching device. Thus there is no way of knowing adequately whether Groome's variation of the action-reflection method actually does what he claims it does. All we have now are empirically unsupported claims.

Some might argue that Groome's "shared praxis" teaching technique is actually a variation of the familiar discursive action-reflection method developed centuries ago by Ignatius of Loyola, the founder of the Jesuits.[84] But in Groome's case the pedagogical method actually becomes one of reflection-reflection, as noted above. In Groome's "shared praxis," the action part of action-reflection is done prior to, outside of, the lesson. It should also be emphasized that this "shared praxis" method is fundamentally a political vehicle born of neo-Marxism and inserted full-blooded into Christian religious education. Through a rather structured and prescribed set of verbal and cognitive activities (his five sequential steps), the learner is supposed to be empowered to unmask oppressive and manipulative forces wherever such forces might be at work. Groome believes that through these cognitive/verbal unmasking activities the learner will be thereby enabled to pursue the life task of bringing God's kingdom (regarded as a political reality) into concrete daily life.

Despite his rhetoric to the contrary, Groome's method remains verbal and cognitive, with little that is either immediately or holistically experiential. This very heavy verbal and cognitive emphasis is a natural outgrowth of Groome's strong dependency on the hypercognitive neo-Marxian Frankfurt School of Critical Theory for the spirit and motor of his theory. Indeed, the aim of Groome's theory of religious education is cognitive awareness. In apparent disdain for the findings of psychology on the weak correlation between cognitive and lifestyle domains of human existence (to say nothing of the outright rejection by almost all philosophers of the hypothesis that knowledge directly produces conduct), Groome makes the centerpiece and axis of his theory the contention that cognition enacted through verbal dialogue will directly enable learners to unmask present oppressive forces and bring about liberation from those forces. In other words, Groome contends that "shared praxis" will directly bring the kingdom of God to earth. Persons reading Thomas Groome are left to wonder: Why is his method so totally verbal? (It must be remembered that unlike most educationists and religious educationists, Groome equates his entire theory with only one solitary teaching method, namely "shared praxis.") If faith is both rational and passional as Groome claims it is, then why is his pedagogical method so completely rational? For Groome, faith is the key; there is little or no discussion by Groome of hope or charity. Of importance in assessing Groome's theory is his identification of faith with politics. Because religious education enables the living out of faith, religious education therefore is necessarily a political activity. Though Gabriel Moran was one of the first Christian religious educationists to write about the politics of religious education, Groome puts politics center stage. Indeed one can fairly say that for Groome politics not only occupies center stage in religious education—it *is* center stage.

Groome cites one of his heroes, Paulo Freire, in asserting that the teacher's activity should be "with" and not "over" people.[85] In this way the students can name their world and through cognitive verbal dialogue freely choose to act creatively on their own personal historical reality. (As a heavy cognitivist, Groome believes that naming one's world is in very large measure creating the here-and-now reality of one's world.) In Groome's eyes, traditional religious education isolates theology from the common people. Echoing James Michael Lee's notion of traditional religious education as a messenger boy for theology, Groome also asserts, though for different reasons than Lee, that traditional religious education regards teaching as a delivery system. This delivery system banks information into passive, empty receptacles. (The banking metaphor is frequently used by Freire.) Groome rejects the proclamation model of traditional religious education because this model simultaneously isolates theology from education and makes theology superior to education. Groome conceptualizes his "shared praxis" method of teaching as engaging theology and education as co-equals in a mutual interactive dialogue. In this dialogue *theoria* and *praxis* maintain a dialectical unity. Groome argues that his "shared praxis" method of teaching requires an ability to participate consciously in group dialogue. Groome's argument about the dialectic between theology and education bears some semblance with Harold Innis's Hegelian synthesis of media-biases in government and religion (see chapter 2). There are also some points of contact between Groome's dialectic between theology and education and James Michael Lee's view of the interaction of theology and education. (Indeed, it is not outside the realm of possibility that Groome borrowed, without citation, some of the general features of Lee's thesis on this matter.) Curiously Lee presses the dialectic between subject-matter content (including theology) and the educational dynamic much further than Groome, even though Lee, unlike Groome, is not a Hegelian in any sense of the term. Lee's view of the dialectic is that in the concrete here-and-now enactment of the lesson itself, religion (including theology as appropriate) interacts with teaching methodology to produce a genuinely new synthesis (Hegelian construct) which results in a fundamentally new reality, namely religious education. Groome also regards theology as the subject-matter content of religious education. Lee, on the other hand, regards lived religion as the subject-matter content, with theology playing a role in this subject-matter content as appropriate. The differential importance accorded to theology by Groome and Lee nicely reflects their respective regard for cognition. Because cognition is wholly cognitive, Groome naturally makes it primary. Because lived religion is holistic and lifestyle in character, it is natural for Lee to place primacy there.

As political unmaskers and as political makers of a new world, learners have the right to speak their own word and name their own reality in the religion lesson, asserts Groome. Teachers have the right to speak their own word too, avers Groome. However, teachers have a concomitant obligation to hear their students' word as well.

In Groome's view, Christian religion education must represent Jesus Christ in service to the community through a political-immanentist ministry of the word. Groome insists that the current task of religious education requires an ongoing synthesis between the orientation of conservation and the orientation of liberation.[86] In this way Groome is struggling admirably to unite the two main orientations in modern Christianity. Notwithstanding, many transcendists are rejecting Groome's theory because it is so heavily immanentistic. For their part, some immanentists reject Groome's position because of its stark reductionism, as for example his reduction of all religious education to politics and his reduction of all religious education to the verbal and the cognitive.

James Michael Lee: McLuhanism and Process Content in Religious Education
Among immanentist religious educationists, James Michael Lee stands out as the most explicit about integrating modern communication theory with the actual concrete activity of religion teaching. Indeed, McLuhanism comprises an integral com-

ponent of Lee's social-science approach to religious instruction. Marshall McLuhan's landmark book *Understanding Media*[87] is explicitly cited by Lee in all three books in his monumental trilogy on religious instruction: *The Shape of Religious Instruction*,[88] *The Flow of Religious Instruction*,[89] and *The Content of Religious Instruction*.[90]

Lee integrates McLuhan's analysis of the communicative act into his paradigm of the religious instruction act. The entire thrust of McLuhan's celebrated thesis that the medium is the message is creatively utilized by Lee to mean that the teaching act (the medium) is itself an autonomous content (a message). In his highly sophisticated macrotheory, Lee states that what is learned in the religion lesson (the total content) is actually made up of two discrete major contents each of which forms a fundamental dimension of the overall content. The first of these two molar contents is what is taught (religion), which Lee terms substantive content. The second of these two molar contents is how the substantive content is taught (the teaching process itself). Lee calls this teaching process structural content. By using the term structural content to describe the teaching process, Lee emphasizes that the medium is a genuine message (content) in its own right, rather than simply a way in which content is taught. Lee states that structural content and substantive content so interact with each other that from this dynamic interaction a new reality is born, namely the religious instruction act considered as a whole. Like McLuhan, Lee forcefully argues that the way we do things (medium, or structural content) necessarily constitutes a major and inextricable dimension of our human activity. McLuhan trenchantly remarks that most people are unaware that the medium is indeed a reality in itself.

Lee insists that though structural content (medium) and substantive content are distinct from one another, they are always united in the religious instruction act. Lee contends that any separation of these two molar contents *as they occur in the here-and-now religious act itself* is not an existential separation but only a logical separation made for purposes of analysis. Lee complains that most religious education theorists down through the centuries falsely separate instructional practice

Communication and the Teaching Act 145

(structural content) and message (substantive content) as though these were two separate entities in the religious instruction act. Such a false separation prevents educators from realizing that the message is not only substantive content but is structural content as well. Indeed, religious educationists who do separate instructional practice from content typically make instructional practice a "messenger boy" or a "translator," to use Lee's own graphic language. Thus Lee's conceptualization of structural content underscores his close parallelism to McLuhanism.

In advancing his highly sophisticated and well-integrated macrotheory of religious instruction, Lee specifically utilizes McLuhan's example of the switched-on light bulb. Indeed, a switched-on light bulb represents as pure process as one can find. Yet even the switched-on light bulb, Lee reminds us, cannot function without being totally tied in with the substantive contents of a filament and a vacuum. In a parallel fashion, Lee insists that there is never a religion teaching act in which substantive and structural content remain ontically separate.[91]

McLuhan's splendid example affords James Michael Lee with an opportunity of illustrating not only that structural content (the teaching act itself) is the medium, but that an inextricable dimension of substantive content is also a kind of medium. After empirical examination of the here-and-now teaching act itself, Lee discovered that there were nine molar forms of substantive content which necessarily occur in every teaching-learning act. One of these molar ever-present substantive contents is process content. Lee defines process content as "the actual moving progressively from one point to another on the road to completion." Thus process content is all substantive content *in via,* a *realite en marche,* as Lee would say. Thus process content is contrasted to its contrary, namely product content. To illustrate his point, Lee gives the example of two times two equal four. The *getting* of the four is process content, while the four which is gotten by arithmetical calculation is the product content. Thus process content (which Lee states is usually more important than product content) is the medium through which all substantive content flows. To use McLuhan's example again, the actual positioning of the light bulb, the structuring of its interior and exterior elements, and turning it on, are illustrations of structural content. The flow of electricity and the interaction of the electricity with filament and vacuum is the substantive process content.

Because substantive content and structural content are necessary complementary forces in the teaching-learning dynamic, each interacts with the other in a kind of shaping manner. McLuhan explores this mutual shaping in depth, and indeed it pervades his entire communication theory. Consequently modern communication theory is integral to Lee's entire way of interpreting religious education. McLuhan's masterful analysis of the effect which the linear process inherent in Gutenberg typeset has exerted on all print cultures plays an important and explicit role in Lee's macrotheory of religion teaching. In its own way, McLuhanism clearly suggests that for religious instruction, as for all other kinds of teaching in both formal and informal settings, there is a basically new role for the teacher, a fundamentally new kind of participation on the part of the student in terms of how this individual pursues learning, and a basic switch from the emphasis on the rational (and ratiocinative) mind to the largely noncognitive and heavily lifestyle-oriented religious way of looking at reality. These three revolutionary basic elements in McLuhanism are major and pivotal elements in Lee's social-science approach.

Lee bids religious educators to heed Marshall McLuhan's seminal distinction between hot and cool media and their powerful effect on audiovisual media of every sort. He reminds religious educators that both the structural content and the substantive process content inherent in media (whether hot or cold) inextricably interacts and shapes the product content so as to make some radio or television or pictorial lessons effective and others ineffective.[92] Religious educators are frequently heard to complain that audiovisual media are often pedagogically ineffective. But the failure lies not in the media but in the fact that they are not discriminatingly used. For example, audiovisual media will always be a failure when television (cool medium) is used to teach linear theology (hot medium). Despite what some theologically oriented religious educators might contend, theology by its very nature is linear.

In Lee's view, a successful religious educator is one who can bring about an efficacious meshing of substantive content with structural content, on the one hand, and of substantive process content and other molar kinds of substantive content, on the other hand. McLuhan describes this interaction in the following manner: A painter learns how to adjust relations among things to release a new perception. A chemist learns how relations among things actually release other kinds of power. In Lee's holistic view, the religious educator is one who deliberatively works to release the total power of an active faith-hope-charity in each learner and in the community of learners.[93]

Lee contends that the prime goal of all teaching is to render learning holistic, namely that learning not remain "inside" the individual but that it be extended so that learning envelops the total individual "inner" and "outer." (It should be noted that Lee vehemently rejects any dualistic or radical separateness between the so-called "inner" person and that individual's "outer" conduct. For Lee, the person is an integer essentially and operationally.) Lee's holistic view of the learning process parallels (though is not dependent upon) McLuhan's concept that all human language represents an outering of the person's less manifest cognitive and affective dynamisms.[94]

From what has been said thus far about James Michael Lee's social-science approach, it is palpably evident that he believes that effective communication is one of the two most fundamentally important capabilities of every religious educator. To be sure, the central importance of effective communication is one of the most critical issues which divides the transcendists and the immanentists. Transcendists regard God as somehow supplying the communication (though it should be noted that many Protestant Evangelical curriculum committees and preachers who are the most ardent proponents of transcendism are the very same persons who utilize modern communication methods the most ardently and pervasively). Immanentists believe that while the power of God pervades all reality, nevertheless the teacher's here-and-now communication is of absolute and indispensable importance. Supporters of James Michael Lee also accept the need for modern communication theory and practice to be inextricably integrated into religious education. Those who do not accept the necessity for such integration reject Lee's social-science approach.

Basic to Lee's social-science approach is that religion teaching is just what its descriptive name implies, namely, the *teaching* of religion. Lee did not come to this position ideologically or in an *a priori* way; rather he carefully examined the religion teaching act itself and found the obvious, namely that teaching is communication. (It is indeed hard to imagine that teaching is not co-essentially communication, but this is precisely what theologically oriented religious educationists claim.) In short, for Lee, awareness and skill are the two principal components in determining the effectiveness or ineffectiveness of teaching. The teacher who is aware of what is communicatively taking place in the here-and-now pedagogical dynamic, *and* who operationalizes this awareness into concrete instructional practices designed to bring about effective communication, will be the successful religion teacher. Conversely, a religious educator who lacks either this kind of communicative awareness *or* the operationizing of this awareness into concrete pedagogical procedures will not be a successful teacher.

The transcendist view postulates that religious education is merely a messenger boy whose task it is to deliver the theological message (kind of product content) to the learners as intact as possible. For the immanentist, on the other hand, the religious educator must necessarily be a skilled communicator who is consciously aware of all the pertinent dynamics occurring in the here-and-now communication act.

It is clear and evident, then, that Lee regards the teaching/learning dynamic as co-essentially an act of communication. For Lee, teaching religion is preeminently an art-science, namely, the art of skillful communication based on the science of communication. Lee illustrates this point by describing a teacher as a person who, like all artists in every field ranging from painters to violinists, play and experiment with new means and innovative modes of arranging experiences. Lee links his position with McLuhan's call for each teacher to make a conscious choice to create a kind of anti-environment, as it were, in order to produce a new consciousness in the learner of how process actually works.[95]

In Lee's view, the teacher must be willing to abdicate total control over the lesson and share both power and authority with the learners. Many contemporary religion lessons are teacher-centered. Indeed even charismatic religion teachers—and especially charismatic religion teachers—are teacher-centered to a strong degree. Charismatic religion teachers are hot media. As such they dominate the lesson and elicit little high-level or authentic participation on the part of the learners. In this type of lesson, the learners become more like a passive audience at an attractive show. They become less responsible, participate less, and have less mutual responsibility with the teacher for the success of the lesson.[96] Even charismatic teachers can be locked into a print mentality. Lee likens such teachers to McLuhan's famous example of those staff generals in the army who are magnificently prepared to fight the previous war.[97] Both Catholic and Protestant communions have an army of religious educators prepared magnificently to fight for or against the Reformation.

Lee believes that learner participation and learner initiation will enable students to approach religious instruction activity with more zest and more heart. Like McLuhan, he adduces the celebrated Hawthorne experiment to support his position. The Hawthorne study found that when individuals are permitted to express their own energies in the process of learning and decision making, the resultant efficiency of activity is phenomenal.[98] Lee insists that the same holds true in religious education.

McLuhan regards verbal language as an extension of a human faculty. Much as the wheel extends the human foot, so language extends the human mind. Thus verbal language and cognition are intimately and inextricably connected, a point made over and over again by James Michael Lee. As one European scholar notes, every word is a linguistic symbol and all cognition can be described as thinking in symbols.[99] Much as the wheel enables the body to move from thing to thing with every greater ease and speed and with *ever less personal involvement,* so too does verbal language extend cognition with greater ease and speed and ever less personal involvement.[100] Although ideal for theological discourse (which is almost totally cognitive and scientific), verbal print language is not nearly as appropriate for teaching religion.

Lee adduces physiological research to conclude that religion appeals to the right side of the brain, the seat of creation and intuition. Verbal language and cognition and print appeal to the left side of the brain, the seat of ratiocination and logic.[101] Both Marshall McLuhan and Pierre Babin, for their part, observe that audiovisual media appeal primarily to the right side of the brain.[102] Once again, from yet another vantage point, one can rightfully conclude that audiovisual communication is more appropriate than print communication for the task of religion teaching.

In summary, James Michael Lee utilizes modern communication theory as a key component of his social-science approach to religious instruction. Lee's social-science approach is characterized by: (1) a recognition that religious instruction is a form of communication; (2) an acknowledgment of the holism of both communication and religion, with a concomitant acknowledgment that cognitive-verbal theology is frequently a necessary resource in the task of teaching religion; (3) a refusal to let theology control religious instruction; (4) a keen awareness that nonverbal, affective, and conduct-centered communication are most efficacious in teaching a Christian lifestyle.

Through his books, scholarly articles, and lectures around the world, James Michael Lee is striving to introduce the social-science approach into religious education. This is a very difficult task since most contemporary religious educationists and educators, both Protestant and Catholic, are only familiar with the language of theology. Lee frequently expresses his keen disappointment at those religious educationists and educators who approach the field from an *a priori* standpoint (theology) instead of examining how religion teaching and learning actually take place. Lee sometimes employs very forthright and candid language to jog the preconceptions of religious educators free from their *a priori* ideologies, and to show the ridiculousness of many of their positions.

Summary: The Religious Education Approach and Modern Communication Theory

The more progressive immanentist religious educationists see religion teaching as primarily an educational enterprise rather than as theological activity *per se*. Although some of the leading exponents of the religious education approach are ordained clergy or professed religious, the lay voice predominates.

Of all the approaches discussed in this chapter, surely the religious education approach is the one most open to the insights and consequences of modern communication theory. The Protestant religious educationist George Albert Coe stands as the first major theorist to be genuinely aware of religious education as an instructional enterprise responsible for the socialization of learners. Among the Catholics, the first major religious educationist chronologically in this century has been Gabriel Moran. Though at first Moran espoused catechetics (the officially sanctioned and theologically controlled form of Catholic religious instruction), he reversed himself completely in 1970 and announced that henceforward catechetics could no longer be the true task of religious education, even in the Catholic church. For Moran, the true task in the contemporary Catholic church is the same as it is in other Christian churches, namely, religious education in all its breadth. Such a religious education is one which strives to enhance the personal freedom of the learners. Moran grounds his contention in his notion of revelation as quintessentially the continuing act of communication between God and humanity. For Moran, the religious educator continues this communicative act in all its pristine freedom.

Though surely a minor player on the landscape of religious education interpretation, Charles Cook demonstrates that workaday religious educators are engaged, in their own way, in synthesizing modern communication theory and revelation-as-communication to build a new view of religious education. In the work of communication theorists Marshall McLuhan and Pierre Babin one can readily discern that McLuhanism and the religious education approach are natural allies. Bruce O'Donnell, an interesting though minor author, links audiovisual communication with religious language, asserting that both possess the power to appeal to humanity's desire for attaining the transcendently spiritual, a state beyond the run-of-the-mill human experience.

Thomas Groome, the neo-Marxist religious education theorist, strives mightily to unite transcendism and immanentism in religious education. But he fails to realize how ontically and operationally deep is the gulf between transcendism and immanentism. His political approach to religious education seeks to reunite theory and practice through praxis. Although Groome frequently alludes to the great value of existential dialogue (sharing of selves in a group) and emotional sensitivity, his theoretical approach and most especially his concrete "shared praxis" methodology never frees itself from the tight bondage of cognition and verbal language. Groome is too committed to his political ideology to recognize what modern communication theory has to offer religious education.

James Michael Lee stands out as the clearest exponent among the immanentist theorists that communication theory, especially McLuhanism, provides one of the major clues as to why traditional religious education has failed so much and so often. Lee is wholeheartedly in tune with McLuhan's central position that the process by which people communicate is an essential component in the overall message of what is communicated. When religious educators fail to realize that the medium is indeed the message, they get lost in replicating (or when creative, in adjusting) print formats that no longer possess optimum power to communicate with contemporary learners. Lee's social-science approach to religious education is clearly parallel to McLuhan's point that controlled discovery learning is the most effective way to teach the modern media-generation.

Theorists who espouse the religious education approach tend to be the most likely to accept modern communication theory and utilize it in the actual activity of teaching religion.

INTEGRATIONISM AND MODERN COMMUNICATION THEORY

To the classic polarities of transcendism and immanentism, Ian Knox creates a third position, namely integrationism. In Knox's view, integrationism is an attempt to synthesize transcendism and immanentism into a third position which reconciles both into a new entity. This new entity incorporates the main advantages and insights of both positions.

It is not altogether clear that Knox, in his important book *Above or Within?*, is really successful in doing what no other religious educationist or theologian has ever done, namely, to integrate immanentism and transcendism in a satisfactory manner. An example of this will serve to suffice. Knox places Randolph Crump Miller, a Protestant, and Marcel van Caster, a Catholic, among the integrationist religious educators. Knox believes that both of these highly influential religious educationists are integrationists. Yet Knox does admit that both exhibit a transcendist orientation, albeit modified, in their work. What is central in the work of both of these scholars is pastoral sensitivity. Yet modern communication theory does not seem to be important to these educationists. Thus one can conclude that with these two examples, at least, Knox does not succeed in demonstrating the validity of a separate integrationist position.

Perhaps a third integrationist position does exist. At any rate, it might be helpful to examine Miller and van Caster.

Randolph Crump Miller: Relational Theology in Process

To use a famous phrase of his own coining, Randolph Crump Miller regards theology as the clue to religious education. Miller does not perceive theology so much as a speculative discipline. Rather, Miller considers theology as the-truth-about-God-in-relationship-to-humanity. He believes theology is concerned with the God/humanity relationship, both as that relationship is revealed in the Bible and as it is incarnated in life situations. A favorite phrase of Miller is that theology must be relevant to the human situation. Relevant theology, as perceived by Miller, allows us to discover God at work in history, in our own generation, and especially in our daily relationships.

Miller appears to be striving to achieve, according to Ian Knox, some sort of equilibrium between the strong and opposing biases of immanentism and transcendism. Miller is searching for a symbiosis between an emphasis on the supernatural, transcendent God who reveals himself and personally confronts each of us, and an emphasis on humanity, which is both divinely confronted and summoned to respond in faith. Miller appears committed to a neo-orthodox Protestant emphasis on a special revelation to Christian believers. At the same time,

Miller also wishes to give credence to the insights of science (particularly that of interpersonal and developmental psychology) and to relate these disciplines to biblical revelation. Miller perceives the God/humanity relationship in a vertical Person-to-person perspective. Yet Miller also emphasizes that this relationship only takes place in the horizontal context of person-to-person relationships. The God-in-relation-to-humanity is a constant theme in Miller's writings. For Miller, the transcendent Other (God) who graciously reveals himself in his mighty acts in history is also the same God who is intimately involved with our own very personal and human development.[103]

Miller does not address the issue of modern communication theory. However, he does not consider formal propositional theological language the most effective means for awakening the concept of the transcendent in learners. For Miller, literature is possibly the most effective language for this task of teaching/learning the reality of the transcendent in human experience.[104] Miller does not address the issue that most young learners actually come in contact with literature through audiovisual entertainment.

Marcel van Caster: A Catechetical Synthesis in the Catholic Tradition

Marcel van Caster, the Belgian Jesuit associated with the catechetical periodical *Lumen Vitae,* is another integrationist. Van Caster has exercised a profound influence on Catholic religious educators the world over through his teaching in Brussels at the International Center for the Studies of Religious Education and through his numerous books and articles. In his earlier works,[105] van Caster followed the kerygmatic pattern of religious education and emphasized the proclamatory teacher-centered transmission of the unique message of revelation. The theological perspective in this type of religious education (which was very popular in Roman Catholic circles in the two decades prior to Vatican II) is focused on the supremely transcendent God who speaks his word to humanity in Jesus his Son, the divine savior.[106] In his subsequent writings, especially after Vatican II, van Caster proposes a new type of religious education synthesis. This synthesis aims at uniting (1) a type of religious education that has its theological emphasis on the spoken revelation of the transcendent God, and (2) a religious education that has its emphasis on human experience.[107]

Van Caster wrote an important series of articles in *Lumen Vitae* from 1968 to 1974. In these articles, van Caster concerns himself with the unity that he claims exists (1) between an emphasis on union with God and an emphasis on human autonomy, (2) between an emphasis on faith in Christ, and an emphasis on commitment to the world, and (3) an emphasis on human values and an emphasis on the content of the gospel. According to Ian Knox, van Caster maintains that this dynamic unity is brought about by a Hegelian thesis-antithesis-synthesis process. Van Caster's own tendency in this dialectical process is to prefer to emphasize the personal "vertical" relationship with God as an important factor in "supernaturalizing" worldly values. Thus, van Caster holds for a sharply delineated distinction between the natural and the supernatural realms. He conceptualizes the supernatural as giving meaning and significance to the natural. On the other hand, he also emphasizes God's immanence in the natural process. He does this to such a great extent, that Ian Knox is unable to facilely place him among the transcendists. Van Caster, like Randolph Crump Miller, does not discuss modern communication theory. His synthesis appears to be an attempt to unify print-biased theological reflection with contemporary human experience. He does not address the issue that the global mass media are the most powerful constituent of contemporary human experience.

On a personal note, the present writer was required in the late 1960s to utilize van Caster's methodology in a religious education program designed for American high-school students. It was the obvious inability of this teaching methodology to produce an effective pedagogy that led the writer to research alternative ways to teach/learn religion. Despite his writings on experiential learning, van Caster remains totally committed to cognition and verbal language in his method of religious education. Visitors to the International Center find van Caster a constant lecturer, not a listener.

Summary: The Integrationists and Modern Communication

Representative educationists among the integrationists include Randolph Crump Miller, a Protestant, and Marcel van Caster, a Catholic. Both have exerted a considerable influence among contemporary religious educators because of their teaching posts and their prolific writings. Miller utilizes print literature as a tool for encouraging a contemporary theological approach to religious education. Van Caster holds that the task of religious education is to unite each learner with salvation history. Intersubjective experiential metaphysics is the philosophical ground for van Caster's approach. In this approach little if any attention is paid to modern communication. For the present author, both Miller and van Caster are too locked into cognition and verbal language as the principal teaching procedures for religious education. They can perceive the printed text as forming vehicles for awakening awareness of the transcendent but cannot recognize that audiovisual forms are much more effective at doing this with contemporary learners.

Conclusion

Principal religious educationists propose four major approaches for the act of teaching: (1) the transcendist, (2) the immanentist-contemporary theological, (3) the immanentist-educational, and (4) the integrationist.

In varying degrees, modern communication theory influences each of these four approaches. Transcendist religious educators steadfastly refuse to accept modern communication theory's imperative to leave behind the product-content orientation of the print culture. Some of these traditional religious education theorists believe that modern media are a universal impediment to the learning of Judeo-Christian values. Others among them believe that it is essential for traditional religious educators to employ the global audiovisual media as a powerful handmaiden in the preaching task of the church.

The immanentist-theological religious educators are more receptive to modern communication theory. They insist, however, that modern communication cannot be allowed to strongly influence or alter the cognitive substantive context of contemporary theology. Yet, paradoxically, some of these representative authors perceive modern communication theory as a strong stimulus for updating theology and traditional Christian humanism. These educators strive to sustain print-based theology within audiovisual forms.

The immanentist-educational religious educators are those theorists who are the most willing to integrate modern communication theory into the teaching act. For these theorists, modern communication theory refutes the alleged duality between content and method, whether that content be regarded as theology or as religion. In this view, educational practice is itself a content, a true content in its own right. These religious educators contend that if it is to be effective then religious education must move away from its historically exclusive reliance on print media and move to a wider and more expansive utilization of all the media available, especially audiovisual media and tactile media. These theorists assert that only a pedagogy grounded in an audiovisual methodology is capable of educating contemporary learners. For them, an exclusive reliance on cognition and verbal language (the essence of the print culture) means that no holistic teaching or learning takes place, because such a method does not educate the whole person.

Integrationist religious educators show no interest in modern communication theory. Contemporary language studies are more applicable to their agenda. Integrationist theorists focus on personal intersubjective communication. Integrationists hold that such a pedagogical method facilitates a receptivity among learners to divine-revelation-as-communication. According to these theorists, language enables each learner to discover his or her own place in the dynamic of salvation history. For integrationists, this discovery is more significant for authentic religious education than any audiovisual experience. Integrationists have yet to break away from lecturing, discussion, and other cognitive linguistic techniques as their principal methodologies for religious education. They *speak* a great deal about experience; they do not recognize the global audiovisual matrix as *the* most significant human experience in the lives of young learners.

This present volume argues that the immanentist-educational approach is the most effective for the act of religion teaching. This is not a matter of opinion or preference. This view is grounded on the empirical evidence of how teaching/learning takes place in religious education.[108]

The present generation of learners, no matter where they live in the modern world, constitute a media-subculture. Audiovisual imaged and amplified sound—especially contemporary music—are the most effective media for communicating with this subculture. Religious educators have only to ponder the vast sums of money that international corporations assign to audiovisual advertising to appreciate how much secular society values the media as the most effective means for altering people's lifestyles.[109] If the goal of religious education is to produce active Christians who live a Christian lifestyle, then the most appropriate means for accomplishing this goal is audiovisual communication, when it is coupled with a pedagogy of media-literacy. If the goal of religious education is merely to produce reflective critical thinkers, then cognitive verbal communication is a very effective means for accomplishing that goal.

Since the theme of this present book is that religious education is a form of communication and that the basic task of religious education is to achieve a Christian lifestyle, the remainder of the book will explore practical procedures for accomplishing this aim.

Notes

1. Quoted in Marshall McLuhan, *The Gutenberg Galaxy: The Making of Typographical Man* (Toronto: University of Toronto Press, 1962), p. 186.

2. Ian P. Knox, *Above or Within: The Supernatural in Religious Education* (Birmingham, Ala.: Religious Education Press, 1976), pp. 4-5. Knox describes the transcendist position as emphasizing the supernatural as above human nature, pp. 55-75 (Cf. Harold William Burgess, *An Invitation to Religious Education* (Birmingham, Ala.: Religious Education Press, 1975), pp. 21-51); the immanentist position as emphasizing the supernatural within human nature, pp. 80-107 (Cf. Burgess, *An Invitation to Religious Education,* pp. 94-121 and then 59-87); and the integrationist position as striving to keep both metaperspectives in equilibrium, pp. 115-144. Although Knox places James Michael Lee in the immanentist tradition, a strong and pervasive case

could be made that the social-science approach enunciated by Lee is actually an integrationist position. In *The Content of Religious Instruction* (Birmingham, Ala.: Religious Education Press, 1985), Lee emphasizes product content as a constitutive element of the content of religious instruction. Lee also notes that the only true way to maintain a conceptualization of the transcendence of God is through immanentist-inspired teaching practices. See Lee, *The Content of Religious Instruction,* pp. 62-63. Lee, however, places himself in the immanentist camp, because he states that the integrationist position does not exist, see *Content,* pp. 713-714, n. 137.

3. Seminal texts articulating the transcendist critique of modern communication are Malcolm Muggeridge, *Christ and the Media* (Grand Rapids, Mich.: Eerdmans, 1978); James Hitchcock, "The Culture Crunch," *The Catechist* 6, no. 4 (January, 1973), pp. 7-9, 15; and George Kelly, *The Battle for the American Church* (Garden City, N.Y.: Doubleday, 1977).

4. William J. Fritts, "The McLuhan Thesis and Its Relationship to Contemporary Christian Apologetics" (Dissertation, Southwestern Baptist Theological Seminary, 1972).

5. Seminal texts articulating the immanentist-contemporary theological position include: Allen Maruyama, "A Theological Critique of Marshall McLuhan's New Man of the Electric Age," (Dissertation Aquinas Institute of Philosophy and Theology, Dubuque, Iowa, 1972), Abstract, pp. 1-6; John XXIII, "The Opening Address of the Second Vatican Council," in *Teachings of the Second Vatican Council: Complete Texts of the Constitutions, Decrees and Declarations* (Westminster, Md.: The Newman Press, 1966), p. 7; "The Church in the Modern World," in the *Documents of Vatican II,* ed. Walter Abbott (New York: American Press, Association Press, Guild Press, 1966), p. 209-215; The Pontifical Commission for the Means of Social Communication, *Pastoral Instruction for the Application of the Decree of the Second Vatican Council on the Means of Social Communication* (Washington, D.C.: U.S. Catholic Conference, 1971); Walter J. Ong, *The Presence of the Word* (New Haven, Conn: Yale University Press, 1967); Carl J. Pfeiffer, "The Church as Multi-Media", *Religion Teacher Journal* 11, no. 3 (April, 1977), pp. 20-22; and finally, Gabriel Moran, *The Catechesis of Revelation* (New York: Herder and Herder, 1966).

6. Seminal texts articulating the immanentist-religious educational approach include George Albert Coe, *A Social Theory of Religious Education* (New York: Scribner's, 1971); Bruce O'Donnell, "Language in Catechetics," *Religious Education* 69, no. 5 (September/October, 1974), pp. 542-557; Gabriel Moran, "Catechetics, R.I.P.," *Commonweal* 93 (December 18, 1970), pp. 299-302; Charles Cook, *Media in Catechesis* (Attleboro, Mass: Marx IV Presentations, 1974); Marshall McLuhan and Pierre Babin, *Autre Homme, Autre Cretien a L'Age Electronique* (Lyons: Chalet, 1977); Pierre Babin, *Le Temps de la*

Communication (Paris: Editions du Centurion, 1985); and Lee, *The Content of Religious Instruction,* pp. 78-128.

7. Knox, *Above or Within?,* pp. 123-126.

8. A stirring fictional account of the John Scopes trial can be found in the play *Inherit the Wind,* by Jerome Lawrence and Robert E. Lee (New York: Bantam, 1969).

9. Marshall McLuhan, "Inside Blake and Hollywood," *Sewanee Review* 55 (October, 1947), pp. 710-715.

10. Muggeridge, *Christ and the Media,* pp. 98, 68.

11. Quoted in ibid., p. 46.

12. For Muggeridge's claim that audiovisual media substitute fantasy for reality, see Muggeridge, *Christ and the Media,* pp. 24, 45, 46.

13. For Muggeridge's claim that audiovisual media reinforce the demonic self-image which is inherently false, see Muggeridge, *Christ and the Media,* pp. 47-48.

14. For a positive approach to eros as a vehicle for Christian love, see Lee, *The Content of Religious Instruction,* pp. 229-244.

15. For Muggeridge's claim that audiovisual media stimulate immoral behavior, see Muggeridge, *Christ and the Media,* pp. 28, 30, 52, 55, and 64.

16. Hitchcock, "The Culture Crunch," pp. 7-9, 15.

17. For an explanation of James Hitchcock's transcendist critique of Chardinian optimism, and, by extension, of modern communication theory, see James Hitchcock, *The Decline and Fall of Radical Catholicism* (New York: Herder and Herder, 1971).

18. Vatican I focused on the papacy as the primary Catholic office for the magisterium, or official teaching authority of the church. Vatican II focused on the bishops in communion with the pope as an essential component of the teaching magisterium. See "The Church in the Modern World," in *Documents of Vatican II,* pp. 37-56.

19. Transcendist Catholics insist that catechetics is under the direct control of the magisterium, or church officials. See Eugene Kevane, *Creed and Catechetics* (Westminster, Md.: Christian Classics, 1977), pp. 209, 253-259.

20. Augustine taught that one sure indication of a Christian truth is *what all the laity believe* as well as all the clergy. See "The Church in the Modern World," in *Documents of Vatican II,* p. 29, n. 39.

21. Pope Paul VI, *Humanae Vitae,* trans. Marc Caligari, 2nd rev. ed. (San Francisco: Ignatius Press, 1983).

22. For Kelly's transcendist critique on the issues of theology, ecclesiology, catechetics, religious education, and audiovisual media, see Kelly, *The Battle for the American Church.*

23. See as an example, Gregory Baum, "Foreword," in Andrew Greeley, *The New Agenda,* (Garden City, N.Y. Image Books, 1975), pp. 11-31.

24. Fritts, "The McLuhan Thesis ."

25. William J. Fritts, letter to author, 21 December 1978.
26. Fritts, "The McLuhan Thesis," Abstract, pp. 1-6.
27. Thomas O'Meara and Donald Weisser, *Projections: Shaping an American Theology for the Future* (Garden City, N.Y.: Doubleday, 1970), p. 4.
28. William Kuhns, *Environmental Man* (New York: Harper & Row, 1969), p. 9.
29. Marshall McLuhan, *War and Peace in the Global Village* (New York: Bantam Books, 1968), pp. 60-61.
30. "McLuhan's Response," in *McLuhan: Hot and Cool*, ed. Gerald E. Stearne (New York: Dial Press, 1967), p. 267.
31. Hughell E.W. Fosbroke, "The Book of Amos," in *The Interpreter's Bible*, ed. George Buttrick, Vol. VI (New York: Abingdon Press, 1956), pp. 765-766.
32. Allen Maruyama's synopsis of his thesis can be found in "A Theological Critique of Marshall McLuhan's New Man of the Electric Age" (Dissertation, Aquinas Institute of Philosophy and Theology, Dubuque, Iowa, 1972 , pp. 1-6.
33. For McLuhan's view that art constitutes an anti-environment to the media-world, see Marshall McLuhan and Wilfred Watson, *From Cliche to Archetype* (New York: Viking Press, 1970).
34. William McSweeney, *Roman Catholicism: The Search for Relevance* (New York: St. Martin Press, 1980), pp. 136, 138.
35. John XXIII, "Opening Address of the Second Vatican Council," in *Teachings of the Second Vatican Council*, p. 7.
36. Marshall McLuhan contends that the so-called message is not the true content of any medium; according to McLuhan, the true content of any given medium is the speed by which it processes information, and thus brings about psychological (individual) change and corporate (societal) change. See Marshall McLuhan, *Understanding Media: The Extensions of Man* (New York: Signet Books, 1964), pp. 23-24.
37. See Lee, *The Content of Religious Instruction*, pp. 280-288.
38. Robert McAfee Brown, "The Church Today: A Response," in *Documents of Vatican II*, p. 310.
39. Mario Von Galli, *The Council and the Future* (New York: McGraw Hill, 1966), p. 299. See also Donald Campion, "The Church Today," in *Documents of Vatican II*, pp. 188-189. For the view that a literate culture fosters introspection, see McLuhan, *Understanding Media*, pp. 136; 265-266.
40. For Karl Rahner's view that Christology is the shaping theological vision for ecclesiology, see Karl Rahner and Wilhelm Thüsing, *A New Christology*, trans. David Smith and Verdant Green (New York: Seabury Press, 1980).
41. "The Church in the Modern World" in *Documents of Vatican II*, pp. 209-215. See also the commentator Adrian Hastings, *A Concise*

Guide to the Documents of the Second Vatican Council II (London: Darton, Longman and Todd, 1969), pp. 16-28. Cf. Walter Ong, *The Barbarian Within and Other Fugitive Essays* (New York: Macmillan, 1962), p. 97 for an explanation of the communication of the Father and the Son in the Trinity; and cf. pp. 66-67 for Ong's view of the connection between personalism and modern communication.

42. Hastings, *A Concise Guide II*, p. 29 See also "The Church in the Modern World," in *Documents of Vatican II*, pp. 315-316. Cf. Jacques Ellul, *The Technological Society,* trans. John Wilkinson (New York: Vantage, 1964), p. 97 and Norbert Wiener, *God and Golem, Inc.* (Cambridge, Mass.: M.I.T. Press, 1964), pp. 29, 54-55.

43. Campion, "The Church Today," in *Documents of Vatican II*, pp. 195-196.

44. Cf. Genesis 1:28.

45. "The Church in the Modern World," in *Documents of Vatican II*, pp. 220-231. See also Von Galli, *The Council and the Future*, p. 299 and Hastings, *A Concise Guide II*, pp. 29-38.

46. McLuhan frequently alludes to the fact that audiovisual media images of Western wealth create dissatisfaction and despair in the Third World natives who cannot hope to achieve such prosperity. When these natives were unaware that such riches existed, they remained relatively content with their lot. See "Hybrid Energy," in McLuhan, *Understanding Media,* pp. 57-63.

47. Ellul, *The Technological Society,* p. 133.

48. "The Church in the Modern World," in *Documents of Vatican II*, pp. 222-248. See also Hastings, *A Concise Guide II*, pp. 41-44.

49. See, as one example, Michael Novak, *The Open Church* (New York: Macmillan, 1964).

50. See Hastings, *A Concise Guide II*, p. 90.

51. The Catholic bishops and their contemporary-theological view on modern communication theory and religious education can be found in the Pontifical Commission for the Means of Social Communication's document, *Pastoral Instruction for the Application of the Decree of the Second Vatican Council on the Means of Social Communication* (Washington, D.C.: U.S. Catholic Conference, 1971), pp. 2, 8, 21-26, 29, 33, 37-39, 43-48, and 53. Although the *Pastoral Instruction* purports to be a commentary on Vatican II's "Decree on the Means of Social Communication," it constitutes a completely new approach to the media. The original conciliar decree, proposing the viewpoint of a very small number of the transcendist bishops, represents an acute embarrassment to any Catholic seriously interested in addressing the issues of the church and the mass media.

52. See Sigmund Freud, *The Basic Writings of Sigmund Freud* (New York: Modern Library, 1938).

53. See Pierre Teilhard de Chardin, *The Phenomenon of Man* (New York: Harper & Row, 1959), pp. 300-310.

54. For Walter Ong's synthesis of Sigmund Freud and Pierre Teilhard de Chardin into his own unique concept of modern communication theory, see Ong, *The Presence of the Word*, pp. 17-110.

55. A synopsis of Walter Ong's synthesis of modern communication theory and immanentist theology, and his application of that synthesis to the task of religious education, can be found in Ong, *The Presence of the Word*, pp. 10, 13-15, 74, 88-89, 96, 100-110, 120, 145, 150, 156, 167, 181-191, 258, 290-297, 300-301, 309, 313-315, and 320-321.

56. Carl J. Pfieffer, "The Church as Multi-Media," *Religion Teachers Journal* 11, no. 3 (April, 1977), pp. 20-22.

57. Gabriel Moran, *Theology of Revelation* (New York: Herder and Herder, 1966).

58. Moran, *The Catechesis of Revelation*.

59. Lee, *The Content of Religious Instruction*, p. 33, n. 98.

60. By way of contrast, James Michael Lee believes that the religious educator can and ought to establish a teaching/learning environment that will bring the learner to God's revelation. For Lee, God works best through the laws of creation (including the laws of learning) which he has created and keeps in being. See James Michael Lee, *The Flow of Religious Instruction*, pp. 144-146.

61. Moran, *The Catechesis of Revelation*, pp. 33, 49, 79-82, 122-123.

62. Burgess, *An Invitation to Religious Education*, p. 108.

63. Fred L. Brownlee, "Social Thought and Action," *Religious Education* 47 (March-April, 1952), p. 82.

64. A summary of George Albert Coe's principal ideas can be found in Knox, *Above or Within?*, pp. 89-90.

65. William Clayton Bower, "Contribution to the Psychology of Religion," *Religious Education* 47 (March-April, 1952), p. 70.

66. Moran, *Design for Religion*, p. 119.

67. A summary of Gabriel Moran's principal ideas about religious education can be found in Knox, *Above or Within?*, pp. 90-91. For Moran's "religious education" approach, see Gabriel Moran, *Design for Religion*, pp. 44-48, 49-71; *Vision and Tactics: Toward an Adult Church* (New York: Herder and Herder, 1968), pp. 52-54; and *Religious Body: Design for a New Reformation* (New York: Seabury, 1974), p. 166.

68. Charles Cook, *Media in Catechesis* (Attleboro, Mass.: Mark IV Presentations, 1974), pp. 5, 7, 11-31.

69. Marshall McLuhan and Pierre Babin, *Autre Homme, Autre Cretien a L'Age Electronique* (Lyons: Chalet, 1977). As of this writing, the text has not been translated into English.

70. Pierre Babin, *Options: Approaches for the Religious Education of Adolescents*, trans. John F. Murphy (New York: Herder and Herder, 1967), pp. 33-34.

71. Pierre Babin, *Methods: Approaches for the Catechesis of Adolescents,* trans. John F. Murphy (New York: Herder and Herder, 1967), p. 65.

72. *Audiovisual Man: Media in Religious Education,* ed. Pierre Babin, (Dayton, Ohio: Pflaum, 1970), pp. 33-54.

73. McLuhan and Babin, *Autre Homme, Autre Cretien,* p. 14.

74. Neil Postman repeats this theme of adults refusing to accept parental responsibility in *The Disappearance of Childhood,* pp. 98-119.

75. Walter J. Ong, "Finitude and Frustration: Consideration of Brod's *Kafka,*" *Modern Schoolman* 25 (March, 1948), p. 178.

76. McLuhan and Babin, *Autre Homme, Autre Cretien,* pp. 15-19, 23-29, 33-46, 51, 68-86, 107-118, 125-149, and 153-162. Plans to translate this text into English were halted because of McLuhan's death in 1982. Pierre Babin and Robert White have collaborated on a 1986 book which incorporates many of the principal ideas in this French text. For readers able to read French, the 1986 volume, Pierre Babin, *Le Temps de la Communication,* is the most recent exposition of the McLuhan-Babin thesis.

77. Bruce O'Donnell, "Language in Catechetics," *Religious Education* 69, no. 5 (September/October, 1974), pp. 542-557. Cf. Postman, *Teaching As A Conserving Activity,* p. 59. Here Postman presents television commercials as inherently a form of religious language.

78. Thomas H. Groome, *Christian Religious Education* (San Francisco: Harper & Row, 1980). Politics is almost universally recognized today as a form of social science.

79. See Rahner and Thüsing, *A New Christology.*

80. Neil Postman, *The Disappearance of Childhood* (New York: Delacorte, 1982), pp. 100-101.

81. McLuhan, *Understanding Media,* pp. 23-35.

82. Jürgen Habermas, *Knowledge and Human Interests,* trans. Jeremy J. Shapiro (Boston: Beacon, 1971).

83. Randolph Franklin Lumpp, "Culture, Religion, and the Presence of the Word: A Study of the Thought of Walter Jackson Ong" (Dissertation, University of Ottawa, Canada, 1976), pp. 63-64.

84. *The Spiritual Exercises of St. Ignatius Loyola,* ed. Lewis Delmage (New York: Joseph F. Wagner, 1968.) The Christian Life Community is the lay organization which trains its members through the Spiritual Exercises. Although Groome does not mention this fact in his text, "sharing faith experiences" began with José Esquivel, a Jesuit priest and Cuban exile. Esquivel worked with the National Federation of Christian Life Communities and served as a consultant both to the American national office at St. Louis and the world headquarters in Rome. Eventually, through his efforts and those of other members of the CLC, thousands of learners made the "Faith Experience," which involves a mutual sharing of one's personal salvation history with a small group of others who also share their faith stories. This method is

now employed in many retreats. Esquivel, who was imprisoned by Fidel Castro, is not at all sympathetic to the Marxist philosophy.

85. Paulo Freire, *Pedagogy of the Oppressed,* trans. Myra Bergman Ramos (New York: Herder and Herder, 1970).

86. Groome's presentation of the dialectical synthesis between personal communication and the church tradition can be found in Groome, *Christian Religious Education,* pp. xii, xiv, 12, 25-27, 51, 59-69, 76, 110-113, 122-124, 137, 146-149, 162, 171-173, 176, 184, 188-193, 200, 214, 228, 246, 254, 263-264, 266, and 272.

87. McLuhan's *Understanding Media* is probably the text most widely read by religious educators.

88. Lee, *The Shape of Religious Instruction,* pp. 57, 89, 216, 223, 305, 314.

89. Lee, *The Flow of Religious Instruction,* pp. 29, 158, 303, 339, and 348.

90. Lee, *The Content of Religious Instruction,* pp. 80, 82, 83, 95, 117, 118, 120, 121, 289, and 358.

91. Ibid., pp. 80-84.

92. Lee, *The Flow of Religious Instruction,* p. 29.

93. Lee, *The Content of Religious Instruction,* p. 95.

94. Lee, *The Shape of Religious Instruction,* p. 57.

95. Lee, *The Flow of Religious Instruction,* p. 216.

96. Ibid., p. 158.

97. Lee, *The Shape of Religious Instruction,* p. 305.

98. Ibid., p. 216.

99. Th. P. van Baaren, "Religious Symbols: Their Essence and Their Function," in *Verbum: Some Aspects of the Religious Function of Words* ed. H.W. Obbink, A.A. van Ruler, and W.C. van Unnik (Utrecht: The Netherlands: Kemink, 1964), p. 22.

100. Lee, *The Content of Religious Instruction,* pp. 289, 358.

101. Ibid., pp. 502-503.

102. McLuhan and Babin, *Autre Homme, Autre Cretien,* pp. 46-48.

103. Randolph Crump Miller, *Biblical Theology and Christian Education* (New York: Scribners, 1956), p. 5. For an exposition of Miller's integrationism, see Knox, *Above or Within?,* p. 124.

104. Randolph Crump Miller, "Linguistic Models and Religious Education," *Religious Education* 65, no. 4 (July/August, 1966), pp. 269-278.

105. Marcel van Caster, *Themes of Catechesis* (New York: Herder and Herder, 1966); Marcel van Caster, *The Structure of Catechetics* (New York: Herder and Herder, 1965).

106. Knox, *Above or Within?,* p. 145, n. 22.

107. Jean Le Du and Marcel van Caster, *Experiential Catechetics* (Paramus, N.J.: Newman Press, 1966), pp. 198-225. For a synopsis of van Caster's integrationist approach to religious education, see Knox, *Above or Within?,* pp. 125-126.

108. The purpose of James Michael Lee's trilogy is to lay a systematic and comprehensive foundation so that an empirical approach may be applied to religious education. See Lee, *The Content of Religious Instruction,* pp. 749-750. It has already been established that the more concrete an experience is, the more effective it is as a pedagogical enterprise. See ibid., p. 689.

109. Vance Packard, *The Hidden Persuaders* (New York: David McKay, 1965).

Part Two:

Varieties of Media Opportunities

4

Audiovisual Materials

The rich varieties of audiovisual media experiences today depend on several different communication devices. These contemporary devices are the practical inventions which developed out of nineteenth- and twentieth-century scientific knowledge about human biology, the physics of light and sound, chemistry, and electrical engineering.

This chapter provides a technological precis about certain audiovisual media. The author has deliberately selected those media which have an immediate application in the teaching/learning of religious education. The telephone, for example, although it is very important for the social life of young learners, is not usually involved directly in teaching/learning, especially in formal settings. So the telephone will not be treated in this chapter. The telegraph, although it is vitally important in the production of newspapers, is also not treated because it is not directly involved in teaching/learning.

Accordingly, the chapter studies those audiovisual media which have an immediate application to teaching/learning. These are: photography, the phonograph, radio broadcasting, motion pictures, television broadcasting, tape recording, and the personal computer.

Photography is the audiomedia replication of human sight. The phonograph is a replication of the human ear and voice. Radio broadcasting is a replication of the human ear, the voice, and feet. (It brings messages over a distance.) Motion pictures replicate the human eye, the voice, the ear, and kinesthesia.

Television replicates the human eye, the ear, the voice, kinesthesia, and feet (cf. radio). Sound tape recorders replicate the human voice, the ear, and memory. Video recorders replicate the human eye, the voice, the ear, and memory. The personal computer, when fully utilized, replicates the human eye, the voice, the ear, memory, and calculation.

Photography

In the photographic process, the light from a subject is collected by a lens, and then is focused onto a light-sensitive material. This material is an emulsion, i.e., a suspension of silver salts in a gelatin solution that has been affixed onto a glass or plastic base. The incoming light causes a chemical reaction in the emulsion, and produces a latent, or invisible image. This latent image is then made visible by a reagent, called the developer. This consequent image is called a negative because it portrays white as black, black as white, and intermediate gray tones in inverse proportion to their actual brightness. This negative is then used as a template to produce a print, or photograph. A film or a sheet of specially treated paper affixed with a light-sensitive emulsion is first exposed to a light which has passed through the negative and then is treated with a suitable reagent. The consequent print is called a positive, since its light and dark areas (the reverse of those on the negative), corresponds to the original subject in terms of black, white, and gray. Color photographic process is essentially the same as that used for producing black-and-white pictures. The principal difference lies in the emulsion. Instead of a single layer of emulsion, there are three separate layers in the color-sensitive film. Each layer is sensitive to a different primary color. Recall that all colors are combinations of the primary colors. These emulsions are developed in a special formula that produces colored-dye images. In this way it is possible to make photographs that possess a fairly faithful representation of the colors of the original subject.

In the "reversal process" a positive is developed directly into the film which has been in the camera. "Reversal negatives" are transparencies. Transparencies are used in slide projectors and film strip projectors, where they are projected onto a large screen for viewing.

The Polaroid company has invented a camera which develops prints (both black and white and color) shortly after the subject is snapped and the film is pulled from the camera.[1]

The Phonograph

The phonograph is an audial device which reproduces sounds. The variations of sound waves are recorded onto the grooves of a rotating record. The recorded sound is then reproduced by a stylus (needle)—or most recently, a laser beam—which vibrates according to the fluctuations of the moving groove. Since its invention in 1877 the phonograph has been the most popular device for reproducing recorded sound. A stereophonic recording is one with a dual track, usually one has the treble sounds and the other has the bass sounds. Improvements in the phonograph include high-fidelity sound, and the compact disk, which is read by a laser beam. A high-fidelity, stereophonic compact disk is currently the most accurate replication of original sound.

The phonograph is normally used to replicate music.[2]

Radio Broadcasting

Broadcasting consists of transmitting intelligible signals via radio or television waves. A radio wave has both length (the amplitude) and a number of cycles per second (the frequency). A hertz is a unit, or one cycle per second. A kilocycle is 1,000 cycles per second. A megacycle is 1,000,000 cycles per second.

The United States Government has assigned specific frequencies for certain types of transmissions on the broadcast frequency band (see chart). Radio waves are part of the electro-magnetic spectrum, which includes visible light, X-rays, gamma rays, and infrared light, and so on.

In radio broadcasting, the microphone converts variations in sound into electrical impulses. These impulses are fed into a transmitter and greatly amplified. The amplified impulses are then broadcast from a large antenna.

THE BROADCAST FREQUENCY BAND		
535-1,605 kilocycles	AM	amplitude modulation
54-88 megacycles	VHF	very high frequency television (Channels 2-6)
88.1-107.9 megacycles	FM	frequency modulation radio
174-216 megacycles	VHF	very high frequency television (Channels 7-13)
470-890 megacycles	UHF	ultra high frequency television (Channels 14-83)

 The amplitude of the carrier wave is altered by the varying voltage produced when sound waves are converted into electrical impulses. Sidebands are caused by the "beating" together both of the carrier wave frequency *and* the various modulating frequencies. A standard AM broadcast channel (see chart) consists of the band of frequencies that contain *both* the carrier frequency *and* the sidebands located on either side of the carrier wave.

 A broadcast station requires both a studio and a transmitter. The studio insures that unwanted external noise is not sent over the radio signal. The transmitter radiates the signals from an antenna in the form of electromagnetic energy over a specified service area. The extent of the service area depends on the wattage of the transmitting station. In amplitude modulation the audio-intelligence signal is superimposed on the carrier signal in the form of amplitude (or voltage) variations, which are called "modulations." The radio receiver eliminates the carrier wave and leaves the audio-intelligence that was placed on the carrier at the transmitter. The demodulator is the heart of the radio receiver. In the radio receiver, the rf amplifier contains a tuned circuit that resonates with the AM band signal. The signal is then made audible by means of a loudspeaker built into the radio console.

Even strong radio signals fade after a certain distance and the government strictly regulates the amount of wattage a station can use to transmit its signal. This regulation is to avoid stations interfering with other broadcasters who are near their band. Network systems enlarge their area by contracting with various local stations to transmit their signal. Networks use microwave relay/systems or telephone cables to link up with stations out of the broadcast range.

Frequency modulation (FM) is a system in which the instantaneous radio frequency varies in proportion to the amplitude of the modulating audio signal and is therefore independent of the frequency. FM signals are more noise-free than AM signals. A high-fidelity stereophonic recording sent on a FM wave and received by an appropriate radio produces a very realistic replication of sounds. Because of this, most FM stations tend to specialize in music and most AM stations in talk or in music of lesser sensitive quality such as rock.[3]

MOTION PICTURES

Motion pictures, or the cinema, consist of a series of photographic pictures on a celluloid strip, with perforated holes for winding and unwinding from reel to reel. When these pictures are projected in rapid succession by a source of light on a suitable reflector (screen), they produce in the observer the illusion of watching continuous motion. The lengths of a film strip determine the duration of the movie. The width of a film strip is measured in millimeters (mm). Seventy mm, 65mm, and 35mm are used in commercial films for showings in theaters. Educational films shown in schools and libraries normally use 16mm. Amateurs making home movies usually use 8 mm.

When a scene is photographed, unexposed film on a reel moves through the film gate in the camera. The shutter opens, exposing one frame of the film to the light passing through the lens. The shutter then closes, the film is advanced to the next frame by the shuttle and the process is repeated as the film moves onto the take-up reel. At the same time, the sound is picked up by a microphone (see radio), amplified, and transmitted to the sound recorder. There are several methods for sound recording. In optical density recording, the sound impulses are fed into a modulator. Changes in the impulses (controlled by the variations in the sound waves) regulate the intensity of a light beam. A lens focuses the light on the film's edge, recording the sound there as a series of light and dark bands. The picture and sound negatives are synchronized. Both sound and picture are then printed onto a third film strip. This third strip is then developed to form the final print.

In the projector, the final print moves from a reel, past a shuttle, to a take-up reel. The shutter opens and closes for each frame, allowing light to shine through the film (recall that all movie pictures are photographic transparencies which can let light shine through) and project the picture onto the screen. Another light shines through the sound track onto a photoelectric cell. The cell, when struck by light, produces an electric current, which varies with the sound waves imprinted on the light and dark bands. These variations in light are converted into sound and amplified through a loudspeaker. The total effect is to recreate the visual and audial components of the original scene. Through sound mixing, multiple audial tracks can be imprinted on the film. Mood music is frequently added to feature films in this manner.[4]

TELEVISION BROADCASTING

Much of television broadcasting is similar to radio broadcasting. In the United States, the radio network companies contributed significantly to the research and development that created and marketed television. The television camera is similar to the microphone. It converts variations in light into electrical impulses (see radio). The television camera uses the "image orthicon" camera tube. The neck of the tube, which holds the source of the electron stream, lies along the long axis of the tube. At the other end of the tube is the optical window. Through this window the scene to be televised is passed. Between them is the optical target that is scanned by the electron beam, and a photocathode that emits electrons when struck by light. The lens system focuses the scene onto the photocathode. Variations in the scene cause variations in the electron beam.

From the television camera the scene is then sent to the transmitter and broadcast out on an assigned FM frequency. Television sound broadcasting is simply radio broadcasting accompanied by a simultaneous kinetic picture.

A television set is both a radio receiver and a visual image receiver. The television set decodes the signal sent by the station, and a beam of electrons sends out variations in impulses which the screen reconverts back into the original image.

Color television works in a similar manner. All color broadcasting is compatible with black-and-white transmission and reception. Any television set, even a black-and-white set, can receive a color signal but cannot fully reproduce what the color cameras record. The fundamental principle behind color television is that the convergence of red, green, and blue light on one spot produces white light. Television had already solved the problem of transmitting white light and darkness (absence of white light). The color television camera actually uses three different camera tubes, all synchronized. By using appropriate filters, one tube responds only to red light, the other only to green, and the third only to blue. When the color television signal reaches the television receiver, there are tiny triangles of red, green, and blue dots on the screen. The beam of electrons causes only those dots to glow that correspond with the original image. The effect is to recreate in a fairly accurate manner the original color scheme of the scene. (This is similar to the color separation process used to reproduce color photographs onto the printed page.)

In the United States the VHF stations are controlled by the three major networks (Columbia Broadcasting System, the National Broadcasting Company, and the American Broadcasting Company), syndicated commercial stations (such as Metromedia), and the Public Broadcasting System. Many major cities also have independent VHF stations. From 1950-1980, VHF broadcasting was the most common form of television for the majority of American viewers. Change in technology and government regulations since 1980 has rapidly changed this situation.

Other forms of television now include the closed circuit, cable television (CATV), ultra-high frequency broadcasting (UHF), and satellite relay television (SATV). Few of these new forms have yet to reach their full potential. Even in major markets, such as New

York City, for example, there are less than ten UHF stations broadcasting, although there are seventy-nine assigned channels. Financial investors are not quite sure which form will succeed in the market and are hesitant to commit huge sums to the development of new stations. UHF stations are often owned and operated by government entities such as states, counties, or municipalities. A decoder on the television set converts the UHF signal into a VHF signal so that the television screen can show the image.

Cable television is the transmission of a television signal over private telephone lines. Several channels can be transmitted since there are no frequency interferences as there are with VHF broadcasts. In the United States, cable television is a private enterprise, and different companies secure franchises to wire established neighborhoods. There have been bitter battles in many parts of the country about which companies will win franchises and this has delayed the development of cable television in some areas. Cable television can send VHF, UHF, and cable programs. The image is usually sharper, since there is no atmospheric or landscape interferences as there is with broadcasting. Subscribers normally pay a set monthly fee which entitles them to use a decoder to receive cable programs. Some cable programs require additional feeds or de-scramblers because they are transmitting first-run movies or special sporting events that have been blacked out of other media or to thwart owners of satellite dishes. Cable television is popular with advertisers since most subscribers are affluent. Parents and teachers are reminded that cable television is considered private communication. It is not controlled by the laws against obscenity that govern public broadcasting. Some parents and legislators, outraged by strong violence and by sexually explicit material on cable television, are attempting to remedy this situation.

In closed-circuit television the transmitted image and sound are limited to certain receivers. Closed-circuit television can be done in a school to televise a religion class or group guidance session. The telephone companies have developed closed-circuit intercity television communication so that corporations can have confidential meetings without the expense of transporting their key executives on costly plane flights.

Satellite relays now make intercontinental broadcasting possible. Broadcasters are no longer limited to the service area range assigned to them by the government.

Communication satellites travel from west to east above the earth in a period of twenty-four hours and so appear to be stationary above the earth. Their television antenna, which receive and then transmit signals, rotate opposite to the rotation of the satellite, so they are always pointing toward the earth. (Recall that the moon always has the same side facing the earth because its daily rotation is equal to the amount of time it takes to revolve around the earth.) A satellite dish can pick up a weak signal from a satellite antenna and convert it into a television image. Satellite viewers have a very broad range of options, since they can receive local broadcasts from a large part of the world.[5]

Tape Recording

Tape recording is a technique for storing information on the magnetic surface of a tape. The recording surface consists of magnetic particles which are uniformly distributed on a thin film of non-magnetic material. *Any form of information that can be translated into an electrical signal can be stored magnetically.* For example, music is transformed into electrical impulses by means of a microphone (see radio). Similarly, pictures may be electrically scanned by means of a television camera (see television), and then converted into a serial stream of electrical impulses. In data processing, binary "ones" and "zeroes" may be represented by voltage or current levels. Thus all of these forms of information may be transformed and then stored magnetically. Magnetic recordings depend on the existence of two phenomena. First, a magnetic field is associated with every electric current. Second, ferromagnetic (highly magnetizable) materials retain magnetization after being placed near a magnetic field. Once this material is stored on a magnetic tape it can be reproduced in its original form by means of a recorder which converts the magnetic configuration back into the electrical impulses and then into sound and/or pictures or data. A sound recorder recaptures from the magnetic tape the original audial signal. A video cassette recorder recaptures the original visual signal. Hard discs are used in computers and replay videos also. They can store larger amounts of magnetic signals in a more compact form.[6]

The Personal Computer

One of the greatest technological advances in the twentieth century for teaching/learning is the personal computer. A personal computer consists of hardware (the devices used to make the computer work) and software (the instructions or programing to tell the hardware what task to perform). Popular American personal computers today are the Apple, the Commodore, the IBM pc, and the many clones of the IBM pc.

The first computers were extremely large—as much as the size of one or two rooms. They weighed thousands of pounds and cost millions of dollars. They used large glass vacuum tubes to function as switches, similar to light switches. Even the earliest electronic computers used electronic codes to process information. Depending on whether a switch is on or off, electronic codes that the computer can read or understand can be created. The development of small metallic transistors replaced the vacuum tubes. This was the first technological advance toward making computers smaller and swifter.

When the integrated circuit was developed, then one little flake of silicon, called a chip, contained tens of thousands of transistors. Computers again shrank in size. Simultaneously, computers became more powerful and more speedy. When a microprocessor (the "brains" of a computer) was put on one chip in 1971, minicomputers and microcomputers were born.

Today there are three main types of computers: the main-frames, the minicomputer, and the microcomputer. Mainframes are the large computers used by large corporations, the government, and universities. Minicomputers are similar versions of the mainframes and are usually used by small businesses.

The computer revolution is being led by the microcomputer, which is also known as the home computer or the personal computer. Unlike the larger computers, the microcomputer is relatively inexpensive. Almost any middle-class American family can afford to purchase a microcomputer, and millions have done so. In poorer neighborhoods, it is common for churches, schools, and libraries to invest in the purchase of personal computers to insure that minority children have access to the technology that will be critical to the future job market.

The usual hardware consists of a computer, a keyboard, connecting cords, a cassette tape recorder or disc drive, a television set, and other peripherals. The keyboard resembles a typewriter with a calculator and other function keys. The cassette tape or floppy disk or hard disk is simply a magnetized set of instructions which can be decoded by the computer. The television set or video display screen translates the computer impulses into visual and audial output to be understandable by the user. Peripherals include several accessories: such as a line printer, a modem to connect the computer by telephone to other computers, an expander to increase its memory, joystick or hand paddles to enable the user to play computer games, and a lightpen for computerized graphic arts.

Software includes a vast array of programed instruction that allows a computer to play video games, do word processing, budgeting, programed learning, graphic arts, and so on. Every day new programing is developed and new uses of the home computer made possible. It is one industry where young learners can compete with seasoned veterans for the education market. All software is protected by copyright laws, just as printed textbooks are. Serious ethical questions have arisen from the piracy of copyrighted software and from the use of modems to crack the security code of businesses and governments. Computer thefts by "hackers" is a serious moral issue today and often parents and teachers are unaware of what their young learners are doing with their personal computers until the police arrive to charge them with theft or breach of security.

Microcomputers tend to create a close relationship between the user and the machine; they allow a great deal of autonomy for the user. Hence they are frequently called personal computers or p.c.'s. The domestic version of the personal computer has many applications, several of which are still in the conceptual state. Possible applications include entertainment, shopping, banking, learning aids, home maintenance, operations, and security.

As instruments of entertainment, computers are widely used

to play video games. Unfortunately, almost all of them are masculine fantasies of violent war-play. Computers can now play chess well enough to defeat 90 percent of all amateur players. One step above computer games are computerized instructional programs that promise to help students learn to read, spell, or do arithmetic. Games themselves can also be educational.

Personal computers can be connected to the living room television set, and through the telephone modem to a network of other users at similar machines in the surrounding area. This has formed into computerized communication known as electronic mail. One aspect of electronic mail is that the recipient does not have to be at home or even have the machine on in order to "read" the mail at a later time.

Employees can now work at home or with others nearby on personal computers connected to the employer's system. This is the so-called electronic cottage-industry. This fundamental change in working style may help alleviate the problems of urban congestion, pollution, and the diminishing energy reserves. It will no longer be necessary for many to commute from their home to work. The automobile had a drastic effect on the lifestyle of many Americans. The loss of the affluent from the urban centers to the suburbs is directly connected to the widespread marketing of the automobile. Personal computers may wield even a greater influence than the automobile.

Soon the personal computer will be as pervasive as the telephone. It will be in large organizations and small ones. Computer illiteracy will mean unemployment and hopelessness for many Americans. Both the executive and the secretary will have personal computers on their desk; they will be out in the field and at central headquarters. Already farmers, doctors, retailers, mail solicitors, supermarkets, truckers, and so on, are using computers. Calculations and simulations will be carried out in planning and budgeting, with input being entered in operation and output being displayed in production and sales. Most large schools have computerized their student records so that they have immediate access to who is teaching whom and whether or not the course has been paid for at registration. An automated office with the capability for instant message transmission and push-button files is the latest communication tool in the global village.

An important application of computerization is word processing. Research papers for both students and teachers are now much easier. Editing and rewriting are no longer the onerous chore of the cut-and-paste era.

Computer models can now do simulations of systems, both physical *and* socioeconomic. If a system can be modeled in precise logical terms, it can be simulated onto a computer. The technique has been important in airplane design, scientific research, war games, economic analysis, and sociometric projections. Obviously the social-science approach to religious education has a ready ally in the personal computer, especially for programed learning.

Some critics are concerned about the negative aspects of the computer revolution. Their fears center on widespread unemployment, the loss of privacy, the avoidance of personal responsibility, computer theft, and the breach of security. Whole financial institutions can readily be thrown into chaos if computers are misused. People who have been dunned for a bill of items they did not order, or have a bank deny they made a deposit so that all their recent checks bounce, or have a school deny they have completed a course needed for graduation are all too aware of what havoc computer misuse can wreak in their lives.[7]

Summary

A rich variety of audiovisual materials are available for contemporary religious educators. The following are most helpful in the religious education teaching/learning environment: photography, the phonograph, radio, the cinema, television, tape recording, and the personal computer. Most teachers and learners have ready access to these audiovisual materials either through the home or via group purchase. Most school systems possess an audiovisual center.

The following tend to facilitate teaching/learning in a religious education setting:

(1) teachers and learners view professionally produced audiovisual material;

(2) teachers and learners discuss audiovisual material after a viewing;

(3) religious educators strive to foster media-literacy in their learners through
  (a) instructing how media-effect takes place
  (b) facilitating media productions on the part of learners.

Subsequent chapters will discuss practical means of achieving these objectives in the religious education setting.

Notes

1. Gail Buckland, "Photography," *Collier's Encyclopedia* (New York: Macmillan Educational Company, 1983), Vol. 18, pp. 735-761. See also: H. Baines and E. S. Bombeck, *The Science of Photography* 3rd rev. ed. (Indianola, Iowa: Fountain Press, 1970).

2. Robert Chipman, "The Phonograph," *Encyclopedia Americana* (Danbury, Conn.: Grolier, 1985), Vol. 21, pp. 958-959. See also Robert Gelatt, *The Fabulous Phonograph, 1877-1977* (New York: Macmillan, 1977).

3. Jerome Kass, "Radio and Television Broadcasting and Reception," *Collier's Encyclopedia* (New York: Macmillan Educational Company, 1983), Vol. 19, pp. 607-620. See also: Abraham and W. Marcus, *Elements of Radio*, 6th ed. (Englewood Cliffs, N.J.: Prentice-Hall, 1972).

4. Loren L. Ryder and Raymond Forey, "Motion Pictures," *Collier's Encyclopedia* (New York: Macmillan Educational Company, 1983), Vol. 16, pp. 595-629.

5. Kass, "Radio and Television Broadcasting and Reception." See also: Bernard Grob, *Basic Television*, 4th ed. (New York: McGraw, 1975).

6. Victor E. Ragosine, "Tape Recording," *Encyclopedia Americana* (Danbury, Conn.: Grolier, 1984), Vol. 26, pp. 278-282. See also: Harry F. Olson, *Modern Sound Reproduction* (New York: Van-Nostrand-Reinhold, 1972); M. Camras, *Handbook of Magnetic Recording* (New York: Van-Nostrand-Reinhold, 1985).

7. Louis Robinson, "Computer," *Encyclopedia Americana* (Danbury, Conn.: Grolier, Inc., 1985), Vol. 7, pp. 474-493. See also Texas Instruments Computer Advantage Club, *TI Basic Student Guide* (Dallas: Texas Instruments, Co., 1983), p. 5. A. Finkel et al. *Vic 20 Programmer's Reference Guide* (Indianapolis, Ind.: Commodore Business Machines, distributed by Howard W. Sams and Company, 1982). Vladimir Zwass, *Introduction to Computer Science* (New York: Barnes & Noble, 1981).

5

Selected Printed Materials on Audiovisual Media

CRITERIA FOR INCLUSION

An overwhelming amount of literature exists today for the religious educator about audiovisual media. The author's experience is that some of the most informative material rapidly goes out of print. Audiovisual printed material is extremely sensitive to the fast pace of current market conditions. The following texts and periodicals were not selected because they represent the finest example of media scholarship. This chapter is not intended to provide titles that can only be found in libraries.

The following criteria were used:

1) The text represents the most recent information. (Texts with early publication dates have been periodically revised, or updated.) This means

    (a) The text is not out of print when the religious educator tries to secure it; and

    (b) The text is not an example of academic information which is no longer relevant, usable, or current.

2) The text provides the religious educator with practical information which can be used in teaching/learning.

3) The text enables the religious educator and the learners to produce their own media work.

4) The text discusses how current media are changing society.

5) The author(s) demonstrate expertise in the field.

6) The price is within the purchasing range of the religious educator. Prices do rise unexpectedly with these texts. An asterisk (*) means that the text is expensive and will require access to

a school, church, or library budget.
Periodicals are selected with the same criteria.

PHOTOGRAPHY: SELECTED BOOKS

How To Use Your 35mm Camera (Sherman Oaks, CA 91413: Alfred Publishing, 1981).

Henry Horenstein *Beyond Basic Photography: A Technical Manual* (Boston, MA: Little, Brown, 1977).

Eastman Kodak Company, ed. K. W. Nineteen *Advanced Black-White Photography* (Rochester, NY: Eastman Kodak, 1985).

Michael Freeman, *Instant Photography: A Creative Handbook* (Salem, NH 03079: Merrimack Publishing Company, 1985).

Eastman Kodak Company, *How to Take Good Pictures* (New York, NY: Ballantine Books, 1985).

Polaroid Corporation Staff, *Photomicrography with Polaroid Land Films* (Stoneham, MA 02180: Focal Press, 1985).

George Wakefield, *Color Films* (Stoneham, MA 02180: Focal Press, 1982).

SELECTED PERIODICALS

Modern Photography, ABC Leisure Magazines, INC. 825 Seventh Avenue, New York, NY 10019; Phone (212) 265-8360. Annual subscription: $15.95. Per issue: $1.75.

Petersen's Photographic Magazine, Petersen Publishing Company, 8490 Sunset Blvd., Los Angeles, CA 90069; Phone: (213) 657-5100. Annual subscription: $11.94. Per issue: $1.50.

American Photographer, CBS magazines, 1515 Broadway, New York, NY 10036; Phone: (212) 719-6265.

Photography Today, Rt. 2, Box 197, Templeton, CA 93465; Phone: (805) 238-1158. Annual Subscription: $36.00. Per issue: $3.00.

THE PHONOGRAPH AND POPULAR MUSIC: SELECTED BOOKS

*Kemps International Music and Recording Industry Yearbook (A Xerox Information Company, New York: Bowker, 1985).

Hewitt Panteleoni, *On the Nature of Music* (Oneonta, NY 13820: Welkin Books, 1985).

K. Blaukopf, *The Photograph in Cultural Communications* (New York: Springer Verlag, 1983).
Jane Leder, *Cassettes and Records*, ed. Howard Schroeder (Mankato, MN 56001: Crestwood House, 1983).
Bert Muirhead, *The Story of a Record Label* (New York, NY: Sterling, 1983).
National Information Center for Educational Media, *Index to Educational Records* (Columbia, SC 29208: University of South Carolina, National Information, 1980).
Diane Rapoport, *How To Make and Sell Your Own Records* (New York, NY: Putnam Publishing Group, 1984).

Selected Periodicals

Phonograph, Cerf Publications, Phonograph Record Magazine, Hollywood, CA 90028.
Popular Music and Society, Sociology Department, Bowling Green University, Bowling Green, OH 43403; Phone: (419) 372-2981. Quarterly. Per issue: $6.00.
The Musical Quarterly, G. Shirmer, Inc., 866 Third Avenue, New York, NY 10022 Quarterly. Annual Subscription: $23.00. Per issue: $7.00.
High Fidelity, High Fidelity/ABC Leisure Magazines, 825 Seventh Avenue New York, NY 10019; Phone: (212) 265-8360. Monthly. Annual subscription: $13.95. Per issue: $1.50.
Music Express, Rock Express Communications, Inc., 37 Madison, Toronto, Ontario M5R 252, Canada; Phone: (416) 964-6624. Annual subscription: $16.00. Per issue: $1.50.
Music in Higher Education, National Association of Schools of Music, 11250 Roger Bacon Drive, Reston, VA 22090; Phone: (703) 437-0700. Per issue $6.00.

Radio: Selected Books

Warren B. Dygert, *Radio As An Advertising Medium* (New York, NY: Garland Publishing, 1985).
J. M. Frost, *World Radio Television Handbook* (Orange, CA 92666: Watson-Guptil Music, 1984).
Susan Gilmore, *What Goes On at a Radio Station?* (Minneapolis,

MN 55401: Carolrhoda Books, 1984).
Louis Sabin, *Television and Radio* (Mahwah, NJ 07430: Troll Associates, 1985).
Rick Sklar, *Rocking America: How the All-Hit Radio Stations Took Over: An Insider's Story* (Los Angeles, CA: Martin, 1984).
Robert McLeish, *The Technique of Radio Production* (Stoneham, MA 02180: Focal Press, 1978).
William B. Levenson and Edward Stanhoff, *Teaching Through Radio and Television* (Westport, CT 06881: Greenwood, 1952).
James M. Theroux, *Effective Educational Radio: An Approach to Analyzing Programs* (Amherst, MA 01003: University of Massachusetts, 1978).

Selected Periodicals

Inside Radio, 1930 E. Marlton Park, Suite C-13, Cherry Hill, NJ 08003; Phone: (609) 424-6800.
Radio Only, Inside Radio, 1930 E. Marlton Park, Suite C-13, Cherry Hill, NJ 08003; Phone: (609) 424-6800. Monthly. Annual subscription: $25.00.
Radio World, Broadcast Equipment Exchange, Industrial Marketing Advisory Services, Inc., 5827 Columbia Pike, Suite 310, Falls Church, VA 22041; Phone: (703) 998-7600. Semi-monthly. Annual subscription: $18.00. Per issue: $2.00.
Journal of Broadcasting, Broadcast Educational Association, Department of Communication, Ohio State University, Derby Hall, Columbus, OH 43216; Phone: (216) 672-2649. Quarterly. Annual subscription: $25.00. Per issue: $6.50.
Journal of College Radio, Intercollegiate Broadcasting Systems, Inc., P.O. Box 592, Vails Gate, NY 12584 Phone: (914) 565-6710. Quarterly. Annual subscription: $12.00.
Better Radio and Television. National Association for Better Broadcasting, 7918 Naylor Avenue, Los Angeles, CA 90045; Phone: (213) 641-4903.

Motion Pictures: Selected Books

*Kemps International Film and Television Yearbook, 1985-1986 (A Xerox Information Company, New York, NY: Bowker, 1985).

Robert Brubaker, ed., *Contemporary Film Criticism* (Book Tower, Detroit, MI 48226: Gale, 1985).
Ian C. Jarvie, *Movies and Society* (New York, NY: Garland Publishing, 1985).
Neil Sinyard *Classic Movies* (Salem, NH 03079: Merrimack Publishing Company, 1985).
Leslie Halliwell, *Halliwell's Filmgoer's Companion* (New York, NY: Scribner, 1985).
Ralph S. Singleton, *Filmmaker's Dictionary* (Beverly HIlls, CA 90212: Lone Eagle Publishing, 1985).
Albert E. Smith and Philip A. Koury, *Two Reels and a Crank* (New York, NY: Garland Publishing, 1985).
Diana Gleamer, *The Movies* (New York, NY: Walker, 1983).
Bernard F. Dick, *The Anatomy of Film* (New York, NY: St. Martin, 1978).
Lewis Jacobs, *The Movies as Medium* (New York, NY: Octagon, 1973).
Eastman Kodak Company, *Cinematographer's Field Guide* (Rochester, NY 14650: Eastman Kodak, 1982).
George Wakefield, *Color Films* (Stoneham, MA 02180: Focal Press, 1982).

SELECTED PERIODICALS

In Cinema, Cinema Magazine, 801 Second Avenue, New York, NY 10019; Phone: (212) 986-5100.
American Film Review, American Educational and Historical Film Center, St. Davids, PA 19087. Annual.
Catalog of 16mm Sound Motion Pictures, Farm Film Foundation, Grange-Farm Film Foundation, 1616 H Street NW, Washington, DC 20006; Phone: (202) 628-3507. Annual: Free.
Films in Review, P.O. Box 589, New York, NY 10021; Phone: (212) 628-1594. Ten times per year. Annual subscription: $16.00. Per issue: $2.00.
Motion Pictures Ratings Review Previews Report, Film Previews Report, Federation of Motion Pictures Councils, 142 N. Trucker, Memphis, TN 38104; Phone: (901) 725-4987. Monthly.
Movie Guide, 450 S 900 E Street 105 Salt Lake City, UT 84102. Monthly. Annual subscription: $9.00. Per issue: $1.00.

Television: Selected Books

Kemps International Film and Television Yearbook, 1985-1986 (A Xerox Information Company, New York, NY: Bowker, 1985).

Robert T. Bower, *The Changing Television Audience in America* (New York, NY: Columbia University Press, 1985).

J. Brent Bill, *Stay Tuned* (Old Tappan, NJ 07675: Revell, 1985).

Robert Hillind and Otto von Ruiden, *Television and Adult Education* (Cambridge, MA 02138: Schenkman, 1985).

Evelyn Goodman, *Writing Television and Motion Picture Scripts That Sell* (Hollywood, CA: Westbourne, 1985).

Kevin Perrotta, *Taming the TV Habit* (Ann Arbor, MI 48107: Servant, 1982).

Ben Logan and Kate Moody, eds., *Television Awareness Training: The Viewer's Guide for Family and Community* (Nashville, TN 37202: Abingdon, 1980).

Edward N. McNulty, *When TV is a Member of the Family* (St. Meinrad, IN 47577: Abbey, 1981).

R. Stavins, ed., *Television Today: The End of Communication and the Death of Community* (Mt. Rainier, MD 20712: Gryphon House, 1971).

Stephen B. Withey and Ronald P. Abeles, eds., *Television and Social Behavior: Beyond Violence and Children* (Hillsdale, NJ 07642: L. Erlbaum Associates, 1980).

Paul Zbar and Peter Orne, *Basic Television: Theory and Servicing: A Text Lab Manual* (New York, NY: McGraw, 1978).

Malka Drucker and Elizabeth Janur, *Series TV: How A Show Is Made* (Boston, MA: Houghton-Mifflin, 1983).

Mat Irvine, *TV & Video* (New York, NY: Watts Franklin, 1984).

Louis Sabin, *Television and Radio* (Mahwah, NJ 07430: Troll Associates, 1985).

William B. Levenson and Edward Stanhoff, *Teaching Through Radio and Television* (Westport, CT 06881: Greenwood, 1952).

Les Brown, *Les Brown's Encyclopedia of Television* (New York, NY: Zoetrope, 1982).

M. Howe, ed., *Learning from Television: Psychological and Educational Research* (Orlando, FL 32887: Academic Press, 1983).

Michael R. Kelley, *A Parent's Guide to Television: Making the Most of It* (New York, NY: John Wiley & Sons, 1983).

Cedric Cullingford, *Children and Television* (New York, NY: St. Martin, 1984).
Sara Lake, ed., *Television's Impact on Children and Adolescents* (Phoenix, AZ 85004: Oryx Press, 1983).
Kate Moody, *Growing Up on Television* (New York, NY: McGraw-Hill, 1984).
Jill M. Schultz, *A Teacher's Guide to Television Evaluation for Children* (Stanford, CA 94305: Stanford University Press, 1961).
Meg Schwarz, *TV For Teens: Experts Look at the Issues* (Reading, MA 01867: Addison-Wesley, 1982)
Joseph Turow, *Entertainment, Education and the Hard Sell: Three Decades of Network Children's Television* (New York, NY: Praeger, 1980).
Robert Sklar, *Prime Time America: Life On and Behind the Television Screen* (New York, NY: Oxford University Press, 1980).

SELECTED PERIODICALS

Inside TV, Macfadden-Bartell Corporation, 215 Lexington Avenue, New York, NY 10016; Phone: (212) 983-5600. Monthly. Annual subscription: $4.00.
Better Radio and Television, National Association for Better Broadcasting, 7918 Naylor Avenue, Los Angeles, CA 90045; Phone: (213) 641-4903. Quarterly. Annual subscription: $6.00. Per issue: $1.50.
Channels of Communication, 304 W 58th Street, New York, NY 10019; Phone: (212) 315-2030. Bimonthly. Annual subscription: $18.00.
Chronicles, National Council of Christian Churches, Church World Service, 475 Riverside Dr, New York, NY 10115; Phone: (212) 870-2250. Monthly.
Dial, Public Broadcasting Communications, Inc., 304 West 58th Street, New York, NY 10019; Phone: (212) 664-7000. Monthly. Free.
Directory of Religious Broadcasting, National Religious Broadcasters, Inc. P.O. Box CN 026, Morristown, NJ 07960; Phone: (201) 540-8500. Annual: $15.00 per.
ETV Newsletter, G.S. Tepfer Publishing Company, Inc., 51 Sugar

Hollow Rd., Danbury, CT 06810; Phone: (203) 743-2120. Bi-weekly. Annual subscription: $135.00.

Emmy Magazine, Academy of Television Arts and Sciences, 4605 Linhershin Blvd., Suite 800, North Hollywood, CA 91602; Phone: (213) 506-7885. Bi-monthly. Annual subscription: $18.00. Per issue: $3.00.

SOUND AND VIDEO RECORDINGS: SELECTED BOOKS

J. Bishop, *Home Video Productions: Getting the Most from Your Home Video Equipment* (New York: McGraw-Hill, 1985).

A. Cristol, *Solid State Video Cameras* (Elmsford, NY 10523: Pergamon, 1985).

Gene B. and Kay Williams, *Chilton's Guide to VCR Repair and Maintenance* (Radnor, PA 19089: Chilton, 1985).

Your Movie Guide to Children's Video Tapes and Discs (New York, NY: New American Library, 1985).

Your Movie Guide to Comedy Video Tapes and Discs (New York, NY: New American Library, 1985).

Your Movie Guide to Classic Video Tapes and Discs (New York, NY: New American Library, 1985).

Your Movie Guide to Science-Fiction Video Tapes and Discs (New York, NY: New American Library, 1985).

John Lebaron and Philip Miller, *Portable Video: A Production Guide for Young People* (Englewood Cliffs, NJ: Prentice Hall, 1982).

Paula Rohrlich, *Exploring the Arts: Films and Videotapes for Young Viewers* (A Xerox Information Company, New York, NY: Bowker, 1982).

Don Harwood, *Video As a Second Language: How To Make a Video Documentary* (Syosset, NY 10791; VTR Publishers, 1979).

Daniel W. Holland et al., *Using Non-Broadcast Video in the Church* (Valley Forge, PA 19482: Judson, 1980).

Mat Irvine, *TV & Video* (New York: Watts Franklin, Inc., 1984).

John Yurko, *Video Basics* (Englewood Cliffs, NJ: Prentice-Hall, 1983).

Peter Lanzendorf, *The Video Taping Handbook: The Newest Systems, Cameras and Techniques* (New York, NY: Crown, 1983).

Printed Materials 191

Matthewson, *Beginner's Guide to Video* (Stoneham, MA 02180: Focal Press, 1982).
Frederick W. Rosen, *Shooting Video* (Stoneham, MA 02180: Focal Press, 1983).
Don Kaplan, *Video in Classroom: Guide to Creative Television* (White Plains, NY 10604: Knowledge Industries, 1980).
National Information Center for Educational Media, *Index to Educational Video Tapes* (National Information Center, Columbia, SC 29208: University of South Carolina, 1980).
Paula Rohrlich, *Exploring the Arts: Films and Videotapes for Young Viewers* (A Xerox Information Company, New York, NY: Bowker, 1982).
James McInnes, *Video in Education and Training* (Stoneham, MA 02180: Focal Press, 1980).
John Lebaron, *Making Television: A Video Production Guide for Teachers* (New York, NY: Teachers College, 1981).
David Lachesabruch, *Video Cassette Recorders: The Complete Home Guide* (New York, NY: Dodd-Mead, 1979).
The Tape Recorder (Austin, TX 78712: University of Texas: Austin Film Library, 1973).
Jane M. Leder, *Cassettes and Records*, Howard Schroeder, ed. (Mankato, MN 56001: Crestwood House, 1983).
Edward F. Dolan, Jr., *It Sounds Like This: How To Use and Enjoy Your Tape Recorder and Stereo* (New York, NY: Julian Messner, 1981).
Finn Jorgensen, *The Complete Handbook of Magnetic Recording* (Blue Ridge Summit, PA 17214: TAB Books, Inc., 1980).
Tape Recording Made Easy: A Programmed Primer (Joliet, IL 60432: G.T. Yeamans, 1983).

SELECTED PERIODICALS

Audio, CBS Publications, 1515 Broadway, New York, NY 10036; Phone: (212) 719-6330. Monthly. Annual subscription: $12.00. Per issue: $2.00.
*Audio Times, CES Publishing, 345 Park Avenue South, New York, NY 10010; Phone: (212) 794-0550. Semi-Monthly. Annual subscription: $50.00.

High Fidelity, High Fidelity, ABC Leisure Magazines, 825 Seventh Avenue, New York, NY 10019; Phone: (212) 265-8360. Monthly. Annual subscription: $13.95. Per issue: $1.50.

Tape Deck Quarterly, Box 1592, 20 Hampton Rd., Southhampton, NY 11968. Quarterly. Annual subscription: $4.50.

Video Magazine, Reese Communications, Inc., 460 West 34th Street, New York, NY 10021. Phone: (212) 947-6500. Monthly. Annual subscription: $15.00. Per issue: $1.95.

*Video News, Philips Publishing, Inc. 7315 Wisconsin Avenue, Bethesda, MD 20814; Phone: (301) 986-0666. Bi-weekly. Annual subscription: $197.00. Per issue: $7.00.

Video Review, CES Publishing, 345 Park Avenue South, New York, NY 10010; Phone: (212) 794-0500. Monthly. Per issue $1.75.

Videoplay, C.S. Tepfer Publishing Company, Inc., 51 Sugar Hollow Rd., Danbury, CT 06810; Phone: (203) 743-2120. Bi-monthly. Annual subscription: $8.25. Per issue: $1.50.

Personal Computers: Selected Books

Jack C. Howard and Paul E. Wilt, *Computer Science for Christian Schools* (Greenville, SC: Bob Jones University, 1985). Teachers edition available.

Dennis O. Harper and James H. Stewart, *Run: Computer Education* (Monterey, CA 93940: Brooks-Cole, 1985).

Brian J. Ford, *COMPUTE! Why? When? How? Do I Need To?* (North Pomfret, VT 05053: David & Charles, 1985).

John E. Savage, *The Complexity of Computing* (Melbourne, FL 32902-9542: Robert E. Krieger, 1985).

N. D. Birrell and M. A. Ould, *A Practical Handbook for Software Development* (New York, NY: Cambridge University Press, 1985).

Bill H. Behrendt, *Music & Sound for the Macintosh* (Englewood Cliffs, NJ: Prentice-Hall, 1985).

Phil Winsor, *Computer-Assisted Music Composition* (Princeton, NJ: Petrocelli, 1985).

Stephen J. Andriole, ed., *Software Development Tools: A Source Book* (Princeton, NJ: Petrocelli, 1985).

Dimitris N. Chorafas, *Interactive Workstations: Software & Hardware* (Princeton, NJ: Petrocelli, 1985).

*Software Encyclopedia, 1986, 2 vols. (A Xerox Information Company, New York, NY: Bowker, 1985).

IBM Software Directory 1985 (A Xerox Information Company, New York, NY: Bowker, 1985).

Van Loves Apple Software Directory (A Xerox Information Company, New York, NY: Bowker, 1985).

Peter A. Gebhardt-Seele, *Computer and the Child: A Montessori Approach* (Rockville, MD 20850: Computer Science, 1985).

Martin Siegel et al., *Computer As a Teacher* (New York, NY: Random House, 1985).

John Conrod, *Computer Bible Games, Book 2* (Accent Books, 1984).

Susan Evans and Peter Clarke, *Computer Culture* (Indianapolis, IN 46202: White River, 1984).

David F. Smith, *Computer Dictionary for Children and Other Beginners* (New York, NY: Ballantine Books, 1984).

Deborah C. Johnson, *Computer Ethics* (Englewood Cliffs, NJ: Prentice-Hall 1985).

Douglas Sloan, ed., *Computer in Education: A Critical Perspective* (New York, NY: Teachers College, 1985).

John A. Vonk and Fritz J. Ericson, *Computer, Society and Learning: Thirty-Six Lesson Plans for Teachers* (Kalamazoo, MI 49005: Learning Publications, 1984).

Selected Periodicals

*Computers and Education, Pergamon Press, Inc., Maxwell House, Fairview Park, Elmsford, NY 10523 Phone: (914) 592-7700 Quarterly. Annual subscription: $140.00. Per issue: $35.00.

Computers in Education, Mooreshead Publications, 25 Overlea Blvd., Suite 601, Toronto, Ontario M4H 1B1, Canada. Annual subscription: $20.00.

Computers in Education (Teaching Electronics and Computing), Electronics Today International, 25 Overlook Blvd., Unit 6, Toronto, Ontario M4H 1B1, Canada. Phone: (416) 423-3262. Irregular. Annual subscription: $25.00. Per issue: $2.95.

Computer in the Schools, Haworth Press, Inc., 28 East 22nd Street, New York, NY 10010. Phone: (212) 228-2800. Quarterly. Annual subscription: $24.00.

Computer and Society, SIGCAS Newsletter, Association for Computing Machinery Special Interest Group on Computers and Society, 1133 Avenue of the Americas, New York, NY 10036. Quarterly. Per issue: $1.25.

Computer Basics, Information Plus, 175 Washington Valley Rd., Warren, NJ 07060. Phone: (201) 560-1510.

Computer Graphics Today, 475 Park Avenue South, New York, NY, 10010.

Computer Instructor, Serbin Communications, 614 Santa Barbara Street, Santa Barbara, CA 93101. Quarterly. Annual Subscription: $6.00. Per issue: $2.00.

*Computer Journal, John Wiley & Sons, Inc., 605 Third Avenue, New York, NY 10158. Phone: (212) 692-6000. Quarterly. Annual subscription: $148.00.

Computer Update, Boston Computer Society, 1 Center Plaza, Boston, MA 02108. Phone: (617) 367-8080. Bimonthly. Annual subscription: $24.00. Per issue: $2.00.

Computer User, MSS Publications, Inc., 12 South 6th Street, Suite 1030, Minneapolis, MN 55402. Phone: (612) 339-7571. Monthly.

Computer User, Tandy/Radio Shack, 16704 Marquendt Avenue, Cerritos, CA 90701. Phone: (213) 926-9544. Monthly. Annual subscription: $24.95. Per issue: $2.95.

6

Learner Media Productions

INTRODUCTION

Good audiovisual media productions are an excellent learning experience for both students and teachers. Religious educators who take the time and effort to facilitate good learner media productions will find that certain traditional truths and values are more easily assimilated. Such knowledge has a better chance of becoming a *realized* awareness rather than merely a *notional* concept. (Realized knowledge is existential; it leads to a religious way of life. Notional knowledge is intellectual and essentialist; it leads to clarity of thought.)

The following guidelines will enable religious educators to facilitate good learner media productions:

(1) Plan carefully. Budget sufficient time and money.

(2) Use *all* learners. This can be done by helping learners realize the value and importance of small tasks. In major media productions, the script-timers, the propmovers, and the grips are as important and as indispensable as the more visible cameraworkers, the actors, and the directors. A visit to a commercial media studio will demonstrate this point very forcefully.

(3) Keep it simple and keep it short. Recall that some of the most effective audiovisual communications in the modern era are thirty seconds long.

(4) Let the ideas and the images come from the learners. Be a guide, not a master.

(5) Teach good editing as an effective tool for creating a powerful effect. Many young learners are deluded—because of the

studied casualness of many media personnel—into believing that audiovisual material can simply be "slapped together." Recall that the most casual rock music star may spend as long as a year to produce a record album with a playing time of eighty minutes.

(6) Teach learners that it is *hard work* to produce a good media effect, but it is also *enjoyable*.

(7) Try to translate a media project into another media, or into a multimedia form.

(8) Know the equipment thoroughly. This includes access to back-up equipment, replacement materials, and ascertaining that there are sufficient grounded electrical outlets available. Ill-prepared educators will discover the mechanical demons of audiovisual media: short circuits, burned-out projector lamps, reels that don't wind, and loudspeakers that whisper.

(9) Know what the learners actually know and do not know about audiovisual media. There may be some very talented learners at your fingertips. On the other hand, many of the media generation can often be quite ignorant about audiovisual materials.

(10) Use each audiovisual production as a learning experience to evoke an awareness of how media-effect takes place. (See the chapter on media literacy.)

(11) Draw up a lesson plan that demonstrates the application of this learning experience in media production to specific themes associated with religious education. Some pertinent examples are provided at the conclusion of this chapter.

(12) If you and your learners are proud of the results, show it to other learners, to other teachers, and to parents.

Required Audiovisual Materials for Learner Productions

Still Photography
  Equipment: camera, developer (or use of commercial developer), display board.
  Supplies: film.

Transparent Slides
  Equipment: 35mm camera, developer (or use of commercial developer), slide projector, slide carousel, table stand, display screen.

Learner Media Productions 197

Supplies: color negative film, developed slides.
Note: Commercial slides can also be rented or purchased.

Film Strips
   Equipment: film strip projector, table stand, display screen. Also: cassette recorder, or phonograph, if needed.
   Supplies: commercial film strip.
   Note: More advanced learners can make their own film strip using a motion picture camera. This process will also require a dark room/developer and a viewing editor.

Phonograph
   Equipment: record player with adequate loudspeakers.
   Supplies: records.
   Note: Music is best heard in a darkened room, with floor mats, or with a soft carpet and minimal furniture.
   More advanced sound systems have stereophonic record players, an AM/FM radio receiver, an 8-track magnetic tape player with a Dolby System, and a single track cassette tape player. Older learners and those in the music ministry will prefer the compact disc with a laser beam because of the excellent quality of replication.

Radio
   Equipment: AM/FM radio, adequate loudspeakers for stereo reception, and a cassette tape player. The tape player should be interconnecting with the loudspeakers to produce a "radio effect."
   Note: For radio music, the same listening room as for the phonograph is appropriate. Radio drama and interviews are best experienced in an open setting with other learners that is similar to a lecture room for an oral presentation.

Motion Pictures
   Equipment: super 8mm camera, or 16mm sound camera, with a microphone system, developer/dark room (or use of a commercial developer), projector, display screen with loudspeaker, spotlights, table stand, large viewing room, tape recorder.
   Supplies: motion picture film, blank tapes for the sound system.

Note: Commercial or educational films can be rented or bought.

The taking of indoor motion pictures requires adequate lighting, so several spotlights will be needed. If a sound studio is not available, the room used should be as free of noise interference as possible.

Television

Equipment: television set with VHF, UHF, CABLE, and, if possible, SATV and closed circuit reception capability; VCR, stand, adequate speaker system, viewing room, video camera/recorder (Camcorder) with microphone system, spotlights.

Supplies: blank tapes.

Note: Television requires very strong lighting for a good effect. If a sound studio is not available, the room should be as free of noise interference as possible.

Audio Tape Recorder

Equipment: stereo tape player/recorder with microphone system; adequate loudspeakers, tape editor/splicer.

Supplies: blank tapes.

Note: Commercial tapes can be bought or rented. The listening room for music can be the same as that for the phonograph. Drama and interviews on tape are best experienced in the lecture room used for oral presentations.

Audio recordings require a sound studio, or a room as free from noise interference as possible. Special safeguards are needed to insure tapes are free of magnetic interference. Diligence is required to avoid erasing a tape or recording over one needed for another project.

Video

Equipment: video cassette recorder, video camera/recorder (Camcorder), with microphone system, television, television stand, adequate speaker system, viewing room, spotlights, video tape editor/splicer.

Supplies: blank tape.

Note: Video requires good lighting. If a sound studio is not available, the room should be as free of sound interference as possible. The 1985 models of Camcorder manufactured by Panasonic operate well in normal room lighting conditions. The Camcorder is recommended as the least expensive type of television camera. It is small, light, and hand-held, and the most suitable for learners in producing television projects.

Personal Computers

Equipment: personal computer, display screen, line printer, phone modem, keyboard, desk top, learner's seat.

Supplies: software tapes/discs, blank tapes/discs, program manual, light pen.

Note: The most effective learning method is to have one computer per learner. Systems which enable the learner to program graphics and music are most suitable for developing media productions. The more sophisticated (the most expensive also) of these systems have an interface—immediate response—between a personal computer and a video screen.

Multimedia Productions

Equipment: television sets, display screens, slide projectors, motion picture projectors, audio tape recorders, video tape recorders, multiple track microphone system, multiple track loudspeaker system, projector room, large video screen interconnected with personal computer input.

Supplies: records, audio tapes, video tapes, color negative slides, film, computer program tapes.

Note: Both learner-produced and commercial a/v presentations may be used. The sound system should be synchronized with one or two of the visual presentations. Dual slide projectors can be set up to dissolve one into another. Some systems can synchronize a dissolve into a film projection. Display screens are available in which the projector works behind the display screen or from the base of an opened briefcase. Some slides and films, if projected from behind the screen, must be placed back-to-front in order to achieve the original effect. This may not be necessary, but is very important if lettering appears on the screen.

Sound Systems

Sophisticated sound systems include an audio studio, and an engineering room with a multitrack sound system. A mixer can be used to "bring up" or "bring down" different sounds. This produces the familiar effect of mood music welling up at a dramatic moment in an audiovisual production and then softening out at a quiet time.

Many recorders and cameras have microphone systems built in. A more sophisticated effect is achieved with stereo microphones leading into track A and track B, or with multiple microphones leading into multiple-tracks. A microphone normally feeds into a dedicated receiver. If all the microphones feed into a single receiver, the total effect can be noisy and unpleasant. One method is to record mood music or voice-overs on a separate tape system, and then play it during the showing of the video or visual portion. Speaking roles require synchronized sound, and this is what should be recorded directly onto the film and/or video tape. Microphones can be single-directional, which means the only sound recorded is from a source the microphone is directly pointing toward. An omnidirectional microphone picks up all of the sound within the reception range.

LEARNER PRODUCTION ACTIVITIES

The following exercises are suggestions and guides for the religious educator. Similar productions can be planned. These are designed to introduce the educator and the learners to audiovisual media productions with a direct application to certain specific themes. The religious educator is there not only to guide in the media-production but also to facilitate a comprehension of the themes associated with the experience.

Level I productions are suggested for learners in the early primary grades (ages 6-9).

Level II productions are suggested for learners in the middle primary grades (ages 10-12).

Level III productions are suggested for learners in the secondary grades (ages 13-17).

Collegians and adults are able to produce their own audiovisual work, and the ideas suggested here should stimulate their own creativity.

PHOTOGRAPHY

A. Photography: Personal Time Line (Level I)
Instructions: Each learner takes a 8½" x 11" piece of construction paper and draws a horizontal line through the center. Set points on the line define important family dates in the learner's personal history. Appropriate photographs are pasted either below or above the specific dates. Learners without photographs are encouraged to do drawings.
Examples: 1950. My father is born (childhood photograph).
1951. My mother is born (childhood photograph).
1978. My parents marry (wedding photograph).
1980. I am born (baby photograph).
1985. My sister is born (baby photograph).
1986. I begin school at _____ (class photograph).

Additional Exercise: The sheet can also be decorated with symbols appropriate to the learner's family, for example, an American flag for someone born in the U.S.A., a boat or plane to represent a member of the family who emigrated to America, other national symbols to represent the country of origin or the race of the learner.
Lesson Application: Uniqueness of each learner, sense of belonging, the people who make up the believing church.

B. Photography: Personal Jesse Tree (Level II)
Instructions: Have each learner draw a tree with several branches on each side of a large oaktag. Photographs of the immediate family and close relatives will be placed on the trunk and the branches. Drawings can be substituted for missing photographs. Deceased members of the family have a black border drawn around the photograph.
Examples: Paternal and Maternal grandparents at the base of the tree trunk.
Learner and brothers and sisters at the top of the trunk.

Paternal great uncles and great aunts on the right lowest branch.
Paternal uncles and aunts on the right middle branch.
Paternal cousins on the right top branch.
Maternal great uncles and aunts on the left lowest branch.
Maternal uncles and aunts on the left middle branch.
Maternal cousins on the left top branch.

Learners without such relatives should be encouraged to create a tree using close friends of the family. Many learners have special family friends who take on the grandparent or uncle or aunt role in their lives.

Additional Exercise: See audio tape for oral history.

Lesson Application: Sense of belonging and place in history as a preparation for the Advent Jesse tree and learning about the ancestors of Jesus.

Sight and Sound

C. *Transparent Slides/Audio Tape and/or Phonograph Portrait (Level III)*

Instructions: Each learner in the class brings in a transparent slide of himself or herself. The teacher takes slides of those learners who do not have their own. Each learner brings in a favorite record or tape with a song or piece of music which is their personal favorite.

The class then makes a carousel of all the slides. A tape is made so that about fifteen seconds of the learner's favorite song is played in the background while the learner gives his or her name and says a few words about himself or herself.

Note: If several learners have the same favorite music the same song can continue playing, while different speakers record their personal statement.

Examples: (Song playing in background.) My name is John Jones. I'm 14 years old, and I live in Smithtown. My favorite sport is hockey, and I think the New York Islanders are the greatest. (Song continues without text.)

(Switch to different song in background.) My name is Debbie Smith, and I just moved to Smithtown. I used to live in Boston. I like bike riding and hot chocolate (etc. . . .).

Additional exercise: A longer version of this can be done on videotape.

Lesson Application: Developing a sense of self-worth, respect for others, practical experience in production activities.

Audio

D. Audio Tape/Phonograph (Level I). The Christmas Story

Instructions: Have a phonograph softly playing Christmas carols, while one learner reads the Nativity story from the Bible. The other learners in the class will make appropriate crowd noises or animal sounds during the narration. The total sound effect is recorded on tape.

Examples: Mary and Joseph searching for a place to stay. (Different voices: "Go away! No room!" Sounds of doors slamming; knocking on doors, more of the same: "No room! Go away!")
Mary and Joseph find the stable. (Animal noises: mooing, neighing, barking)
Jesus is born. (Baby crying)
The shepherds come to worship. (Baaing)
The angels glorify God. (Singing)

Additional Exercises: Have the learners listen to the tape with their eyes closed and visualize what is happening in the gospel story. Do the sounds enhance their imagination?

Lesson Application: Reality of the humanity of Jesus, this early rejection foretells of the rejection that led to the cross.

E. Audio Tape/Phonograph (Level II). The Passion Story

Instructions: Have a phonograph softly playing hymns of Jesus' crucifixion, while different learners recite the passion story. The Catholic liturgy for Palm Sunday and for Good Friday provides a traditional selection of voice roles for this narrative: One learner is the narrator, one is the Lord Jesus, one is the single voice, and the remainder are the crowd. Additional sound effects can include soldiers' feet marching, the crack of a whip, a hammer hitting nails, etc.

Examples: "After saying these things, Jesus went forth with his disciples across the Kidron valley, where there was a garden, where he and his disciples entered" (Jn 18:1). (Silence, walking steps, the opening and closing of a door, yawns, sounds of men falling asleep, etc.)

Additional Exercise: The role can also be mimed while the narrators are speaking and the action videotaped or filmed.

Lesson Application: The power and reality of the suffering of Jesus.

F. *Audio Tape/Phonograph: (Level III). Remembrance/Meditation*
Introductions: Have learners sit or lie on the floor, assume a relaxed position, close their eyes and empty their thoughts of distracting images. Tell them to let the experience happen and to help each other by remaining silent. Music without words plays softly in the background. The leader speaks slowly, pausing frequently to achieve the full effect.

Example: Let us go back in time, recalling special moments in our lives, try to see the image suggested, hear the sounds, recall the sense of touch, the feelings experienced at the time. If memory fails, use your imagination to reconstruct the scene suggested.

> Getting up and coming here this morning (pause).
> The face of your best friend (pause).
> The faces of your parents, brothers and sisters (pause).
> The day you graduated from grammar school (pause).
> Confirmation (pause).
> First Communion (pause).
> First Penance (pause).
> The first day of school (pause).
> The earliest memory of your father (pause).
> The earliest memory of your mother (pause).
> The first time you realized I am me, I'm different than everyone else (pause).
> Baptism (pause).

Note: Those Christian churches which do not have major sacraments for young members may wish to substitute appropriate religious experiences, such as: reading of the Bible, the first time in church, first hearing of a sermon, first sense of belonging to a fellowship, earliest memory or image of God, and so on.

Because some memories for some learners may be very unpleasant, it is a good practice to "bring them back to the present," by mentioning each memory in reverse order, more quickly, and concluding, "Feel what it is like to be in this room, now, with these people, listening to this music. Now, when you feel ready, gradually open your eyes, and look around you."

Additional Exercise: Host a discussion in which the learners are invited (not forced) to share their key experiences with one another. The group may wish to re-create a particularly humorous one. This sharing or re-creation can also be videotaped or filmed.

Lesson Application: Appreciation of self-worth, place in God's plan, incipient instruction in meditation techniques.

G. Audio Tape (Level III). Oral History

Instructions: Have each learner prepare a cassette recorder and a blank tape. The purpose of this exercise is to learn living history by interviewing and speaking with older relatives and neighbors about their part in key past events. The tape is then played to the group as part of a sharing/discussion. Learners should edit before such a presentation.

Examples: Each parent about the day the learner was born and what happened.
Each parent about the day the learner was baptized and what happened.
A grandparent about what they did during the Depression, World War II, etc.
An older relative about how they emigrated to the United States.
An older relative about school when they were a child.
A pastor about how a church or mission was started.
A neighbor about how the town grew, what it was like fifty years ago, etc.
Different peers about what they did during a recent crisis, such as a hurricane, a flood, major fire, etc.

Additional Exercise: The group may re-create a particularly moving experience and videotape or film it.

Lesson Application: A sense of history, self-esteem, the religious educator can use this as a model for showing how the gospels are "oral history" written down.

Sight and Sound

H. The Story Board (Level II). The Good Shepherd
The Story Board is an excellent way to prepare for a film or videotape. Story Boards can be simple cartoons in sequence, or more elaborate images, with slides or mime enactments.

It is suggested that each scene be sketched on a piece of oaktag, with an appropriate text written below, and an audio tape made of the music bridge.

SCENE 1: Shepherd with many sheep. (Long Shot)
Text: The Good Shepherd knows his sheep.
Music: Paul Quinlan's *The Lord is My Shepherd* from the album *It's a Brand New Day* © Brophy Dad's Club.
SCENE 2: Shepherd with one sheep. (Medium Long Shot)
Text: He knows each of them by name.
Music: Continue: *The Lord is My Shepherd.*
SCENE 3: Shepherd feeds grass to sheep. (Long Shot)
Text: He feeds them with wholesome food.
Music: Continue: *The Lord is My Shepherd.*
SCENE 4: One sheep wanders away from flock. (Medium Close-Up)
Text: Then one day one of the sheep lost his way.
Music: Weston Priory's *O Lord Be Not Far* from the album *Wherever You Go* © Weston Priory Productions.
SCENE 5: A sheep lost in the woods, with wolves in the distance. (Long Shot)
Text: The sheep became lost and frightened. Danger lurked everywhere.
Music: Continue: *O Lord Be Not Far.*
SCENE 6: The shepherd seeks the lost sheep. (Close-Up)

Text: The Good Shepherd looked everywhere for the lost sheep.
Music: Continue: *O Lord Be Not Far*.

SCENE 7: The shepherd finds the lost sheep. (Close-up)
Text: The Good Shepherd looked until he found the lost sheep.
Music: *Eight-fold Alleluia* from the album *Hymn of the Universe* © The Word of God.

SCENE 8: The shepherd carries the lost sheep on his shoulder.
Text: The Good Shepherd brings the lost sheep back to the flock.
Music: *Eight-fold Alleluia* continued.

Other appropriate music can be substituted. The text would be narrated by a single speaker, placed on an audio tape, with the music bridge in the background. Scenes can be drawn or placed on slides. The Story Board acts as a guide-map in developing the film or videotape. Camera ranges are suggested in the parentheses.

Visual

I. Film or Videotape (Level III). Modern Retelling of the Good Shepherd

Using the Story Board above, restructure the Good Shepherd story and translate it into a modern idiom. For example, the Good Shepherd can be the father of a family, the flock the brothers and sisters, and the lost sheep a runaway teenager. The runaway gets lost in a large city, and the father seeks out the child.

Music bridges can be contemporary rock music.

Lesson Application: The importance of penance and divine forgiveness.

Audio

J. Audio Tape/Records/Radio (Level I). Disc Jockey

Have learner select excerpts from favorite records or tapes and introduce each one with a short statement.

Additional Exercise: Do this with church hymns.

Lesson Application: The influence of music on our moods and attitudes.

Sight and Sound

K. *Video Tape/Television or Audio Tape/Radio (Level II). Talk Show*

Have learner interview other members of the class about their family, their hobbies, their future plans.

Additional Exercise: Have an interview about the meaning of the sacraments, such as an upcoming Confirmation.

Lesson Application: The value, uniqueness, and importance of each individual.

L. *Video Tape/Television or Audio Tape/Radio (Level III). Meeting of Minds*

Have learners set up a talk show in which the interviewer meets and discusses important issues with figures from the past. One example would be a discussion about faith and religion with the great religious leaders of the world: Moses, Jesus, Mohammed, and Buddha.

Additional Exercise: This interview can have more immediacy if local pastors and rabbis can be included and use this opportunity to explain the meaning of faith in their different churches and synagogues.

Lesson Application: Origins of religion, ecumenism, and fostering of interfaith dialogue.

Audio

M. *Audio Tape/Radio (Level I). Broadcast Radio Public Service Announcement*

All radio stations to serve the public interest must during the course of their broadcasts include public service announcements. Have the class write one, record it, and try to place it on a local radio station.

Suggested Text: A message of love and concern from the _____ Christian Community. Faith in God can carry you through many problems. When you do not know where to go and your problems seem too much, turn to God. His love and care will see that you do well.

Additional Exercise: Visit the radio station to see how the message is made part of the daily broadcast.

Lesson Application: The message of Jesus must not only be believed but publicly preached. The power of radio to reach many people.

Visual

N. Video Tape/Television (Level II). Broadcast Television Public Service Announcement

All television stations on the VHF and UHF bands to serve the public interest must broadcast public service announcements. Have the learners write and produce one.

Suggested text: A close-up of one of the learners, speaking into the camera: "It's 10 p.m. Do you know where your children are?" (Written text as postscript): A message of love and concern from the _____ Christian Community.

Additional Exercise: Have the class visit the local television station to see how the tape is made part of the broadcast.

Lesson Application: The message of family life must be strengthened and nurtured on the television medium. The power of television to reach many people. The effort and work needed to get a message onto television.

Sight and Sound

O. Video Tape/Television or Audio Tape/Radio (Level III). Broadcast of Carols

Many radio and television stations want to broadcast local people during the Christmas holidays. Prepare a thirty minute program, with scriptural text reading and the singing of Christmas carols. Remember to give credit at the end to the various roles played by members of the class.

Make arrangements with a local radio station or television station to broadcast the program during the holidays. Some stations may prefer to tape the program themselves in order to control the quality of the sound or video. Follow timing directions very carefully, because of the tie-ins with network programs, or contracts with advertisers, the station may require twenty-seven minutes instead of thirty minutes, and so on.

Additional Exercise: Try to schedule an interview with a talk show host about the making of the program.

Lesson Appreciation: The work and effort required to make a good media production; the value of witnessing to the faith; the sharing of a Christmas present with many others.

COMPUTATION

P. Personal Computer/Audio Tape: (Levels, I, II). Days of Creation.

Note: The following exercise is done with a Vic Commodore Personal Computer. An audio tape can be made of the first chapter of Genesis, which lists the six days of creation. Computer graphics are geared to correspond with each day's creation. The first day: The creation of night and day.

Program: 1. FOR x=8 to 9
2. POKE 36879, X
3. PRINT "(Clear Home) POKE 36879," X
4. FOR T=1 to 1000
5. NEXT T
6. NEXT X
7. GOTO1
8. END

This program creates an endless loop, where the screen alternately flashes white and black, symbolizing the creation of Night and Day. The program can be stopped by pushing the Run/Stop key.

The second day: The creation of the firmament and the waters.

Keyboard Punching	*Effect:*
1. Shift (Clear Home)	The screen is clear; the cursor is at the top left corner.
2. POKE 36800, Control, Blue, instant delete back to the start.	The cursor turns blue, all directions are erased, the cursor is back to the starting point.

3. Command Key (C=), + key, for six continuous lines	A blue net box appears, and turns each line into a blue background, when six lines are complete, a sky or firmament has been made. The cursor is now at the beginning of the seventh line.

The third day: The creation of the land and of the plants.

4. POKE 36800, Control, Green, instant delete back to the start.	A green cursor appears, all directions are erased, and the cursor is at the beginning of the seventh line again.
5. Command Key (C=), + key, for 14 continuous lines.	A green net box appears, and turns each line into a green background, when the 14 lines are complete, the land has been made. The cursor is now at the beginning of the 21st line.
6. POKE 36800, Control, Black, instant delete back to the start.	A black cursor appears, all directions are erased, and the cursor is at the beginning of the 21st line again.
7. Move cursor up 6 spaces, and right 5 spaces.	The cursor is now in the green land.
8. Shift, X; Shift, X; cursor right 5 spaces; Shift X; Shift X.	Four small trees will appear in the green land.

The fourth day: The creation of the sun, the moon, and the stars.

9. Cursor up 12 spaces.	The cursor will be in the blue sky.
10. Shift U, Shift I	The top half of the sun will appear.
11. Cursor back two spaces, down one space; Shift J, Shift K	The bottom half of the sun will appear, forming a complete circle.

12. Cursor right 6 spaces, up 3 spaces. * Cursor 2 spaces right * Cursor 2 spaces right *.

Three stars will appear in the sky.

13. Cursor down one space, left 2 spaces Shift W.

The small moon appears in the sky.

The fifth day: The creation of the animals.

14. Cursor down 10 spaces, cursor left 5 spaces.

The cursor will be in the green land, but not on the same line as the plants.

15. Command key (C=),R, Command key (C=),R, Shift W.

The top half of an animal appears, with the head facing right.

16. Cursor down one space, left 3 spaces.

The cursor is directly below the top back of the animal.

17. Shift -, Shift -.

The feet of the animal appear.

18. Cursor left five spaces; Shift W, Command Key (C=),R, Command Key (C=),R.

The top half of a second animal appears with the head facing left.

19. Cursor down one space, left 2 spaces, Shift -, Shift -.

The bottom half of the second animal appears.

The sixth day: The creation of a human being.

20. Cursor left 10 spaces, up 4 spaces.

The cursor is on the green land, but not on the same line as the plants or animals.

21. Shift M, Shift W, Shift N

The head and the arms of the human being appear.

22. Cursor left one space, down one space, Shift -,

The torso of the human being appears

23. Cursor left one space, down one space, Shift -,

The lower trunk of the human being appears.

24. Cursor left two spaces, down one space, Shift N, Shift E, Shift M.

The legs of the human being appear.

Additional Exercise: Have a learner program the following into a second Vic Commodore Personal Computer. It will create a musical background to the creation theme, with a science-fiction mode.

1. Poke 36878,11
2. FOR I=128 to 200
3. POKE 36875,I
4. FOR D=1 to 100
5. FOR M=201 to 255
6. POKE 36876, M
7. NEXT D
8. NEXT I
9. NEXT M
10. POKE 36875,0.

Lesson Application: Learners can achieve a sense of wonder and appreciation of the effort and love that went into the creation of the universe.

Level III: Older learners can take the above exercise and program it in such a way that the different objects of creation appear in sequence. This can be done with a light pen, or with a program.

In another method, the learner or religious educator can place questions and answers into the program with "if . . . then" statements in such a manner that each object of creation only appears if the correct answer is given by the learner.

Conclusion

Learner media production activity can awaken an interest and love in religious education. From the experience of media production, the religious educator can also guide the learner into recognizing the analogy between God's work with humanity and the learner's work with the media. Some examples follow:

MEDIA EXPERIENCE	ANALOGY WITH RELIGIOUS EDUCATION THEME
PRODUCTION	CREATION

FAILURE	SIN
EDITING	SALVATION
STORYBOARD	BIBLICAL NARRATION
PERSONAL AND FAMILY HISTORY	SALVATION HISTORY
CAUSE/EFFECT	GOD/CREATION
MUTUAL COOPERATION TO CREATE PRODUCTION	CHURCH/HUMAN SALVATION
ENHANCEMENT OF ORDINARY EXPERIENCE	REDEMPTION

7

Religious Broadcasting

Religious educators need to be familiar with religious broadcasting. For many learners, religious broadcasting is an especially powerful stimulus for living a religious life. The potency of religious broadcasting raises some vital questions. Does it lead to more involvement or less involvement with the local church? Does religious broadcasting have an intellectual component, or does it merely cause a response on the part of the learner to an emotional stimulus?

Religious broadcasting may be defined as the explicit or implicit preaching of the gospel message over radio and/or television. Christian leaders are very divided over the value and the impact of religious broadcasting. Pessimistic transcendists, such as Malcolm Muggeridge, deny that broadcasting in any form assists the Christian mission.[1] Other transcendists, notably Evangelical Protestants, do not speak with one voice about religious broadcasting. Some Evangelicals, such as John Stott, an English clergyman, argue that the failure of commercial mass media to portray gospel values is due to neglect by Christians of the arduous task of producing edifying radio and television programs.[2] The majority of Evangelical Protestants, however, remain very optimistic about radio and television. Optimistic transcendists, such as the immensely popular Billy Graham, an Evangelical Protestant preacher, assert that radio and television are powerful allies of the Christian churches in their task of bringing the world to belief in Jesus Christ.[3]

Immanentists are just as divided as the transcendists about

religious broadcasting. The immanentist communication theorist, Neil Postman, for example, is extremely pessimistic about religious broadcasting. According to Postman, each television Evangelist is simply creating another mass-media personality cult. In Postman's eyes, religious broadcasting represents a complete avoidance of serious theology and does not inspire a true commitment to the authentic Christian tradition.[4] Thomas H. Clancy, a radio and television director who is an immanentist Catholic priest, offers a cautious optimism about implicit religious broadcasting. Clancy, however, remains pessimistic about explicit evangelism. He asserts, nevertheless, that broadcast news is a natural ally of the Catholic church.[5] Ellwood Kieser, a well-known media producer and an immanentist Catholic priest, is very optimistic about religious broadcasting. Kieser believes that all media programs which strive for the humanization of the audience (the basic task of preevangelization) are much more effective than those programs which limit their scope to explicit evangelization.[6]

THE TRANSCENDISTS AND RELIGIOUS BROADCASTING

Malcolm Muggeridge is convinced that the mass media constitute the most powerful communicative influence in contemporary society. In his view, the mass media exert an incomparable force on social, economical, and cultural levels. Writing as an Evangelical Protestant before his conversion to Catholicism, Muggeridge castigates the mass media for saturating the public with fantasy, because such media-fantasy turns people away from the truth of Jesus Christ. Muggeridge argues that the depiction of evil deeds by attractive people in the media make such sinful acts appear charming, and harmless. He complains that often news events are depicted in such a devious manner by the mass media that truth is totally obscured and only lies are communicated to the viewers. Screen images mesmerize the viewers, and frequently turn the public away from good and toward evil. Muggeridge lists the following as explicitly endorsed by the mass media: the trivialization of human death, blatant commercialism, the encouragement of sexual promiscuity, the acceptance of abortion as convenient and proper, the abdication of moral responsibility for evil deeds, and the glorification of the banal.

According to Muggeridge, the pernicious influence of the mass media is so pervasive that authentic religious broadcasting is simply an impossibility. He maintains that Christ is not the Lord and Master of the contemporary mass media; Satan is. He also notes that no one is quite sure what will or will not capture the public's fancy when it appears on the mass media. Something religious may become a fad, or a trend, or simply not be noticed at all. Muggeridge fears that this is the destiny of the Christian message on the mass media: The Word of Christ is swept away by the vast ocean of Satanic images which permeate the airwaves.[7]

Another transcendist, the Evangelical Protestant clergyman John Stott, is not as negative about mass media as is Muggeridge. Stott notes that historically Christians are always debating their proper role toward the non-Church world. Christians ask: Is it the Christian vocation to deny the world? To renounce the world? To affirm the world? To transform the world? To change the world? The mass media currently represent the non-Church world, according to Stott. For Stott, the problem with the mass media is not that worldly people control the mass media. Rather, the real problem is that Christians are not being the "salt" intended to cure the rotten meat. By this gospel metaphor, Stott suggests that Christians are meant to refine, to reform, and to rescue the mass media for Jesus Christ. In Stott's eyes, Evangelical Christianity stresses the reality of Christ in a media-world that has totally succumbed to fantasy. John Stott believes that Christians possess the skill to reform the mass-media world. Unfortunately, at the present time, Christians lack the will to do so.[8]

Billy Graham, the famous Evangelical Protestant preacher, is extremely optimistic that the message of Christ can and should be communicated via the mass media. He notes that Americans have many more opportunities to preach evangelism over the airwaves than do Europeans. Graham asserts that there are thousands of people whose lives have been changed by seeing a television program which presented Christ's gospel. Many of these same people would never have gone to a church or attended an Evangelical crusade. Graham contends that the world is tragically affected by the reality of sin. Consequently, the world's values are opposed to those of the Kingdom of God. Graham insists that the Christian's goal is to live for the glory of God, not for worldly values. Therefore, any problem with the mass media is a symptom of a much deeper problem, namely the alienation of the human heart from God. Consequently, only a radical transformation in Christ will solve the major problem. Once that transformation occurs, the mass media become a vehicle for glorifying God and not a stimulus for evil behavior.[9]

THE IMMANENTISTS AND RELIGIOUS BROADCASTING

The immanentist communication theorist Neil Postman argues that the medium of television has totally and universally conquered the culture associated with the print medium. For Postman, print culture is characterized by the slowed-down process of thought which is encouraged by written exposition. The television culture, by way of contrast, is characterized by the fast-tempo responses which are required by a visually entertaining show. Hence, as an example of this, the creators of the Public Broadcasting System's *Sesame Street* readily admit without any reservation, not only that learning is not obstructed by entertainment, but on the contrary, the learning is *indistinguishable* from entertainment. This breezy attitude is a total reversal of the print culture's traditional insistence that learning is hard and often unpleasant work. According to Postman, the television culture continually blurs distinctions. Consequently, the material and the spiritual realms are jumbled together on television. Such a confusion easily leads to the power and influence of television's evangelists. In Postman's view, each television evangelist constitutes one long and loud television commercial indistinguishable from all of the other inducements to use and to buy.

Just as the science-fiction shows give the audience "a message from outer space," Postman contends, the television evangelists give their listeners "a message from God." Postman insists that this slick presentation of the God-message is as banal and as manipulative as the other commercials for soap or cars.

Postman claims that television commercials have infantilized theology. Commercials do this by casting themselves in emotive language, that is, the commercials use narratives to appeal to the emotions. Postman insists that television evangelists do exactly the same thing. Television converts everything into a Las Vegas revue. The evangelical religion show is visually entertaining, emotionally appealing, and totally void of solid intellectual content. The viewer is presented with a handsome blow-dried evangelist, who speaks with a pleasant and authoritative voice, who is often surrounded by a beautiful family, who is applauded by an adoring audience, and who is accompanied by well-orchestrated music. Postman reminds us the television evangelist is not on a pulpit, but on a stage. The audience is not a congregation, but gawkers at a show. Postman castigates this whole operation, arguing that no dogma, terminology, logic, ritual, or tradition is called upon to burden the minds of the viewers. The viewers are merely asked to respond to the charism of the preacher.[10]

Mainline Protestants often denounce Evangelicals with this same charge. For many mainline Protestants, such a use of the mass media remains simply and primarily a personality cult. Furthermore, many mainline Protestants (and many Catholics also) are suspicious of the "abstract Christianity" fostered by the television evangelists. According to these non-evangelists, Christianity is meant to be experienced within a local community, with all of the problems inherent in many people existentially struggling together to achieve a common purpose. The television congregation only has to respond to a charismatic preacher. The effort of creating a community of believers who live and work together and thus form a church is not needed.[11]

Thomas H. Clancy, an immanentist Catholic priest who directs radio and television programs in New Orleans, presents a cautious optimism about religious broadcasting. In an article intended to encourage Catholics to get more involved in radio and television, Clancy states that religious broadcasting is unquestionably a booming enterprise. Quoting Ben Armstrong's *The Electric Church*,[12] Clancy notes that in an average week 47 percent of the American public turn to radio or television for at least one religious program, while only 42 percent attend a church service. The average weekly audience in America for religious programs on the radio is 114 million people. This is a staggering statistic, since it represents almost half of the population of the entire country. The television audience per week for religious programs is 14 million. By 1980 more than thirty television stations and more than 600 radio stations were exclusively devoted to religious broadcasting. The number of religious television stations has dramatically increased since that time, because many new cable stations are now exclusively religious in content. Almost all of these broadcast stations are owned and operated by Evangelical Protestants. Consequently, the radio and television programs are primarily Protestant and Evangelical.

Clancy believes that such Evangelical religious programs offer Catholics and other mainline Protestants an excellent opportunity to learn more about the deep religious values held by their brother Christians. Clancy also claims that listening to Evangelicals would constitute a step forward in ecumenism for mainline Christians.

Catholic religious broadcasting is also booming, according to Clancy. Writing in 1979, before the widespread expansion of the Catholic Television Network, Thomas Clancy noted that there are many Catholic sponsored religious programs on the air. In Clancy's own New Orleans market, Catholic radio programs were on the air eleven hours per week, and Catholic television programs were on the air an hour and fifty minutes per week. In Birmingham, Alabama, Mother Angelica, a dynamic nun in late middle-age, established a religious television station which is carried all across the nation by local cable companies. It is estimated that 10 million persons each day tune into Mother Angelica's EWTN daily (Eternal Word Television Network). As is usually the case with its Protestant counterparts, programing on EWTN tends to be quite conservative religiously and theologically.

Thomas Clancy does not believe that explicit verbal preaching constitutes the most effective form of religious broadcasting. Explicit preaching has limited audience appeal. In Clancy's view, the best religious broadcasting is that which is integrated with standard news reports. The reason for this is that almost all electronic media feature news programs of one kind or another and the general public by and large watches these programs. News programs draw a far larger audience than do Evangelical television preachers.

Clancy claims that papal deaths, papal elections, and papal visits to foreign countries constitute natural media events of a character which are at once newsworthy and religious. Such media-events bring the message of the Catholic church to countless millions around the world. John Paul II is exceptionally adroit in utilizing mass media for religious purposes. Even non-Catholics acknowledge and admire his skill in presenting the Catholic church on television.[13]

In Clancy's view, the awesome potency of television news is that it possesses the power to make anything important. The fact that the pope appears on television makes the pope important and, by inference, makes religion important in the galaxy of pressing world concerns. Clancy is quick to admit, however, that television news, by virtue of the very nature of the media, is more person-oriented and less issue-oriented. He readily concedes that there is always a danger of a personality cult. At the moment, religionists should rejoice in this fact since perhaps the greatest television personality in the world (globally speaking) is a religious figure, namely the pope. John Paul II is a global media event in himself. Christians will be more effective in promoting religion in this television age if local media produce local religious leaders who can themselves become local media events.

In an observation characterized more by parochial concerns and less by an ecumenical vision, Clancy asserts that Catholics possess a distinct advantage over Protestants in the successful utilization of electronic media. Protestants tend to center their television activities on preaching the Word, and this more often than not results in dull television. Catholics, on the other hand, tend to center on liturgical action; such kinetic and action-oriented worship with many in-built affective variables makes for appealing television.

On the other side of the coin, however, Clancy believes that Protestants are much more skilled than Catholics in effectively utilizing religious music. Gospel songs are exceptionally popular today. There are three major Gospel styles with much crossover: soul gospel music, which is connected with black rhythm and blues; traditional gospel, which is linked to country and western; and contemporary gospel, which is linked to adult popular music. It is in this last style that major Catholic artists are beginning to emerge. Clancy cites the St. Louis Jesuits, the Dameans, Carey Landry, and the Weston Priory as examples of contemporary leaders in popular Catholic gospel music. Clancy also believes that Catholic programs should use the rich store of Protestant gospel music.

Clancy maintains that religious programing should not be long and tedious. In religious broadcasting, less is more. He strongly recommends the use of succinct, high-quality commercials for a religious message. On a negative note, Clancy does not believe that long Evangelical Protestant programs are effective in converting an unchurched audience to belief. He admits that substantive religious programing might appeal to the already converted, but he denies that it has any appeal for the unchurched or the unevangelized.

Although most Protestant Evangelicals favor what is called the "talking head" format, Clancy states that this method is not effective. Evangelicals contend that such a format can cover the most substantive points of religion and of the Bible. This is the style favored by these Evangelicals affiliated with the National Religious Broadcasters. Clancy, however, insists that it is difficult to justify this "talking head" procedure by an appeal to the four gospels. Normally, Jesus' teaching was subtle. Jesus employed parables, and he usually didn't explain them. This is the storytelling format. Jesus used symbols to tease the minds of his listeners. He did this to spark his listeners to actual thought and reflection on his message. Clancy notes that, although there are a few long discourses in the gospel by Jesus, most of these speeches are simply not as dynamic as the presentations by many contemporary radio and television preachers. Jesus was not as anxious to cover a great many points in his discourse. Clancy also points out that St. Paul had a completely different style, more attuned to the present Evangelical method.

Clancy asserts that no one is actually converted by the mass media. He understands "conversion" to denote the original New Testament Greek word *metanoia*. *Metanoia* is the turning of one's life around in order to seek God or to establish a closer union with God. Clancy notes that commercial advertisers use the electronic media, not to sell a product, but to put the customers in contact with a salesperson who will do the actual selling. Consequently, in regard to religious conversion, Clancy argues that the electronic media can only raise the God-question which is *ultimately resolved by consulting a person*. Clancy argues that current research demonstrates that the majority of people do not form an opinion on an important question (such as religious belief) by reading about it in a newspaper or hearing about it on radio and television. Decisions of such a nature are made after people personally consult with a more informed member of their peer group, who has also been exposed to the same media information. Information thus flows in two steps, from the mass media to opinion leaders, and then from opinion leaders to the members of the peer group.

Clancy continues that, using the findings of such research, the Christian churches really should use radio and television to raise the "God-question" in the minds of the audience. Then the Christian producers should hope that, once the issue is raised, the question will be decided in favor of God in a later discussion among peers. According to Clancy, Christians should and can expect that religious broadcasting can raise the "God-question" for millions of the unchurched. Clancy considers this an urgent mission.

Clancy claims that money is the key to successful religious broadcasting. In 1977 it is estimated that religious broadcasters, mostly Evangelical Protestants, bought $500 million worth of air time. (Most radio and television stations will give religious broadcasters free air time in early morning nonprime-time program slots. For the most part, prime-time slots have to be purchased at premium prices.) Four basic costs are involved in broadcasting: time, production, promotion, and market research. Once a religious broadcaster has gained time on the air waves, the next step is to have a program to put on the air. While a religious program is on the air, the Christian producer must advertise the show. (This usually entails purchasing additional commercial air time.) After the religious program is seen, then the producer needs to find out if the program achieved the desired results.

In May, 1980, the American Catholic bishops began the National Catholic Communication Collection. For the first time in the history of the United States, the Catholic hierarchy made an institutional commitment to finance and to upgrade the religious broadcasting of the church. The initial target for this first collection was $7 million, which Thomas Clancy did not think at the time was really an adequate budget for such a major media enterprise. (Such a figure pales in comparison with the $500 million spent by Evangelical Protestants which only includes purchasing of air time, not production costs). Clancy believes that Catholic producers need to learn from the Evangelicals about the mechanics of financing major media productions. Catholics should systematically request funds from the audiences of their television and radio programs. Clancy insists that Catholic producers need to overcome their reluctance to request funds from their viewers and listeners. He adds that if the Catholic church can beg for schools, for the missions, and for the poor, surely it can also beg for the mass media work. To some extent, this advice has been heeded by the American Catholic bishops, who now conduct an annual appeal to raise funds for the mass media work of the church.

Writing in 1979, Clancy does not concur with many Catholic leaders who believe the purchase of cable stations is the most effective form of religious broadcasting. To be sure, he does admit that on cable television Christian producers do have complete control of the programing, and that is very appealing. The same producers also have the headache of putting something on the air continually, and according to Clancy, this is a nightmare. The Christian church should strive instead, in Clancy's view, to gain access to the broadcast networks which reach the major portion of the population.[14] Neither Catholics nor Protestants have heeded this advice, and today religious programing on cable television is a major enterprise of the Christian churches. There is a primary reason for this: Cable television enjoys what the market researchers call "good demographics," meaning that cable television is normally found in the homes of affluent opinion leaders. This is the very audience that religious broadcasters want to reach.

Ellwood Kieser, the Paulist Catholic priest who once produced the famous *Insight* series for television, presents an optimistic immanentist view about religious broadcasting. In an article intended to urge Catholics to become more involved in religious broadcasting, Kieser reminds his readers that in the past the

American Catholic church was primarily concerned with meeting the needs of the vast immigrant population. Such an enterprise forced the American Catholic church's vision inward. Consequently, all of the energies of the American Catholic church in the first half of the twentieth century were consumed in meeting its own needs. Accordingly, with few exceptions, there was little emphasis on a missionary outreach to others. The American Protestant church, on the other hand, was composed primarily of an indigenous population. The Catholic church, unlike the Protestant church, was not consumed with a burning desire to have a missionary outreach, or to serve the world, or to evangelize the unbeliever. Although all of these are essential elements of the Christian community, they atrophied in the early part of this century within the Catholic community. Protestants, not having to undergo the process of assimilation, however, were free to nurture such a missionary outlook. So Protestants took the initiative and became deeply involved in religious broadcasting.

Kieser notes that some serious problems face the contemporary American Catholic church. Of 61 million Catholics, 12 million are estranged from the church. There are 72 million churchgoing Protestants, and 11 million members of non-Christian religious—Judaism, Buddhism, and Islam. Sixty-eight million Americans remain unchurched, with no religious affiliation whatsoever. Kieser states that if we add 12 million estranged Catholics and 62 million unbelievers there are now 80 million people in America, or 40 percent of the total population, who do not enjoy the meaning, freedom, and love made available to humanity through Jesus Christ.

The issue for the Catholic church, in Kieser's view, is how do we lead such people to faith? The mass media provide the clue. Kieser insists that millions of Americans, especially the young, are currently fascinated by things of the spirit, especially by the very essence of religion: the experience of God. Such a media-generation is thereby especially receptive to the gospel.

Kieser surmises that this heightened spiritual sensitivity may be rooted in the souring of the American dream. Americans once erroneously thought happiness could be found in the possession of things, the good life of affluence, as if human fulfillment could be found in rising production and consumption.

Toward the end of the 1970s after much national disillusionment, Americans began to return to spiritual matters. For example, between 1975 and 1977, approximately 7 percent of American Catholics began to feel "more positive" about their own faith.

A new lay Catholic now exists in the Catholic church, according to Kieser. Energized by the theological metaperspective of Vatican II, such Catholics are no longer part of the traditional inward attitude associated with the immigrant church. The new lay Cathoics want to share their faith and vision with relatives and friends. This sharing results from a conversion experience undergone by many of these new missionaries. The new mission field of the contemporary church is the mass electronic media.

Kieser defines conversion as a "transformation of consciousness." This transformation brings about a reordering of goals and values and a redirection of energies. Most important of all, this transformation includes a total surrender of one's personal life to the God who has broken into human history in the person of Jesus Christ.

In Kieser's view, the sharing of this specific conversion experience is precisely what evangelization is all about. (Explicit evangelism is the preaching of the gospel message; implicit evangelism is the impetus toward authentic humanization, which is fully realized in the light of gospel salvation.) Consequently, anyone who is engaged in genuine evangelization will attempt in one way or another to reveal Jesus to his or her hearers. Evangelization involves preaching the details of Jesus's life, death and resurrection, but it includes not only saying what Jesus said but doing what Jesus did.

Jesus was the most powerful person in history in bringing about the humanization of people. Consequently, believers understand that God wills people's total humanization. This humanization, Kieser asserts, is the preoccupation of the authentic evangelist. For Kieser, unlike the early Malcolm Muggeridge, Christian values and human values converge and strengthen one another. Kieser insists that any time people help fellow human beings to take charge of their lives and to affirm their dignity, any time people help fellow human beings understand what it means to be human, any time people responsibly exercise their freedom by protesting unjust social conditions, any time people urge others to reach out in love to one another, then such people are doing what Jesus did. Precisely in this manner, Kieser claims, people are evangelizing.

Traditionally, Kieser reminds us, American Catholics have been reluctant to discuss publicly their relationship with Jesus Christ. God talk, Jesus talk is, for many Catholics, too personal, too intimate. By way of contrast, lay Protestants are three times more likely to engage in such missionary activity. (The Catholic charismatic movement, however, has changed the attitude of many lay Catholics, who now are very similar to other Christian evangelists.)

An important vehicle for the church in the evangelization of the unchurched, for Kieser, is the mass media, especially radio and television. Contemporary culture, he maintains, is preeminently a media culture. Increasingly, electronic media, especially television, dominate the culture. Television has created a new set of symbols by which Americans think; so television forms new role models for people. Only the family can rival contemporary television's power to shape attitudes, to communicate values, and to form consciences.

In Kieser's view, television is, after the family, the greatest of the humanizing vehicles. Television can therefore be a providential tool, put into believers hands by God, for the evangelization of the unchurched.

Television is fundamentally, for Kieser, a storytelling, myth-making medium. He also considers television an experiential medium. Television has the power to elicit a depth experience. Television can communicate with a nonbeliever in the privacy of the home, where he or she does not feel threatened in any way.

Kieser points out that television is truly a mass medium; only television can possibly touch all of the unchurched.

He enunciates six principles to insure that the Catholic church will truly be effective in its use of the mass media. Though Kieser's statements are specifically directed to Catholic media efforts, his views are equally beneficial for the media activities of other Christian denominations.

(1) Preaching the gospel and doing public relations for the

Catholic church are not identical. (Thomas Clancy misses this point.)

(2) Church activity on the media should reflect an immanentist orientation. Program presentation should be profoundly humanistic. Programs should include doing what Jesus did in exploring what it means to be human.

This immanentist perspective means programs that inspire liberation, motivate love, and unify the human family. The unique contribution of the Catholic communion is to lay bare the transcendent dimension of the humanization process. Thereby Catholic programs reveal God's immanent presence in the human and propel people to the full flowering of their humanity.

(3) Media work means collaborating with many non-Catholics who share the Church's vision about the welfare of humanity.

(4) At times, when using the mass media, the Catholic church should choose to be direct and explicit in talking about Jesus. At other times, the Catholic church should choose to be less direct, and more implicit. In its implicit stance, the Catholic church will seek to lead viewers to an experience of God's presence in the human. Both approaches are valid, and both approaches can produce evangelical results.

(5) Diverse media presentations will be needed for the diverse American public.

(6) Finally, the Catholic church should produce high-quality programs that can survive in prime-time slots and not content itself with early Sunday morning low-budget, small-audience projects.

Kieser concludes by calling upon the American Catholic bishops to make a unified effort to improve dramatically the Catholic church's media evangelization. He reminds the bishops that the Catholic church can no longer afford to be second-best in religious broadcasting. He specifically recommends:

(1) A research institute to study the evangelical impact of present-day electronic media. Such an institute can also formulate ideas, criteria, and principles by which communicators and audience can evaluate both secular and religious programing.

(2) Communication departments at Catholic universities and colleges which will produce theologically motivated, humanisti-

cally committed, professionally qualified communicators.

(3) Special pastoral care for professional communicators, especially in the mass media centers of Los Angeles, New York, and Washington.

(4) Collaboration with professional communicators who strive for humanization programs. The institutional church leadership needs to affirm those professionals who most fully communicate human values and so relate the insights of the Judeo-Christian vision of the human condition to contemporary life.

(5) Public confrontation of those programs that contribute to the dehumanization of people. There are too many crass producers in the mass media business who respond only to government intervention, or to the pressure of negative public opinion, or to the threat of losing lucrative advertising revenue.

(6) Media literacy for the American viewing public, so that people can recognize what is dehumanizing and what is humanizing in the mass media.

(7) Mobilization of the viewing public to create substantial support for humanizing programs and substantial opposition to dehumanizing programs.

(8) Recognition of the gospel imperative to maintain a Christian church presence at the communication subcommittees of both houses of Congress, and at the Federal Communication Commission (FCC). Many problems in American broadcasting can only be remedied by sophisticated political action.

(9) Development of national spokespersons who can bring the light of the gospel to bear on contemporary issues.

(10) The Catholic church requires adequate financing for the offices of national media operations. (This suggestion was taken up a year after the article was originally written, when the bishops inaugurated the national collection for mass media work in 1979.)

(11) Placement of high-quality evangelical programs in the broadcasting time-slots that are now opening upon the airwaves.

(12) Establishment in every diocese of a media center to produce radio and television programs and to act as an information center, a point of contact with the secular media.

All of these efforts, according to Kieser, will begin a dialogue whereby all believers can wrestle with the issue: How can the church best fulfill its mission to humanize and evangelize through the mass media?[15]

SUMMARY

Religious broadcasting is highly controversial among many Christian leaders. Both transcendists and immanentists argue strenuously about its true effectiveness. Evangelical Protestants, such as Billy Graham, believe that religious broadcasting is an especially effective tool for bringing people to a belief in Christ. Transcendists, however, have varying opinions about the mass media. Malcolm Muggeridge is convinced that the mass media are a powerful ally of Satan and so undermine the inculcation of Christian values in the public on a global scale. John Stott argues in turn that mass media will reflect the values of the gospel only if and when Christians strive to drastically reform contemporary programing.

In the United States, Evangelical Protestants have developed a vast and powerful network of religious broadcasts. Most Evangelical Protestants insist that such programing spreads the message of Jesus Christ and teaches people the truths of the Bible.

Most immanentists and many Catholics are uneasy about explicit evangelism on radio and television. The Catholic church in America did not commit much of its resources to religious broadcasting until the end of the seventies.

Neil Postman represents a strong protest against television evangelism. He thinks such an endeavor does nothing more than trivialize religion, stripping religion of intellectual content and rational thought.

Ben Armstrong sees another danger in television evangelism: the emergence of a personality cult that is not centered on Jesus, but on the preacher. He also contends that television evangelism produces an "abstract Christianity." In such an "abstract Christianity" believers do not have to existentially wrestle with the everyday problems of forming a genuine community where conflicting viewpoints often clash and need to be resolved.

Thomas Clancy is somewhat optimistic about religious broadcasting. Clancy sees an ecumenical opportunity: Catholics and

Protestants can learn more about each other through religious broadcasting. Catholics, for Clancy, are fortunate to have explicit liturgical action and papal ceremonies which appeal to the cinema and to television news. Clancy does not believe that explicit evangelism is effective on television. He does admit, however, that once the God-issue is raised by the mass media, the unchurched may be more willing to accept the Christian message from a peer group leader whom they respect and admire.

Ellwood Kieser is the most optimistic of the immanentist writers about the effectiveness of religious broadcasting. He notes that Catholics have a great deal to do to catch up with the sophisticated methods of the Evangelical Protestants, who have been committed to religious broadcasting for fifty years. He does not believe explicit evangelism is very effective on the mass media. He strongly believes in the effectiveness of programing which is intended to "do what Jesus did," namely, strive for the humanization of the audience. Kieser believes that the Catholic church needs to commit much more money and more human resources to religious broadcasting.

NOTES

1. Malcolm Muggeridge, *Christ and the Media* (Grand Rapids, Mich.: Eerdmans, 1978), p. 15.
2. John R.W. Stott, "Chairman's Speech," in Muggeridge, *Christ and the Media*, pp. 121-123.
3. Billy Graham, "Foreword," in Muggeridge, *Christ and the Media*, pp. 5-7.
4. Neil Postman, *The Disappearance of Childhood* (New York: Delacorte, 1982), p. 116.
5. Thomas H. Clancy, "Nine and a Half Theses on Religious Broadcasting," *America* (April 7, 1979), pp. 271-275.
6. Ellwood Kieser, "Evangelization through Electronics," *America* (May 6, 1978), pp. 358-361.
7. Muggeridge, *Christ and the Media*, pp. 15-16.
8. Stott, "Chairman's Speech," pp. 121-123.
9. Graham, "Foreword," pp. 5-7.
10. Postman, *The Disappearance of Childhood*, pp. 116.
11. Ben Armstrong, *The Electric Church* (Nashville: Thomas Nelson Publishers, 1978).
12. See Clancy, "Nine and a Half Theses on Religious Broadcasting," p. 271.

13. Bert Quint, "Television and the Pope: A Perfect Match," *TV Guide* (September 29, 1979), pp. 4-6; 8.

14. Clancy, "Nine and a Half Theses on Religious Broadcasting," pp. 271-275.

15. Kieser, "Evangelization through Electronics," pp. 358-361.

Part Three:

Media Appreciation

8

The Development of Media-Literacy

When an actor or actress can hold an audience spellbound, the performer has reached the peak of his or her career. When a college professor has more and more students clamoring to register in his or her courses, the teacher has become a true educator. When a preacher draws a larger and larger congregation each succeeding Sunday, then that person has become an authentic proclaimer of the Word of God. The theme of this book is that when media-literacy is truly mastered, the religious educator becomes genuinely effective and will find a receptive audience.

Talent alone does not make a great actor, a great teacher, or a great preacher. Each must hone his or her art with study, practice, and hard work. A really effective religious educator is a master of communication. In the present age, genuine communication requires a keen understanding of media-literacy, both for the religious educator and for the learner. Media-literacy enables the educator and the learner to recognize what media-effect is, when media-effect contributes to the enhancement of a religious lifestyle, and when media-effect undermines a religious lifestyle.

Media-literacy is a skill by which one recognizes how one is being directly or indirectly influenced to think, act, or feel in a determined way. Media-literacy includes the ability to accept or to reject this media-effect in the light of a Judeo-Christian value system which transcends socio-media codeterminism.

Since all media constitute an enhancement of human emotions, media possess an innate power to make *anything* seem more important than it really is. In the face of constant media-hype, many people simply withdraw into self-absorption and deliberately ignore many media-events. To overcome this resistance, media-advertisers use all forms of depth psychology techniques to win the public's attention and trust in their products and services. These psychological techniques do not address the rational mind. Associations of humor, pathos, passion, and pride are used to appeal to the emotions. The rational mind knows well that there is no connection whatsoever between smoking and being young, athletic, and beautiful; still the tobacco industry spends millions of dollars to insure that the public's emotions will make such a connection.

Different media in different ways extend a human faculty, replicate a human experience, enhance a human emotion, and establish a psychological association.

The *photograph* extends the human eye, replicates human vision capabilities, enhances nostalgia, and establishes an association of familial attachment.[1] The *phonograph* extends the human ear and voice, replicates human hearing, enhances moods, and establishes an association of home comfort. Moods generated by the phonograph include patriotism, romanticism, nostalgia, and so on.[2] The *radio* extends the human ear, the human voice, and the human foot. It replicates traveling to deliver an aural message. The radio enhances a sense of belonging. It establishes a psychological association of being identified with a specific group. According to Marshall McLuhan, broadcast radio was a key component in creating World War II, because the radio inflamed nationalistic loyalties.[3] The *cinema* extends the human ear, the human voice, the human eye, and human kinesthesia. It replicates human dreaming. The cinema enhances human admiration. It establishes a psychological association of desiring to imitate idolized celebrities.[4] Television extends the human ear, the human eye, the human voice, the human foot, and human kinesthesia. It replicates a human being present at an event; television enhances human participation. *Television* establishes a psychological association of being conscious of the globe.[5] It has the power to eliminate sequential time constraints and logical verbalization. Rapid-fire images simulate the extended consciousness associated with drug trips or certain forms of consciousness-expanding activities such as meditation and so-called "mind control."[6] The *audio tape recorder* extends the radio and the phonograph. It replicates human memory. The tape recorder enhances sound replication. It establishes a psychological association of retention. The *personal computer* extends the human eye, the human ear, the human touch, human planning, and human thinking. It replicates human intelligence. The personal computer enhances successful problem solving. It establishes a psychological association of satisfaction in one's own achievement. Marshall McLuhan considers the computer the key to reestablishing holistic knowledge.[7]

As a first step in teaching/learning media-literacy, learners need to experience how the media can bestow great importance on something insignificant. As an exercise, have two learners address the class. Learner A is to use a loudspeaker for every sentence spoken. Learner B is not. Learner A is to say inane statements, such as: "Cereal comes in boxes." "My house has a sink." "Books have pages and covers." After each statement, Learner B is to counter with a sentence of great religious significance, such as: "Jesus died for all of us." "Faith in God brings true happiness." "The Bible is the word of God." After this exercise, have the learners discuss the media-effect. Which speaker easily grabbed the attention of the audience? Which statements were *enhanced*? Which sounded *as if* they were unimportant? Lesson application: Excellent substantive content can be utterly lost by a low-grade structural content. Conversely, inane product-content can be greatly enhanced by a high-grade process content. Media-literacy includes the ability to recognize if the substantive content is intentionally related to the structural content.

Media-Literacy for Religious Educators

Religious educators cannot teach/learn what media-literacy is until they recognize that the modern media have had a powerful impact on all aspects of religious education. John Culkin, a Catholic priest who is a specialist in communication theory, provides religious educators with a key for media-literacy in their own field. Heavily influenced by Marshall McLuhan, Culkin persuasively argues that structural content alters the substantive content to which it is conjoined. Furthermore, certain kinds of structural content have a natural affinity for certain kinds of compatible substantive content. Every substantive content is therefore a content in structure, a content which is mediated by another content, namely structure. In this sense, the structural content, or medium, is a co-message along with the substantive content. This interactive, inherent relation between substantive content and structural content is very similar to James Michael Lee's theory of religion teaching.

Culkin attributes the following consequences of modern communication on contemporary religious education: (1) Ecumenism prospers, since particularistic faith formulations cannot survive in the global village; (2) biblical studies concentrate on the early oral contents and the cultural contexts associated with those contents; (3) the use of audiovisual communication does not mean the reinforcement of values associated with the print culture; (4) there is a new emphasis of the whole human race as the mystical body of Christ. Consequently, racism, sexism, and ageism approach their sunset; (5) there is an emphasis on inner psychological experiences; (6) there is a stimulus for liturgical participation; (7) there is a growth in Pauline charity, which is universal and not exclusive; (8) the essentialist God of Isaac Newton is near death; the existential God of personalism has a bright future; (9) teachers are witnessing the end of bureaucracy in the church, in the school, and in society; (10) values are to be discovered by learners, not dictated to the learners.[8]

John Culkin wrote this analysis of media-effect on religious education in 1969. Since that time, despite some set-backs, religious educators have witnessed: (1) interfaith cooperation in religious education (e.g., scholarly books such as this one are deliberately aimed at an ecumenical audience); (2) research into the oral base of the biblical narratives; (3) the weakening of many of the values associated with the print culture; (4) more and more efforts within the profession of religious education to address the wrongs done to women, the aged, and minorities; (5) the use of inner psychological experience as a methodology for teaching/learning spiritual consciousness; (6) increased lay participation in the liturgy, especially within the Catholic communion and in mainline Protestant denominations; (7) a new emphasis on charity for the world poor, the homeless, and the marginal in society; (8) a greater use of personalism as a philosophical and theological resource for teaching/learning a religious lifestyle; (9) some initial attempts on the part of the clergy to involve the laity more in the administration of church-sponsored religious education programs; and (10) the emergence of value clarification and discovery learning within the discipline of religious education.[9]

Media-Literacy for Learners

Since the modern world is a media-environment, a special effort is required to make learners aware of media-effect. A total environment becomes so much a part of a learner's mental map that it becomes, for all practical purposes, invisible. In his lectures around the world, Marshall McLuhan frequently alluded to the fact that trying to convince moderns that they live in a media-environment was like trying to convince fish they live in water. A fish only recognizes the specific nature of its world when it is taken out of it. In a similar way, modern learners only recognize a media-environment when they achieve media-literacy. A working test of media-literacy is taking a learner out of the total media-environment so that the learner can assess the impact of media-effect. This is the reason some retreat directors insist on learners being cut off from the media-world. The traditional rationale for a retreat is that a learner cannot hear the call of grace if the learner is constantly distracted with media-noise, a noise which unconsciously motivates the learner to think and to act in a determined way. These retreat directors hold that an authentic response to grace requires personal freedom, and a media-determined learner is not yet free to respond fully to God's call.

Media-literacy requires six constitutive elements:

(1) Awareness of the source of the substantive content (e.g., a novel, a biblical narrative, a news story, etc.);

(2) recognition of the structural genre (e.g., fiction, fantasy, document, commercial, etc.);

(3) knowledge of the target audience (e.g., general public, children, adults, senior citizens, residents of a specific geographic area, an ethnic group, a racial group, men, women, blue-collar workers, students, etc.);

(4) the intended effect (e.g., provide information, evoke a specific emotion);

(5) the actual effect (which many times is directly opposite to the intended effect, e.g., a commercial advertisement intended to encourage the purchase of a product may turn potential customers away; a satire meant to entertain may cause widespread anger);

(6) the learner's freedom to choose, to accept or reject, the intended effect. One of the hardest lessons for young American learners to grasp is that self-worth and peer acceptance is *not* associated with material possessions. Media-commercials have so affected youth's values that it is exceptionally difficult for youth to acknowledge this basic truth.

Awareness of Substantive Content. Religious educators need to guide learners to comprehend the original source of the substantive content in each of the media. Specific examples enable this awareness to take place. A written novel, for example, might be the source of a movie, such as Charles Dickens, *A Christmas Carol*. A movie such as *M*A*S*H* might be the source of a television series. A news event such as the American space program can be the source of a book and a movie, such as *The Right Stuff*. Once learners grasp how one medium can be the substantive content of another medium, and which one is the original source, then learners can more readily perceive the other elements: genre, target audience, intended effect, actual effect, and, of course, the learners' freedom to choose to accept or reject the intended effect.[10]

Substantive content in photographs can be (1) family and friends, (2) news events, (3) art, or (4) an advertisement. Substantive content in phonographs and audio tapes can be (1) instrumental music, (2) vocal music, or (3) speech. Substantive content in the cinema can be (1) family and friends, (2) news events, (3) art, (4) advertisement, (5) animation, (6) theatrical performance, or (7) information. Product content on the radio can be (1) news events, or (2) whatever can be placed on phonograph records or

The Development of Media-Literacy 241

audio tapes. Substantive content on television/video can be all of the above. Substantive content in a personal computer varies with the software, but the most common forms are video games, financial calculation, and word processing.

Recognition of the Structural Genre. Photography genres are (1) personal, (2) journalistic, (3) artistic, or (4) commercial. The genres in phonographs and audio tapes are (1) verbal or (2) musical. Verbal genres include (1) the factual or (2) the fictional. Musical genres can be (1) instrumental, (2) vocal, or (3) vocal-instrumental. Verbal genres can be dramatic or comedic; recorded speech can be (1) a monologue, (2) a dialogue, or (3) polyvocal. Musical genres in America include (1) classical, (2) popular, (3) rhythm and blues, (4) disco/dance, and (5) country and western. Specific genres also include youth rock and roll, Hispanic salsa, and gospel.

Cinema genres consist of the (1) personal home movie, (2) news documentary, (3) artistic, (4) commercial, (5) cartoon, (6) feature film, and (7) educational. Feature films can be (1) dramatic, (2) comedic, or (3) musical. Dramatic forms are murder-mystery, biographical, historical, romantic, horror, etc. Comedic forms are satire, farce, slapstick. Musicals can be any of the dramatic or comedic forms but usually involve a happy ending.

Radio genres include (1) newsreporting, (2) entertainment, (3) discussions, and (4) call-ins. Radio newsreporting includes sports events. Radio entertainment includes variety, music, drama, and comedy. In the past, the most popular form of the radio drama was the soap opera, which chronicled the problems of a fictional family or community. Discussions normally involve a moderator and experts on a specific subject. Call-ins permit the listeners to phone in their opinions and have their opinions broadcast also.

Television and video include all of the forms available in the media listed above. Television genres include the time of day: (1) morning programs, (2) day-time programs, (3) prime-time evening programs, and (4) night programs. Television stations broadcast their most recent and their best programs (at least as they see it!) during prime time. Popular television genres include the game show (which is a programed news event), the soap opera, situation comedy, the mini-series, the variety show, the action show, a major news event such as a presidential election or space flight, a major sports event, such as football's Super Bowl, documentaries, and, of course, commercials. Video is a new method for selling records to youth and thousands of videos are now made by major record companies and singing acts. Videos have been praised for being a totally new form of nonsequential imagistic communication. Videos have also been denounced for emphasizing sex and violence.

Genres in the personal computer vary with the many forms of software available. For our purposes, principal genres in the personal computer include programed learning, computer games, and graphic arts.

Knowledge of the Target Audience. A personal photograph is intended for a small circle of relatives and friends. A newsphoto is intended for the general public. An art photograph is intended for a special audience of those who appreciate such aesthetic material. An advertisement photograph is intended for a specific group of consumers.

A music phonograph or audio tape is intended for the record-buying public. Certain types of music are aimed at specific buyers, as for example, adults, youth, music students, blacks, Hispanics, the aged, and so on. Verbal reenactments are normally intended for educational purposes. Comedy records are aimed at that segmnt of the public who enjoy certain types of humor.

Radio audiences tend to be very specific. Programs are aimed at (1) the driving public, (2) people at work, (3) women at home, (4) youth, (5) the aged, (6) specific ethnic groups, and (7) people who live in a particular geographic area. Sports programs are aimed at baseball fans, or football fans, and so on. Certain all-news programs are aimed at executive decisionmakers.

Learners can discover what specific audience a radio station is targeting its programs for by writing and asking for the demographic profile of the listeners. Advertisers select what stations they use on the basis of these reports.

Until 1980, television aimed its programs at the widest possible audience, concentrating its prime-time programs on affluent, middle-aged Americans, 25-38, who were starting their families and buying their own homes. This audience constituted the largest segment of the consumers in the United States. With the advent of the video cassette recorder and cable channels, the upper-income portion of this audience began to slip away. Broadcast television responded by upgrading the quality of much of its programing, so that prime-time television is managing to hold on to some of this audience. Like radio, television aims its programs during the day at specific narrow audiences, such as homemakers, the aged, and children. The Public Broadcasting System aims its prime-time programs at the educated, while most sports events on the other networks are intended for blue-collar workers. Network executives use the Nielsen and Arbitron systems (a statistical sample of certain home-viewers) to determine the demographic appeal of their programs. Many excellent programs have been taken off the air because they appealed to the young or to the aged, rather than to the middle-aged with the greatest amount of purchasing power. The emergence of cable and UHF stations now means that television is becoming more of a medium for a narrow audience and less of a mass medium for the largest audience.

Until 1960, most cinema was aimed at adults. When most adults subsequently stayed home to watch television, the cinema redirected its target audience. Today most movies are intended for a youth audience, 18-25. The most successful films, however, are those with the broadest appeal, with a story line and excellent action that attract adults as well as youth. Sex and violence are frequently used in the cinema to maintain the interest of the youth audience. Some storylines are quite well done, but others are sophomoric and tasteless. Because of the heavy expenses involved, today's cinema tends to be either very good or very bad. It is rare today to have an "average" movie in terms of quality.

Computer companies are specifically designing their personal computers to be used by the widest group of people possible. Most popular with young males, the personal computer is becoming part of the everyday life of students, homemakers, women, even factory workers and farmers. Although a personal computer is designed for a single user, software is intended for large segments of the computer-literate public. Obviously, specific software is aimed at specific audiences such as business executives, writers, financial managers, students, secretaries, merchants, graphic artists, and so on. Electronic mail and telephone modems are intended to link computer users and to create a computer-savvy public in constant intercommunication.

Recognition of the Intended Effect. All media intend to (1) provide information and (2) evoke an emotion. Totally objective information, which has no emotional intent, is almost impossible, since both the creator and the editor select material that they expect will evoke a response.

The personal photograph, for example is not meant merely to record a family event but also to evoke a response such as love, caring, joy, and the like. A few news photographs are intended to provide only information. Usually, however, news photographs also have an emotional appeal. During World War II, the news photograph of the marines on Iwo Jima struggling to raise the American flag in a strong crosswind became a patriotic symbol. Art photographs are intended not only to replicate a visual scene but to evoke an aesthetic response from the viewer. Commercial photographs are designed to motivate the consumer to desire the product or service portrayed.

Verbal replication on the phonograph or on tape is usually aimed at providing cognitive information. Dramatic reenactments are intended to entertain and to evoke certain responses. Vocal music provides a minimum of cognitive information and is mainly concerned with evoking an emotional response. Instrumental music is primarily concerned with stimulating an aesthetic response, with specific emotional overtones. Religious educators can guide learners in the recognition of intended emotional responses by playing certain forms of music, and after the learners have listened in silence, ask the learners to state the principal emotion they felt. Although there will obviously be some variation, the religious educators will find that a majority of the learners had similar responses: (1) a love song is intended to evoke a romantic response, (2) a blues song is intended to evoke sadness, (3) a military march is intended to evoke patriotism, (4) most classical music is aimed at evoking relaxation and thoughtful reflection. In the verbal genre, a comedy record is intended to evoke laughter.

The Development of Media-Literacy 245

In the cinema, most home movies are intended to replicate family scenes and evoke a sense of belonging and caring about one another. Most news documentaries replicate facts but are also designed to create a sense of belonging to a community, or being angry at a foreign invasion, or feeling pity for the poor, and so on. Artistic cinema works are intended to evoke an aesthetic response. Commercial cinema is aimed at appealing to the desire of potential consumers to possess a product or service. Commercial cinema is considered to be exceptionally effective because the medium makes people and products look better than they actually are. Animated cartoons are normally intended to provoke laughter. Theatrical performances in feature films evoke the whole spectrum of emotional responses, including: anger, horror, patriotism, romanticism, sadness, pity, and so on. Most features focus on one specific emotion, though many films appeal to several emotions.

Emotional responses to the same feature can vary with a specific audience. Older people watching a silent comedy made in the twenties may experience nostalgia, since the movie reminds them of their youth. Young people, with no recollection of the same era, may concentrate on the comedy and find it humorous. Feature-length documentaries not only provide information and serve as educational tools but almost always have an emotional intent. A film biography of Abraham Lincoln will evoke a sense of patriotism in Americans. Many blacks, viewing a film of Lincoln, will feel a sense of gratitude, an emotional response which would be rare in a white audience.

Broadcast radio shares the same effects as the phonograph and audio tapes. In addition, sound commercials have a unique ability to stimulate the imagination of the viewer. Such commercials have a powerful emotional impact, and if well designed can widen the appeal of an advertised product. It is the nature of the radio medium to stimulate a sense of belonging in the listeners. Pride in a community, or in a state, or within a specific group of people, or in a region, or in a nation can readily be attained by radio forms which link large groups of people together. Unfortunately, radio can also be used to pit generation against generation, race against race, one national group against another. Radio is a powerful medium for bringing people closer together; it can also alienate one group from another and stimulate fear and hatred of those who are different.

Television possesses the same range of cognitive information and emotional appeal as the phonograph, the photograph, the cinema, and the radio. In addition, television is the great unifier of people. It is the one medium uniquely designed to evoke a sense of unity within the entire human family. While the depiction of war on the cinema normally evokes a sense of patriotism and hatred of the enemy, a news documentary on television about war normally evokes a sense of repulsion at actual violence and, concomitantly, a certain sympathy for the enemy. Soviet television documentaries on the 1980s war in Afghanistan are carefully edited so that the Russian people will not see the damage their troops are doing to civilians or the losses their army is enduring. The British government refused to permit television crews to film the Falkland Islands war so that the people in England would not be repulsed by the horror of fighting the battle to regain possession of the territory. Print and news photographs in the past could easily be edited by government officials, so that only the desired information got out to the public. By way of contrast, no government official can erase the pain of watching a television scene of a civilian seeing his burned-out home and his children shot by the soldiers of a nation. Once such a scene is televised to a nation's public, the public's support of their armed interventions evaporate. In the United States, television is the principal reason why the American public stopped supporting the intervention in Vietnam.

The personal computer provides a wide range of cognitive information and a full range of emotional responses. Unique to the personal computer is a sense of pride in accomplishment and a feeling of mastery or control of a specific environment.

Recognition of the Actual Effect. Media are designed to make people think and act in a determined way. The actual effect of the media is to create people who do not think for themselves but react as they are programed to do so. True personal freedom can only be gained when a learner acknowledges what is actually happening to him or her because of the media. Media-effect works on the unconscious; therefore, it is as hard to discover the actual media-effect as it is for depth psychology to penetrate to the actual source of emotional behavior in the psyche.

COMPARISON OF MEDIA-EXPERIENCES AND ACTUAL EXPERIENCES

Actual Events	*Media-Events*
1. Listening to someone say he or she loves you.	1. Listening to a singer saying he or she loves you.
2. Driving a car.	2. Watching a car commercial.
3. Being hugged and kissed by a loved one.	3. Watching two actors hug and kiss.
4. Army training.	4. Watching a war movie.
5. Playing a sports game.	5. Watching a sports game.
6. Making a faith commitment.	6. Watching a preaching of the gospel.

All media-events are vicarious experiences and do not have the full power to involve the whole person. Although the singer on the record may have a more beautiful voice, be accompanied by romantic music, and have an appealing personality, he or she does not love the listener as a lover but as a consumer. The car commercial is designed to create a sense of pride in possession, freedom, and mastery on the road. An actual driver must obey all of the traffic laws on the book or wind up in jail or dead. The car commercial emphasizes the driver as master, but in actuality is directed at the driver as car buyer. The actual driver is controlled by the community's driving laws and neglects them at his or her peril. A person who hugs and kisses you may not be as beautiful or as appealing as the cinema star but loves you for yourself. The actor and actress are pretending to be lovers and are primarily interested in advancing their careers, not making love to one another. Boot camp for any soldier is a hard and disciplined life. It is intended to make the soldier into a professional killer who is willing to die for his or her country. Soldiers in a feature film are dodging blank bullets and running away from smoke screens. Film soldiers pretend to fight and die for their country. Actual soldiers do fight and die. A war movie is normally intended to evoke patriotism and military pride; an actual war means widespread death and destruction. The war movie typically does not portray the soldier as victim but as victor. The war movie audience is supposed to forget the horror and concentrate on the glory.

One of the most popular entertainments in America today is watching trained athletes play a sports game. Any amateur athlete knows how hard it is to play even the simplest game well. The illusion is created that these professional athletes play hard and well out of sheer love for the game. The whole purpose of a sports event is not to have an athletic competition but to sell sports equipment, beer, and shaving cream. Most of the products advertised at sporting events, if fully used, would make the purchaser unable to perform the simplest athletic function. Media-sports are played, not for the sportsmanship, but for the marketing.

One of the hardest things in life to do is to accept God as one's master in life. A true religious commitment means a complete change of heart. It means that one's lifestyle is no longer for self but for others. It also means that one no longer sees the self as a purchaser but as a person. In other words, a true religious lifestyle means the end of mass-media *determination*. The truly free person is not boxed in by the false promises of the mass-media. Too often, media-preaching does not lead to this freedom. Media-preaching can lock a listener into the same determined pattern as other commercials. The media-believer can mouth Christian truths, but, like an adolescent's love for a rock star, the conversion is a vicarious experience, not a real one.

The Learners' Freedom. Any freedom comes after hard work and effort. The American Revolution cost lives and money but earned the United States its freedom. The Judeo-Christian tradition is rooted in personal freedom. The Exodus means the end to Hebrew slavery. The passion, death, and resurrection of Jesus, for the Christian, means freedom from sin and social-determination. The Protestant Reformation, for all the pain it caused all

Christians, is intended to free believers from oppressive church authority. Within the Catholic communion, Vatican II is a sincere effort to promote freedom within the church.

The first requirement of freedom is the recognition that one is not free but a slave to determined behavior. The second requirement is to recognize how technology is employed to keep one subservient. The third is to exercise one's freedom to choose.

Religious educators need to guide learners carefully so that they can recognize how media determine their behavior and how they can be free to accept or reject such media-determination. A guidance in personal freedom means precisely that; it does no good to substitute one form of control for another. This present volume is intended to help religious educators to guide learners, not to dictate to them.

As one exercise in choice, ask the learners to purchase two boxes of the same food: a nationally advertised brand and a no-frills one. Cover the boxes with heavy construction paper and have each learner sample the two products. Can anyone tell the difference? Why does the advertised one cost more than the no-frills one? Why do so many people buy the more expensive one if it is exactly the same thing? Are people exercising freedom or simply going along with the crowd? Why do people pay more for the same thing?

Summary

Media-literacy requires an ability to recognize substantive content, genre, target audience, intended effect, actual effect, and the freedom one has to accept or reject the intended effect.[11] Most major media forms are intended to encourage the purchase of products and/or services. Religious educators can foster media-literacy in their learners by doing instructional exercises which make them conscious of the six elements. Media-literacy is exceptionally difficult to teach/learn since most learners are unconscious of media-effect and do not believe they are determined to act and to think in a set way. One method retreat directors use to free learners from media-effect is to cut off all media-noise during the time of the retreat.

Notes

1. Marshall McLuhan, *Understanding Media: The Extensions of Man* (New York: Signet Books, 1964), pp. 169-181.
2. Ibid., pp. 241-248.
3. Ibid., pp. 259-268.
4. Ibid., pp. 248-259. See also: John Phelan, *Mediaworld* (New York: Seabury, 1977).
5. McLuhan, *Understanding Media*, pp. 268-294.
6. Robert Masters and Jean Houston, *Mind Games: The Guide to Inner Space* (New York: Dell, 1972).
7. McLuhan, *Understanding Media*, pp. 300-311.
8. John Culkin, "A Guide to McLuhan," *Religious Teacher Journal* (October, 1969), pp. 26-29. See also James Michael Lee, *The Content of Religious Instruction* (Birmingham, Ala.: Religious Education Press, 1985), pp. 78-128.
9. Andrew Greeley, *The New Agenda* (Garden City, N.Y.: Doubleday, 1973), pp. 150-180.
10. The written sources for these three productions are: Charles Dickens, *A Christmas Carol* (New York: St. Martin, 1979); Richard Hooker, *MASH* (New York: Pocket Books, 1982); Tom Wolfe, *The Right Stuff* (New York: Farrar, Straus and Giroux, 1979). Much of modern biblical criticism is based on making learners aware of these six elements. Most of the misunderstandings about the Bible stem from a failure to recognize the six elements, so that, for example, the Book of Jonah is read by some Christians as if it were a historical account, while it was intended by the sacred author as a fictional satire on the complacency of the ancient Hebrews.
11. The following texts will assist the religious educator in becoming more conversant with the principles of media-literacy:

> David C. Czitrom, *Media and the American Mind: from Morse to McLuhan* (Chapel Hill, N.C.: University of North Carolina Press, 1982).
>
> Everette E. Dennis and John C. Merrill, *Media and Contemporary Society* (New York: Macmillan, 1984).
>
> Peter M. Sandman, et al., ed., *Media: An Introductory Analysis of Mass Communication*, 3rd ed. (Englewood Cliffs, N.J.: Prentice-Hall, Inc. 1982).
>
> Tony Schwarz, *Media: The Second God* (New York: Random House, 1982).
>
> Robert H. Stanley and Charles S. Steinberg, *Media Environment: Mass Communication in American Society* (Ardmore, Pa.: Hastings Books, 1976).
>
> Robert Stein, *Media Power: Who Is Shaping Your Picture of the World?* (Boston: Houghton-Mifflin, 1972).

9

The Development of Motion Picture Appreciation

Feature films have an enormous impact on the lifestyle of many Americans, especially adolescents and young adults. Films influence fashion, purchasing, how we look at ourselves as a people, how we love, how we hate, how we raise our children, how we treat our parents, and so forth. In our mediaworld, movie-makers are much more influential than educators, church leaders, or politicians. Because of mass media, film celebrities are often the focus of people's attention. Film celebrities can win our attention and secure our loyalty. On the one hand, film celebrities can inspire us to be better than we are; on the other hand, they can corrupt us to be worse than we are. Some film stars can lead some impressionable people astray into an immoral lifestyle by promoting promiscuous sex, irresponsibility, illicit drugs, and unnecessary conspicuous consumption. Other film stars can also encourage people to live a Judeo-Christian lifestyle by championing the cause of the poor, by fighting corruption in public life, and by supporting various worthwhile charities. Ronald Reagan, a president of the United States, was a former movie actor.

With proper guidance from religious educators, young learners can discern when a film is affirming a Judeo-Christian lifestyle or when it is denying such a lifestyle. Motion picture appreciation, or cinema-literacy, means, among other things, that sometimes a movie that explicitly preaches the gospel may be so poor as a movie that it actually undermines the Judeo-Christian lifestyle. By way of contrast, sometimes a film about people who do not live a Judeo-Christian lifestyle may be so well done as a movie that the film clearly reveals that such evil behavior is wrong. Accordingly, sophisticated discernment is required of any religious educator who uses cinema-literacy as a resource in the teaching/learning of a religious lifestyle.

Print and other media criticisms can assist a religious educator in understanding a film. The best way, however, to learn to appreciate a movie is to watch the film and then discuss it with professional peers or with learners. An excellent film requires several viewings to discover how subtle nuances are used to expound the theme. Films depend on rapid visual images and synchronized sound for their total impact. Many times important clues to the overall effect are missed if the viewer watches the film only once. Some poor films, however, are simply not worth that investment in time and effort.

Cinema-literacy requires an awareness of several key elements: the target audience, the intended effect, the actual effect, and the viewer's freedom to accept or to reject the effect. This chapter will concentrate on the key elements of cinema-literacy: (1) the stages of a film, (2) the sources of a film, (3) key personnel in movie-making, (4) historical periods, and (5) the genre of the film. Awareness of these five elements can enable the religious educator and the learner to develop a sophisticated cinema-literacy. Such cinema-literacy can serve as an excellent resource in the teaching/learning of a religious lifestyle.

THE STAGES OF A FILM

Films begin with a *concept*. A concept is a key storyline or a central image that so grips the imagination that the movie-makers predict the film will attract a mass audience. By way of example, the opening session of the Supreme Court of the United States is usually not material for an exciting movie. A story about the first woman to join the Supreme Court, however, is an exciting story. The movie *First Monday in October* predates the appointment of Sandra Day O'Connor, the first woman Supreme Court justice. In some ways, the film prepared the American psyche for this historical change, even to the point of predicting

The Development of Motion Picture Appreciation 253

that the first woman justice would be a champion of a conservative interpretation of constitutional law.

The *script* is written to develop the concept more fully. A script includes the visual scenes, the dialogue, and usually recommends in a general way camera angles. A *storyboard* is based on the final written script, or in some cases may predate a written script if the concept is based more on a series of visual images.

Financing is secured to insure that all of the expenses of the movie to be made will be paid. Feature films are expensive and indeed quite risky since many do not make a return on the initial investment. A small group of wealthy people or a large corporation must so believe in the concept and in the box office appeal of the major performers that they are willing to risk the large sums of money involved. Movies with a large cast and many special effects can cost $25 to $50 million. An average feature film today costs $5 million to make.

The financial backers select the *producer,* who is responsible for the executive administration of the movie production. Some producers work for major studios; others are independent. The producer chooses the *director,* who then *casts* the movie. Some producers insist on deciding which major performers will act in the movie instead of letting the director choose. The director converts the concept and the written script into a series of film images. The director runs the rehearsals, blocks out positions, manages the shootings, and reviews the daily rushes (the scenes that have been shot that day). Scenes are almost never shot in the written order of the script, but according to the availability of performers, weather conditions, studio times, and so forth.

After the principal actors and actresses are on contract to do a film, the *casting director* selects all of the other performers for the remaining parts. Performers rehearse scenes, the director blocks out positions, and then the acting is done before the camera. The same scene may be shot many times, from different camera angles, and with different cameras. At the daily rushes, the director selects the combination of film scenes that are to be in the master print.

Shooting a film takes a long time. A ninety-minute movie on the screen usually requires six to nine months of shooting. The rigors of movie making can be quite demanding on the actors and actresses. For example, standing in very cold weather they may have to pretend that they are sweating on a hot, August day. After a leisurely break, they may have to pretend that they are being pursued by gangsters.

When a film is completed, the prints are *spliced*, usually by a film editor. The master print is then spliced in such a way that the entire feature, which has been shot in bits and pieces, is now in finished form, following the continuity of the written script.

The master print now goes to the sound engineer for *mixing*. Sometimes voices have to be redubbed because the sound levels or vocal enunciations were not exactly correct when the original recording took place during the shooting. Mood music is also mixed into the sound track at this stage, and the sound engineer also decides when to have the music swell, go soft, or die out.

The master print now goes to the film editor for *editing*. The film editor decides what scenes to cut from the master print. A director may send a two-hour movie to a film editor, whose producer wants a ninety-minute feature. This means that thirty minutes will have to be cut from the master print.

After editing, the final cut is sent to the producer for *approval*. Once a master print is approved, then thousands of copies are made from the master print. A feature film is copyrighted like a book and so becomes a protected property. This means that the producers own the film and have the right to sell or rent the film. Licenses are required to show the film on another medium. Usually producers send the film copies to a *distributor*. The distributor then rents the film throughout the world to commercial theaters, for public showings for a limited amount of time, such as one week. Once having paid to rent the film, then the theaters can charge a price of admission to the public to see the movie. In this way the ticket prices reimburse the investors for their initial outlay of money. Large box office receipts mean that theaters want to extend the rental time or that other theaters want to rent the film. The more such tickets are sold, the bigger the national and worldwide gate receipts. A hit movie selling

The Development of Motion Picture Appreciation 255

millions of tickets can recoup a $5 million investment in less than a week and from then on earn profits for the financial backers. On the other hand, if the public stays away and the movie bombs, then no theaters want to rent it. In such a case the investment money may be totally lost.

It is the policy of most major studios to stop all public showings at a certain date (such as six months from the premiere). All of the copies are then collected and locked in a vault. After a period of time has elapsed, the producers can then reissue the film. Reissues can be (1) a second run of theatrical showings, (2) a license to a television network to show the movie once or several times, or (3) issuing a videotape of the film for private buying and/or renting.

After a period of time, certain movie titles are considered by their producers to have exhausted their mass appeal. At this point, these movies are sold to distributors who specialize in stocking vintage films. They can then be sold or rented to retrospective theater houses, libraries, schools, and the like. The large-scale emergence of videotapes has greatly reduced this practice.

THE SOURCES OF A FILM

A film can have an *original* script or be an *adaptation*. An original script means that the material was designed specifically for the film. An adaptation means that the concept for the movie comes from a non-film source. Common sources for films include: historical events, the biographies of famous people, news events, novels, Broadway plays, Broadway musicals, record albums, comic strips, singing acts, sports events, vaudeville, and so on. Some examples are listed at the end of this chapter.

Sometimes an old movie is the source for a new film. *The Wiz*, for example, is a movie based on a Broadway musical. The Broadway musical, however, was in turn based on the original movie *The Wizard of Oz*. So the movie *The Wiz* had its source in the original movie *The Wizard of Oz*. Sometimes a new movie is simply a new version of an older movie. *Heaven Can Wait* is a modern retelling of the older movie *Here Comes Mr. Jordan*. Mel

Brooks' *To Be or Not To Be* is a comedy about Polish Shakespearean actors who are struggling to survive during the Nazi occupation. The movie is a retelling of an older Jack Benny comedy.

Key Personnel On A Film

Certain producers and directors over the years become identified with quality film. These movie-makers also repeat certain themes over and over again. When religious educators become familiar with certain directors' work, they will know what to expect and will also be able to select what movie-makers will be best suited for showings in a religious education class. Some prominent directors-producers and the recurrent themes found in many of their films are listed at the end of this chapter.

The production of a feature film requires many other skilled people besides the producer and the director. A few productions represent very personal works, with one individual acting as producer, director, and star. This is unusual and rarely succeeds. Successful feature films require an extensive range of technical skills and a producer or director who can inspire the staff to excel at their work. See the list of key personnel at the end of this chapter.

Historical Periods Of A Feature Film

Two important historical questions about a feature film are: (1) *when* was the film made?; (2) *what historical period* is the film depicting? Major feature films have been produced in the United States for eighty years. To a certain extent, movies mirror both the technology and the time period to which they belong.

The Development of Technology in the Movies. Sound synchronization did not begin until 1929, so that movies made prior to that time were designed as visual mimes. Music scores for a piano were sent to the theaters with the film copy to accompany the showing. Placards were displayed on the screen to depict the unheard spoken words of dialogue. After 1929, sound synchronization was used in all major films. Color films with consistent quality began in 1933, and after that date most major features were filmed in color instead of black and white. In the early fifties new technology added the wide screen, stereophonic sound, and 3-D to feature films. Movies tried a variety of innovations to lure adults back to the theaters after the extensive use of television. 3-D quickly faded, but the other new technologies remained. More recent developments include Dolby sound for excellent aural replication, new color dyes to improve visual representation, better lenses for improved resolution, special films which do not require intensive lighting, and miniaturized cameras which are lightweight and very mobile. The widespread use of videotape also means that classic films once subject to rapid deterioration can last much longer.

Movies as a Reflection of Specific Time Periods. Movies frequently mirror the prevalent attitudes of the age. The 1920s were times of exuberance and self-confidence in America. Accordingly, the feature films of that time mirror this optimism. The 1930s saw the economic Depression, and so movies portrayed strength of character, or offered pure escapism from the troubles of the day. The 1940s were the years of World War II, and so the films of the time stressed bravery, patriotism, and the problems faced by returning soldiers. The 1950s were years of conformity, peace, prosperity, but also included a hysterical fear of Communist nations taking over the West. Movies showed Americans enjoying their wealth and prosperity, or struggling with the demands of waging the cold war with the Soviets.

The 1960s were a time of rebellion against tradition and authority, and accordingly movies reflected this iconoclastic attitude. Sexual permissiveness began to be a frequent theme in movies. Major films became more explicit in their portrayal of physical lovemaking. At the same time, film evaluation services became less strict in their ratings of such material. In the 1970s America faced a period of disillusionment, uncertainty, and increased self-awareness and self-centeredness. Many adult Americans found it hard to make commitments, accept responsibility for their actions, fall in love, or stay with a routine. The movies reflected these personal concerns. The 1980s witnessed a rebirth of patriotism, of family responsibility, and of romantic love. All of these concerns are now being treated in contemporary films.

Movies About Other Historical Periods. Contemporary movies can also be about earlier historical periods. *Ben Hur* is about ancient Rome. *Camelot* is about medieval England. *Revolution* retells the story of the American Revolution in the eighteenth century and its aftermath in the lives of people. Westerns depict life in nineteenth-century America when the prairie states were settled. Some movies depict several past decades of the twentieth century, such as *The Way We Were*.

Nickelodian tells about the origins of moviemaking prior to 1920. *The Great Gatsby* shows the lifestyle of wealthy Americans in the 1920s. *Singing in the Rain* is a romantic valentine to moviemaking in the 1920s and 1930s. *Annie* portrays how poor Americans struggled to cope with hard times in the Depression. *A Bridge Too Far* depicts both the heroism and the stupidity of the Allies during the world war. *The Man in the Gray Flannel Suit* is regarded as an excellent and accurate portrayal of the pressure on American males to conform in the 1950s.

The Beatles' *Yellow Submarine* is an animated cartoon extolling the youth rebellion of the 1960s. *All The President's Men* shows how the Nixon White House was torn apart by the Watergate scandal in the 1970s. *Back to the Future* shows the problems faced by a contemporary teenager who travels back to the time when his parents were teenagers in the 1950s.

The Genres of Feature Films

The various genres of feature films were discussed briefly in the previous chapter. These principal genres in the cinema include the documentary, drama, comedy, and animation.

The documentary is usually not a full-length feature. A so-called docu-drama, which is a fictionalized account of an actual event, is a popular form. For example, *Norma Rae* is a composite of several female union organizers who struggled to unionize the textile mills in the South. Both *Silkwood* and *Marie* are biographies of brave women who fought against corruption, but the film versions romanticize their lives and their struggles.

Drama and comedy represent the most common genres in feature films. Popular dramatic genres include the murder-mystery, biography, historical reenactments, melodrama, romance, horror, fantasy, and science-fiction. In the murder-mystery, the audience becomes a detective grappling with the problem of solving who is responsible for a crime. *Murder on the Nile* is an example of this genre. A biography tells the life story of a person. It can be a well-known person, such as Sigmund Freud, whose story is told in *Freud*. It can be a relatively obscure person, such as Karen Silkwood, whose fight against radioactive environments in the workplace is told in *Silkwood*. It can be a fictional person, such as *Norma Rae*, who is a composite of several female union organizers rather than a real person. Historical reenactments are frequent in movie dramas. World War II is a popular historical event and has been the source of many fine films such as *The Great Escape*. Melodrama concentrates on plot and action but not on characterization. *Raiders of the Lost Ark* is an excellent example of a good melodrama. The romance is a love story; the French film *A Man and A Woman* represents a good example of this genre. The horror film usually features some fantastic creature threatening people. It has been a perennial favorite of Hollywood for over fifty years. *Frankenstein* is the classic example of this genre. A fantasy presents pure escapism; it takes the viewers to a world of the imagination which can never exist in reality. *Mary Poppins* is an example of this genre. Science-fiction is a plausible fantasy, that is, once a single imaginary premise is accepted the whole story which follows is logical and consistent. Science-fiction often makes predictions of what our lifestyle will be like in future generations. Frequent themes in science-fiction include: traveling through time (e.g., *The Time Machine*; *Back to the Future*), traveling to alternate worlds (e.g., *The Planet of the Apes*), the human race inventing interstellar spacecraft, (e.g., *Star Trek: The Movie*), aliens from outer space visiting the earth (e.g., *E.T.*, *Close Encounters of the Third Kind*), or nonhuman aliens dealing with the same problems that humans must cope with, such as fighting to gain political freedom (e.g., *Star Wars, The Empire Strikes Back, The Return of the Jedi*). In the nineteenth century, science-fiction novels prepared the human psyche for the lifestyle of the twentieth century. Perhaps twentieth-century science-fiction films are preparing the psyche for the lifestyle of the twenty-first century (when most of twentieth-century adolescent learners will live their adult lives).

Comedic genres include satire, farce, and slapstick. Satire is a witty, intentional expose of human vice and folly. *Take The Money And Run* is a satire of the gangster film. A farce is a lighter form of humor. A farce puts normal people in a ridiculous situation (e.g., *Foul Play*), or ridiculous people in a normal situation (*A Night at the Opera*). Slapstick is visual comedy. Slapstick shows car chases, pies in the face, pratfalls, and doors slamming in peoples' faces. Stan Laurel and Oliver Hardy were masters of slapstick.

Animated features are usually fantasies about talking animals or journeys to imaginary worlds. *The Lion, The Witch and the Wardrobe* is an animated version of C. S. Lewis's children's tale which tells the story of creation and redemption on a parallel world. *Fantasia* is considered one of the best animated feature films ever made.

SUMMARY

Motion picture appreciation, or cinema-literacy, requires a knowledge of several key elements, including: (1) the stages of film-making, (2) the original source of a feature film, (3) the role of the key personnel in movie making, (4) historical periods, and (5) genres. Religious educators can guide learners *to actively bring a value system to movie watching instead of passively learning a value system from movie watching*. Religious educators can develop their own cinema-literacy by watching movies and then discussing these films with professional peers, or with their learners. Cinema-literacy includes, as well as the elements cited in this chapter, an awareness of the target audience, the intended effect, the actual effect, and the freedom to choose whether the viewer will accept or reject the effect.

Learners require careful guidance to discover how certain feature films affirm or deny Judeo-Christian values. Religious educators require sophistication, so that they do not believe, on the one hand, that a movie which contains explicit preaching is automatically worthwhile, or, on the other hand, that a film which depicts an evil lifestyle automatically means it is a bad movie.

At the conclusion of this chapter, there is a list of selected feature films and some television mini-series. These titles were

The Development of Motion Picture Appreciation   261

selected because the films can serve as excellent resources for the teaching/learning of religious themes. The major theme of the film, as understood by the present writer, is also cited. Religious educators need to engage in group discussions with their learners to discover the actual effect of each film. Careful listening to the learners' viewpoint will assist the religious educator in learning how a targeted audience actually responds or does not respond to the intended effect. Every watching experience and every group is different, so many interpretations will emerge. Classic movies, however, like classic books, have a wide and perennial appeal.

Religious educators can help learners to discover the theme of a movie, not by telling the theme to them, but by cueing learners on how to watch a film critically. Is *A Bridge Too Far* a war movie, or is it a plea for pacificism? Is it a critique of other war movies, or is it a correction of the simplistic view that the Allies were always right and just in World War II? Religious educators can instruct their learners to watch the clues to the behavior of the major characters and from that they will learn the theme of the movie. Younger viewers will be excited by the explosions and the fighting. Wiser viewers will soon discern that there is a vast amount of unneeded loss of life and damage to property portrayed in this campaign.

Is George Stevens' *King of Kings* an accurate portrayal of the Jesus of the gospel? Is it a sentimental approach that makes Jesus Christ appear weak and unmanly? Is *Jesus Christ Superstar* blasphemous? Or does it reveal the humanity and caring of Jesus? Does the *Ten Commandments* make Moses out to be a lesser or grander man than he is in the Hebrew Bible? Does the film concentrate on the miracles and lose sight of the reality of the Exodus? Or does the film make the scriptures come alive with meaning and power? The answer to these questions is not in this text, but in the audience.

SOME EXAMPLES OF THE VARIETY OF ORIGINAL SOURCE MATERIAL FOR FEATURE FILMS

FILM TITLE	ORIGINAL SOURCE
Star Trek I: The Movie	Television series
Superman	Comic book

FILM TITLE	ORIGINAL SOURCE
Bang the Drum Slowly	Baseball games
Camelot	Broadway musical
Agnes of God.	Broadway drama
The Ten Commandments	Hebrew Bible
A Christmas Carol	Novel
Freud	Biography of Sigmund Freud
Jesus Christ, Superstar	Record album
A Hard Day's Night	Beatles' singing act
A Bridge Too Far	World War II
King of Kings	The four gospels in the Bible
The Delta Force	News event: plane hijackings
E.T.	Original script
Henry V	Shakespearean play
Rabbit Test	Nightclub comedian's act
Clue	Board game
Grand Prix	Sportscar racing
The Sunshine Boys	Vaudeville
All That Jazz	Choreography
Snow White and the Seven Dwarfs	Folk tale
King Solomon's Mines	Original movie of same title
The Turning Point	Ballet
Carmen	Grand Opera
All The President's Men	Newspaper investigation
I Led Three Lives	American espionage

SELECTED DIRECTORS, SAMPLE FILMS, THEIR NATIONALITY, AND RECURRENT THEMES

DIRECTOR/NATION	SAMPLE FILM TITLES	RECURRENT THEMES
Woody Allen/ American	*Sleeper* *Take the Money and Run*	Excels at satirizing the anxieties of urban life, or other film genres.
Richard Attenborough/British	*Gandhi* *A Chorus Line*	A master at an autobiography or biography.
Ingmar Bergman/ Swedish	*The Seventh Seal* *The Virgin Spring*	Depicts dark visions of human sinfulness and the need for redemption.
Mel Brooks/American	*To Be or Not To Be* *Blazing Saddles*	Is a master of comic farces.

The Development of Motion Picture Appreciation

DIRECTOR/NATION	SAMPLE FILM TITLES	RECURRENT THEMES
Luis Bunuel/Spanish	The Milky Way Viridiana	Creates biting satire on the pretensions of political and church officials.
Frank Capra/American	Mr. Smith Goes to Washington It's A Wonderful Life	Extols the natural goodness of the individual rising above the crowd.
Charlie Chaplin/British	City Lights The Dictator	A master of slapstick and comic satire on human foibles.
Francis Coppola/American	The Godfather Apocalypse Now	Criticizes Americans' love for violence by making movies with very violent action sequences.
Cecil B. DeMille/American	The Ten Commandments King of Kings	Dramatizes religious themes such as God's love for humanity on an epic scale.
Michael Douglas/American	Romancing the Stone The Jewel of the Nile	Specializes in melodramas with humor and fast-paced action.
Blake Edwards/American	Pink Panther Victor/Victoria	Satirizes various film genres, such as the detective story, the musical comedy.
Frederico Fellini/Italian	8½ Juliet of the Spirits	Uses autobiography to comment on lifestyle, filmmaking, human frailty, and pretension.
John Ford/American	Stagecoach	Set the stage for a slew of exciting Westerns as a successful film genre.
Jean Goddard/French	Jules and Jim Something I Know About Her	Does biting social commentaries on the lifestyles of amoral French contemporaries.
Alfred Hitchcock/British	Vertigo North by Northwest	Excels at the telling of a murder mystery.

DIRECTOR/NATION	SAMPLE FILM TITLES	RECURRENT THEMES
George Lucas/ American	Star Wars Raiders of the Lost Ark	Is a master of fast-paced action-adventure stories.
Mike Nichols/ American	The Graduate Carnal Knowledge	Uses humor and satire to show the shallowness of many adult Americans.
Tony Richardson/ British	A Taste of Honey The Loneliness of the Long-Distance Runner	Recreates the hard life of the lower class in England.
Ronald Thomas/ American	Splash Cocoon	Uses fantasy to extol exuberance and love of life.
Francois Truffault/ French	400 Blows	Bittersweet autobiography about growing pains during adolescence.

Especially Suitable for The Young Learners:

Walt Disney/ American	Snow White and the Seven Dwarfs Pinocchio	Master of animated stories for children and the young-at-heart.
Steven Spielberg/ American	E.T.	Focuses on the natural goodness of children and their conflicts with the world of adults.
Harve Bennet/ American	Star Trek III: The Search for Mr. Spock	The leaders of the starship *Enterprise* risk their careers to restore Mr. Spock. The theme of resurrection is an important part of the film.

KEY PERSONNEL ON A FEATURE FILM

JOB TITLE	FUNCTION
Executive Producer	The administration of personnel and budget for the film.
Director	Converts the original concept and script into a film. Supervises actors, rehearsals, shooting and selection of prints.
Writer	Converts a concept or other source material into a screenplay.

The Development of Motion Picture Appreciation

JOB TITLE	FUNCTION
Principal Cameraworker	Supervision and coordination of camera crew, cameras, and cinematography.
Principal Sound Engineer	Supervision and coordination of sound staff, sound equipment, and sound-mixing.
Lighting Director	Supervision and coordination of all lighting staff, lighting equipment. Selects lights, filters, and angles for illuminating a scene.
Grips	Move cameras back and forth on dollies for close, medium, and long shots.
Featured Actor	Principal male role in the film.
Featured Actress	Principal female role in the film.
Supporting Actor	Male who acts as a foil or friend to the principals.
Supporting Actress	Female who acts as a foil or friend to the principals.
Cast	All actors and actresses with speaking roles.
Stand-ins	Staff used to test equipment, especially for blocking, lighting, and sound level.
Stunt Staff	Trained athletes who do the action stunts for a film.
Extras	All actors and actresses with nonspeaking roles in the film.
Hairdresser	Styles the hair of the performers.
Make-up Artist	Does make-up and cosmetics for the performers.
Script-timer	Insures that shooting stays on schedule and that each sequence fits the continuity of the story line.
Costumer	Insures that all wigs and costumes are authentic, well-made, and fit the performers.
Special Effects Team	Use a different studio equipped with special equipment to create visual and audio effects.

JOB TITLE	FUNCTION
Film Editor	Splices film prints together to create the entire master print. Edits the final print to stay within a time slot.

SELECTED FEATURE FILMS AND TELEVISION MINI-SERIES WITH RELIGIOUS EDUCATION THEMES

TITLE		THEME
1. A BRIDGE TOO FAR	*	The allied invasion of Europe in World War II sets the stage for a denunciation of the futility and waste in war.
2. A.D.	II	First generation Christians struggle to overcome the evils of pagan Rome.
3. AGNES OF GOD	*	Three women engage in conflict of ideas on faith, delusion, religion, and psychiatry.
4. BARABBAS	*	The thief freed in place of Jesus endures his own passion and redemption.
5. BECKET	II	The Archbishop of Canterbury is martyred by Henry II of England for choosing church over state.
6. BEN HUR	II	A first-century Jew finds faith in Jesus Christ.
7. BROTHER SUN, SISTER MOON	II	St. Francis of Assisi and his cousin St. Claire leave a life of wealth to follow Jesus in religious life.
8. CAMELOT	I	Arthur unifies England as a Christian nation, then endures rejection, death, and salvation.
9. CARDINAL	*	A worldly priest rises in the hierarchy and struggles with human love and celibacy.
10. CAROUSEL	I	A carnival barker dies and comes back from heaven to help his teenage daughter.
11. CLOSE ENCOUNTERS OF THE THIRD KIND	I	Aliens in UFOs are inviting human beings to higher consciousness and a spiritual reawakening.
12. THE CRUCIBLE	*	Puritan witch trial forces a community to come to terms with conscience and faith and the meaning of justice.

The Development of Motion Picture Appreciation

TITLE		THEME
13. DAVID AND BATH-SHEEBA	*	A popular retelling of the king of Israel and his forbidden love.
14. DAYS OF WINE AND ROSES	*	A husband and wife battle with alcoholism. A strong recommendation for AA in the film.
15. EAST OF EDEN	*	John Steinbeck's brittle story of two brothers fighting for a father's love retells the Cain and Abel theme.
16. E.T.	I	A frightened alien from outer space is adopted by three children who protect him from adults.
17. THE EXORCIST	*	A young priest plagued with self-doubts is called in to exorcise an evil spirit from a young girl.
18. GANDHI	II	The heroic founder of modern India uses nonviolence to end British colonial rule.
19. GODSPELL	I	The Gospel of St. Matthew set to mime and music.
20. GOSPEL ACCORDING TO ST. MATTHEW	II	This film, by an Italian Marxist, emphasizes Jesus championing the poor.
21. GREATEST STORY EVER TOLD	I	The story of Jesus's public ministry, passion, death, and resurrection.
22. GRAPES OF WRATH	II	A Depression family leaves the dust bowl to find a new life in California.
23. THE HEART IS A LONELY HUNTER	II	A deaf mute and a young girl struggle to express love to each other.
24. HEAVEN CAN WAIT	I	A young football player becomes an angel too soon and is allowed to return to earth.
25. HENRY V	I	Shakespeare's ideal king fights France for the glory of God and England.
26. HIGH NOON	I	A sheriff must face an outlaw seeking revenge when no one in his town will help him.
27. INHERIT THE WIND	II	A retelling of the Scopes trial, with creationists and evolutionists battling over the meaning of the Bible.

TITLE		THEME
28. JESUS CHRIST, SUPERSTAR	I	The Passion of Jesus, told as if it happened to a contemporary rock star.
29. JESUS OF NAZARETH	I	Franco Zeferelli's masterful retelling of the life of Jesus. Historically and biblically accurate.
30. KING OF KINGS	I	A romanticized interpretation by George Stevens of the life of Jesus. Cecil B. DeMille's version is in an epic style.
31. LA DOLCE VITA	*	A bitter denunciation of the empty lives led by the wealthy of modern Rome.
32. THE LEFT HAND OF GOD	*	An American outlaw escapes hit men by pretending to be a Catholic priest in pre-Communist China.
33. LILIES OF THE FIELD	I	A Baptist black helps German nuns to set up their American mission.
34. LION, WITCH, AND WARDROBE	I	An animated feature, C.S. Lewis's modern fairy-tale which is a retelling of the biblical themes of creation and redemption.
35. THE MAGICIAN	*	Ingmar Bergman's traveling magician is a modern version of Jesus as a miracle worker.
36. A MAN FOR ALL SEASONS	II	Thomas More chooses loyalty to the Catholic church over fealty to Henry VIII of England.
37. MARIE	II	A woman in the State of Tennessee discovers she is in the center of a corrupt government and fights for justice.
38. MR. SMITH GOES TO WASHINGTON	I	A young Congressman fights corruption and complacency in national politics.
39. O GOD	I	George Burns as God visits John Denver, an unbeliever, in a modern version of the Moses story.
40. THE OLD MAN AND THE SEA	I	Ernest Hemingway's story of a Cuban fisherman is a retelling of the passion of Jesus.
41. ON THE WATERFRONT	II	A young stevedore fights corruption in the dock unions.

The Development of Motion Picture Appreciation

TITLE		THEME
42. OUR TOWN	II	A young woman returns from the dead to visit her family for one day.
43. PLACES IN THE HEART	II	A young widow struggles to keep her farm and family together. Her only help is a black farmer and a blind boarder.
44. QUO VADIS	I	The retelling of the story of St. Peter whose faith in Jesus conquers his fear of martyrdom.
45. RAISIN IN THE SUN	I	A black family struggles to survive after the father dies. American racism makes their struggle more difficult.
46. RED BADGE OF COURAGE	I	A soldier's wound, given when he was fleeing battle, becomes a symbol of his true courage.
47. ROOTS	I	Seven generations of an American black family struggle with slavery, poverty, racism, and assimilation.
48. THE SCARLET LETTER	I	A Puritan woman who has a child out of wedlock must endure the taunts of her neighbors.
49. THE SEVENTH SEAL	*	Ingmar Bergman has a personified Death bringing the plague to medieval Europe.
50. 1776	I	John Adams, Thomas Jefferson, and Benjamin Franklin team up to create the United States of America.
51. SHAME	*	Ingmar Bergman's bitter denunciation of the effects of war on a couple and their home.
52. SOMETHING BEAUTIFUL FOR GOD	I	Malcolm Muggeridge tells the story of Mother Teresa of Calcutta.
53. THE SONG OF BERNADETTE	I	An adolescent girl's faith in the Virgin Mary leads to the miracles at Lourdes.
54. THE TEN COMMANDMENTS	I	Cecil B. DeMille's mammoth re-creation of the story of Moses and the Exodus.
55. TESS OF THE D'URBERVILLES	II	Thomas Hardy's story of a Welsh girl whose life is a tragic reenactment of a pagan sacrifice.

TITLE		THEME
56. TO KILL A MOCKINGBIRD	I	A young girl watches her father fight racism and hatred in the American South.
57. TRUE CONFESSIONS	*	An ambitious priest's career ends when he becomes associated with the brutal murder of a prostitute.
58. THE VIRGIN SPRING	*	An adolescent girl is raped and murdered; her father is bent on revenge; the site of her death becomes a source of healing and faith.

* These titles are recommended only for older adolescents or adults because of explicit violence or sexual material which may be too strong or confusing for younger learners.

I Level I, recommended for young learners in the early primary grades.

II Level II, recommended for learners in the middle primary grades.

10

The Development of Television Appreciation

INTRODUCTION

For both learners and religious educators, trying to be objective about television is as hard as attempting to be objective about a beloved member of the immediate family. Since 1950, television has been the dominant communication medium in almost every American home. Most Americans today have two or three television sets in their home. It is not unusual for a child to be given his or her own television by the age of five or six. As of 1986, one-third of the American homes have a video cassette recorder, or cable reception, or both. By 1992, at least 75 percent of the American homes will be so equipped.

The development of television appreciation—for both religious educators and learners—requires a special training in objectivity. Neil Postman recommends a thorough grounding in the principles of the print culture as the best antidote to a total media-determinism.[1] The thinking viewer can "talk back" mentally to the pervasive media-effect of television.

Religious educators often have a difficult time cultivating media-literacy in regard to television because this medium so dominates their own lives. Any religious educator under thirty-five has had television as a constant companion for his or her entire life. Religious educators are just as media-saturated as the young learners. It requires vigorous mental discipline to break the hypnotic hold of television.

Television appreciation grows with a knowledge of the following: (1) content, (2) time slot, (3) target audience, (4) ratings, (5) demographics, (6) advertising techniques, (7) the programing policy of the major networks and the local stations, (8) genre, and (9) the use of critical reviews.

The present volume does not recommend that religious educators take upon themselves the task of regulating the viewing habits of young learners. This is a responsibility for parents, who unfortunately often abdicate their task. Religious educators are more effective by acting as guides and emphasizing the good programs, which, in their view, contribute to the building of a rich Judeo-Christian lifestyle. Recall the sophistication required about the cinema. Religious educators need the ability to understand that simply because a television program engages in explicit preaching does not necessarily mean that it contributes to building up a Judeo-Christian lifestyle. On the other hand, simply because a television program depicts people who do not live a Judeo-Christian lifestyle does not mean that it will corrupt young learners.

Nine Steps to Television Appreciation

Religious educators can assist young learners in the nine steps needed to develop an appreciation of television. Such a skill will enable the learners to recognize which television programs contribute to the building up of a religious lifestyle, and which ones do not.

Content. In the television medium, content may be: (1) a live transmission, (2) videotape, (3) film, (either from the cinema or made-for-television), and (4) computer input.

Content on the major television networks comes from the first three sources. When the content of television is either cinema or a made-for-television movie, then the principles of cinema literacy, which were treated in chapter 9, apply. Live television today is usually limited to news and sports. Most programs are videotaped prior to transmission. Videotape permits the producers to edit, check quality, and reshoot errors.

Television content can be (1) original, or first-run, and (2) a repeat, or rerun.

For the major networks, first-run prime-time original programs

The Development of Television Appreciation   273

are broadcast only during the season, which runs from September to April. After April, prime-time normally consists of reruns. Outside of prime-time, original programs are normally the news, discussion shows, game shows, and soap operas. Game shows and soaps also return to reruns after April.

Time-Slots. Television networks plan their programing according to the time-slots discussed in chapter 8. Original well-made programs are usually broadcast during the prime-time hours. Reruns or shows with limited audience appeal are normally broadcast in the morning, afternoon, early evening, or late-night hours. For example: Early morning shows are aimed at adults before they leave for work; morning and afternoon shows are geared for women homemakers or preschool children; late afternoon shows are intended for children who have come home from school; evening shows are intended for the entire family to be watched by both the children and the adults who have returned from work; and late evening shows are intended for adults who are watching after the children retire. Since some adults work unusual hours, some stations repeat prime-time programs again during odd hours.

Saturday morning programing is aimed at children. Weekend afternoons are geared to sports fans, usually working men who are home at that time.

Target Audience. Network broadcasting is meant for a general mass audience. Prime-time shows and sports championship matches are examples of broadcasting where the television station is deliberately trying to appeal to as many people as possible. The term "narrowcasting" means aiming for a specialized audience. Narrowcasting is intended for a specialized, limited audience such as preschoolers, blacks, Hispanics, business executives, and so forth. Religious broadcasting is considered narrowcasting, since the networks do not think of believers as a mass audience, but a very specific one. Hence religious producers find it very difficult to secure access to prime-time television but find it easy to obtain other time-slots.

The following matching test will enable learners and religious educators to determine how well they understand the concept of a target audience. They key to the matching test is at the end of this chapter.

Match the television program with the audience for which it is targeted:

Television Program
1. Monday Night Football
2. Sesame Street
3. The Cosby Show
4. American Bandstand
5. The Lawrence Welk Show
6. Masterpiece Theatre
7. Another World
8. Sunday Mass
9. The Tonight Show
10. He-Man and the Masters of the Universe
11. Wall Street Week

Target Audience
A. School children
B. Senior citizens
C. Catholics
D. The entire family
E. Business executives
F. Sports fans
G. Preschoolers
H. Adults
I. Teenagers
J. College-educated adults
K. Homemakers

Ratings. Ratings are used by the networks and the local stations to gauge a program's popularity. Good ratings normally mean a program will remain on the air and poor ratings mean that a program will soon be taken off the air. Ratings determine how well a program is doing in comparison with other programs which are being aired at the same time. Networks usually subscribe to a ratings service such as Arbitron or Nielsen. These services set up special boxes attached to television sets in homes which have been randomly selected. From these samples, the rating services calculate the total audience ratings for a particular show or time-slot. The services report on a weekly basis to the networks and stations: (a) the ratings, that is, the number of television sets tuned on to the program, and (b) audience share, that is, the percentage of those people watching television who are tuned on to the program. If a program receives a 33 1/3rd rating and an audience share of 54, this means that one-third of existing sets are tuned into this program, and 54 percent of the people watching television are tuned to this program. Advertising rates are determined by the ratings, audience share, and demographics (see below). Programers want to garner the largest share of the mass audience in order to bring in the highest return on the advertising dollar. Ratings can have a devastating effect on quality programs, which appeal to limited audiences. Such programs are often taken off the air to make way for shows with a mass appeal.

Rating services have always been criticized by educators who believe that too frequently the services encouraged networks to lower their programing standards. Criticism of the rating services is now prevalent among the broadcasters also. Broadcasters are finding that too often the rating services have widely divergent numbers for the same program and are calling into question the sampling techniques currently used. Future plans call for the use of special electronic sweeps, which will be more accurate in informing networks and stations on how many people are actually tuned into their program. The television audience is also becoming much more critical of television fare. The audience has a wide choice now of cable and UHF stations. The video cassette recorder means that viewers can record a program, and not be home at the time. There is therefore a great deal of pressure on the networks to produce quality shows.

Demographics. Rating services also inform television networks and local stations about the demographics of their viewers. This is a very important component in deciding on the retention of programing. Demographics reveal the age, sex, education level, geographical location, income, and purchasing habits of the typical viewer. A usual profile would state that a typical viewer of a program is a white, urban male, aged thirty-four, married with two small children, with an annual income of $35,000, college educated, and about to make a major purchase (such as an automobile or home). This information is extremely important to advertisers and companies. If a company makes a child's toy, it will want its advertisement to run during a program aimed at young children. On the other hand, a car manufacturer will want the advertisement to run when adults are watching, and so on.

Low demographics, even with high ratings, can kill a program. *The Lawrence Welk Show* is extremely popular with senior citizens, but since this age group does not make major purchases, the national networks refused to keep the show on the air. However, since many local stations wanted to secure this age group, a syndication of independent stations kept the program going.

The favorite demographic group for advertisers today are

young, urban professionals, nicknamed "Yuppies," who have high salaries and make major purchases. Many of these people are beginning their families and so will be buyers for many years to come. Programs today are aimed at such people. By way of contrast, popular programs in the 1950s such as *The Honeymooners* and *I Love Lucy Show* appealed to the blue-collar worker. Today, popular shows like *Mary* and *Foley Square* are intended for college-educated professionals.

Advertising Techniques. When religious educators and learners are alert to advertising techniques, their media-literacy improves greatly. Television commercials are intended to make the consumer aware of and happy about a product and/or service. Objective information aimed at the rational mind is rarely, if ever, used. Persuasion, or an appeal to the emotions, is the most common technique in television commercials. [2] Psychological association is employed so that the viewer will unconsciously link the product and/or service with a well-liked celebrity or with a delightful image. Actors and actresses are carefully selected to match the product. Ordinary-looking people appear in commercials for household products. Beautiful models are used in advertisements for jewelry, perfume, and high fashion. Athletes endorse sports equipment and sportswear, and so on. Emotional appeals are made to the consumer's basic psychic drives: pride, envy, fear of rejection, guilt, sexual attraction, and so on. Companies spend millions of dollars so that viewers will immediately recognize the firm's logo or the color of the package, feel good about the product, and be pleased with themselves for buying the nationally advertised brand. After a generation of millions of such commercials, it is very rare to find anyone who is immune to such pressure. It takes an heroic effort for adults to conquer this insistent demand for buying products and services advertised on television which they do not need and cannot afford. Too many adults in the United States say that God and religion come first in their lives, but actually many such adults live a lifestyle which shows that conspicuous consumerism is really their greatest value. This makes it exceptionally difficult for religious educators and young learners to teach/learn that an authentic religious lifestyle does not agree with the media-determinism of conspicuous consumption.

The Programing Policy of the Major Networks and Local Television Stations. What a television network or local television station broadcasts during prime time indicates the programing policy. This is when the television producers are reaching the largest percentage of the audience. Special shows for narrowcasting normally draw from their larger pool of viewers.

During 1985-1986, major changes took place in the national networks, which have affected current programing policy. Up to that time, the Columbia Broadcasting System (CBS) aimed its programing at Middle America, that is, mid-aged, mid-income, and mid-west. CBS News had a fine reputation for objectivity and tenacity. The National Broadcasting Company (NBC), a division of the Radio Corporation of America, had a programing policy of appealing to upper-income, urban sophisticates who resided in major cities. The American Broadcasting Company (ABC) targeted its programs at an audience who liked simple unsophisticated entertainment: adolescents, sportsfans, and blue-collar workers. The Public Broadcasting System (PBS) aimed its programs at students, educators, and the intellectual elite. Metromedia and other syndicated networks tried to reach a distinct audience by appealing to a range of interests and by concentrating on local news and local programs outside of prime time. Syndicates gained their own audience by offering something distinct: sports when the other networks show situation comedies, news when others have movies, movies when others have first-run shows, and so on.

Corporate take-overs and changes in the policy of the Federal Government also affected network programing policy in 1985-1986. It is difficult even now to gauge all of the changes which have occurred and will occur. Some information about the new owners or the new policies of the networks will help religious educators and learners to appreciate the current approach. CBS had to fight off a take-over attempt by a coalition of political and religious conservatives who claimed their news programing was slanted toward liberalism and that too many of their prime-time shows were unsuitable for children. CBS successfully defended itself by drastically cutting down its news research staff and using the money saved to buy back its own stock, thereby becoming too expensive for corporate raiders to take over. CBS executives claim that they have not nor will not change their programing policy. However, disinterested observers do feel that the network has become somewhat more sensitive to conservative viewpoints and that more of its programs in prime time will be suitable for family viewing. This means that less emphasis on sex and violence will probably be the new norm. NBC fought off a potential corporate takeover by merging with General Electric. GE has never before been involved in network programing, so some knowledgeable observers believe that there will be no major change in the network's policy. ABC defended itself from a potential hostile corporate takeover by merging with Capital Cities Communications. Capital Cities has been a fiscally conservative company with an emphasis on holding tight on the purse strings. Observers believe Capital Cities/ABC will cut down on staff and expenses. Although the network will aim its programs at the same audience as before, commentators also believe there will be less blatant sex and/or violence and more family programing. PBS is not a government-owned network, but depends on federal grants for its basic funding. Federal policy has been to cut down more and more on such grants. Membership fees and corporate and foundation grants have not kept pace with expenses, so many PBS stations now show mini-commercials from corporate sponsors. This is irritating their traditional viewer-supporters, and many PBS stations are now finding it harder to raise local dollars. Cutbacks in programs and broadcasts appear inevitable. PBS stations have also been severely criticized by American producers and actors for broadcasting so many British-produced shows during prime time. PBS shows no willingness to change this policy, but battles on this important issue will continue to be fought during the next few years. Commentators believe more American-produced shows will appear on prime-time PBS television. Metromedia was bought out by Rupert Murdoch, a well-known Australian press tycoon. He also controls Twentieth-Century Fox, a movie production company. He intends to use the Metromedia syndicate as the basis for developing a new national network. He also has a movie company to supply his network with first-run movies. Murdoch has publicly stated that he intends to make Metromedia a quality network aimed at the family and at the more educated viewer. Murdoch owns many newspapers which, under his direct personal supervision, emphasize sensational stories of sex and violence, so many observers doubt that he will fulfill his public promise.

Television Genre. Television networks and local stations have three divisions: news, sports, and entertainment. The news and sports shows are usually first-run, original programs. Entertainment can be either (1) original or (2) a repeat. News programs present local, regional, or national news. Sports programs broadcast daily games or special championships. Entertainment is very varied. Entertainment shows can be situation comedies, action-adventure, drama, comedy, variety, soap opera, talk-shows, the cinema, cartoons, and so on. A program can be broadcast daily, weekly, monthly, or on a special occasion. The most watched television shows are the situation comedies which appear once a week and have a regular cast of popular actors and actresses. Gentle family comedy generally attracts a large following. Thus *The Bill Cosby Show* consistently ranked at or near the top of the ratings in its heyday. Specials can attract a huge audience on a once-a-year basis. *The Super Bowl* is an example of a special championship game which attracts a huge number of viewers, including many who do not normally watch a sports event.

Religious educators should remember that some excellent television programing is available outside of prime-time. Such shows lend themselves more readily to the teaching/learning of the Judeo-Christian lifestyle. Video tapes have also made it possible to secure and show programs to learners without waiting for a broadcast.

The Use of Critical Reviews. Major newspapers, television guide booklets, magazines, and some religious organizations provide critical reviews of television programs. Some television news programs do critical reviews of television fare. Sometimes a network or corporate sponsor may provide a study guide. Such reviews normally concentrate on the story line, the quality of the acting, and whether or not the reviewer found the program appealing. Such reviews do not normally refer to whether or not a program agrees with the Judeo-Christian lifestyle, but a religious educator can usually tell very quickly from the story line, the time of the broadcast, and the source of the story. Again, a certain amount of sophistication is required. *Something About Amanda* is a television movie about incest. Most religious educators will find it an excellent production, not at all titillating, and a tool for opening up a discussion about sexual abuse in the home. *Jesus of Nazareth* and *A.D.* are fine movies for helping a young learner to understand the first century, when Christianity began. On the other hand, a game show like *Wheel of Fortune,* while entertaining, is not a good vehicle for the teaching/learning of a religious lifestyle. Such shows really are intended only for enjoyment.

The following television shows frequently have themes which allude to the nurturing of a Judeo-Christian lifestyle:

ORIGINAL 1985-1986 TELEVISION SHOWS	FREQUENT THEMES
1. The Bill Cosby Show	1. Love and respect within a family.
2. Mr. Rogers Neighborhood	2. Coping with emotions.
3. Punky Brewster	3. Overcoming sexism about girls.
4. Mary	4. Ethics in the workplace, and in relations.
5. Different Strokes	5. Overcoming peer pressure to do wrong.
6. Webster	6. Honesty with parents and with children about difficult topics.
7. Smurfs	7. Cooperation to achieve a goal.
8. Foley Square	8. Integrity in the work place.
FREQUENT RERUNS OR SPECIALS:	
9. Charlie Brown Christmas Special	9. The real meaning of Christmas for children.
10. Original V mini-series	10. How adults sustain or abandon values when threatened.
11. Mork and Mindy	11. Mindy frequently teaches Mork about kindness, caring, overcoming prejudice, etc.
12. The Waltons	12. How family members can support one another.
13. Star Trek	13. The need to understand what values are negotiable and what ones are essential for a responsible leader.

FREQUENT RERUNS OR SPECIALS:	FREQUENT THEMES
14. Lou Grant	14. Integrity in the workplace.
15. Brady Bunch	15. Cooperation within blended families.
16. Happy Days	16. The value of completing an education.
17. Insight	17. Value-clarification at times of conflict.

Summary

Television appreciation is a form of media-literacy which requires training. Religious educators can help young learners to develop this skill by making them aware of the nine steps toward television appreciation: (1) understanding the content, (2) recognizing the significance of the broadcast time-slot, (3) knowing what the target audience is, (4) comprehending television ratings, (5) understanding how demographics are used to measure the appeal of a program, (6) being conscious of how television commercials work, (7) learning the new programing policy for each television network, (8) recognizing the genre, and (9) using critical reviews as guides for television viewing. Some television programs are excellent tools for developing a teaching/learning of the Judeo-Christian lifestyle. Others are simply entertainment and cannot be used for this purpose. A sophisticated religious educator will quickly learn which television shows lend themselves to the teaching/learning of a religious lifestyle. As with cinema literacy, television appreciation is best developed by viewing a show and then conducting a discussion with professional peers and/or with young learners. The most difficult task is to teach/learn how television commercials undermine the Judeo-Christian lifestyle.

Notes

1. Neil Postman, *Teaching As a Conserving Activity* (New York: Dell, 1979), pp. 185-198.
2. Vance Packard, *The Hidden Persuaders* (New York: McKay, 1957).

The Key to the Matching Test: 1—F, 2—G, 3—D, 4—I, 5—B, 6—J, 7—K, 8—C, 9—H, 10—A, 11—E

Index of Motion Picture and Television Titles

A Bridge Too Far, 258, 261, 262, 266
A Christmas Carol, 240, 262
A Chorus Line, 262
A.D., 266
Agnes of God, 262, 266
All That Jazz, 262
All the President's Men, 258, 262
American Bandstand, 274
Annie, 258
Another World, 274
Apocalypse Now, 263
Back to the Future, 259
Bang the Drum Slowly, 262
Barabbas, 266
Becket, 266
Ben Hur, 258, 266
Brady Bunch, 281
Brother Sun, Sister Moon, 266
Camelot, 258, 262, 266
Cardinal, 266
Carmen, 262
Carnal Knowledge, 264
Carousel, 266
Charlie Brown's Christmas Special, 280
City Lights, 263
Close Encounters of the Third Kind, 259, 266

Clue, 262
The Crucible, 266
Cocoon, 264
The Cosby Show, 274, 279, 280
David and Bathsheeba, 267
Days of Wine and Roses, 267
The Delta Force, 262
The Dictator, 263
Different Strokes, 280
East of Eden, 267
8½, 263
The Empire Strikes Back, 259
E.T., 259, 262, 264, 266
The Exorcist, 267
Fantasia, 260
First Monday in October, 252
Foley Square, 276, 280
400 Blows, 264
Foul Play, 260
Frankenstein, 259
Freud, 259, 262
Gandhi, 262, 266
The Godfather, 263
Godspell, 267
Gospel According to St. Matthew, 267
The Graduate, 264
Grand Prix, 262
The Grapes of Wrath, 267
The Great Escape, 259

283

The Great Gatsby, 258
Greatest Story Ever Told, 267
Happy Days, 281
A Hard Day's Night, 262
The Heart Is A Lonely Hunter, 267
Heaven Can Wait, 255, 267
He-Man and the Masters of the Universe, 274
Henry V, 262, 267
Here Comes Mr. Jordan, 255
High Noon, 267
The Honeymooners, 276
I Led Three Lives, 262
I Love Lucy, 276
Inherit the Wind, 267
Insight, 281
It's a Wonderful Life, 263
Jesus Christ Superstar, 261, 262, 268
Jesus of Nazareth, 268
The Jewel in the Nile, 263
Jules and Jim, 263
Juliet of the Spirits, 263
King of Kings, 261, 262, 263, 268
King Solomon's Mines, 262
La Dolce Vita, 268
Lawrence Welk Show, 274, 275
The Left Hand of God, 268
Lillies of the Field, 268
The Lion, the Witch and the Wardrobe, 260, 268
The Loneliness of the Long Distance Runner, 264
Lou Grant, 281
The Magician, 268
A Man and a Woman, 259
Man For All Seasons, 268
The Man in the Gray Flannel Suit, 258
Marie, 258, 268
Mary, 274, 280
Mary Poppins, 259
M*A*S*H, 240
Masterpiece Theatre, 274

The Milky Way, 263
Monday Night Football, 274
Mork and Mindy, 280
Mr. Rogers Neighborhood, 280
Mr. Smith Goes to Washington, 268
Murder on the Nile, 259
Nickelodian, 258
A Night at the Opera, 260
Norma Rae, 258, 259
North by Northwest, 263
O God, 268
The Old Man and the Sea, 268
On the Waterfront, 268
Our Town, 269
The Pink Panther, 263
Pinocchio, 264
Places in the Heart, 269
Planet of the Apes, 259
Punky Brewster, 280
Quo Vadis, 269
Rabbit Test, 262
Raiders of the Lost Ark, 259, 264
Raisin in the Sun, 269
Red Badge of Courage, 269
The Return of the Jedi, 259
Revolution, 259
The Right Stuff, 240
Romancing the Stone, 263
Roots, 269
The Scarlet Letter, 269
Sesame Street, 274
The Seventh Seal, 262, 269
1776, 269
Shame, 269
Silkwood, 258, 259
Singing in the Rain, 258
Sleeper, 262
Smurfs, 280
Snow White and the Seven Dwarfs, 262, 264
Something Beautiful for God, 269
Something I Know about Her, 263

Index of Motion Picture and TV Titles

The Song of Bernadette, 269
Splash, 269
Stagecoach, 263
Star Trek, 280
Star Trek: The Motion Picture, 259, 261
Star Trek III: The Search for Mr. Spock, 264
Star Wars, 259, 264
Sunday Mass, 274
Superman, 261
The Super Bowl, 279
Take the Money and Run, 260, 262
A Taste of Honey, 264
The Ten Commandments, 261, 262, 263, 269
Tess of the D'Ubervilles, 269

The Time Machine, 259
To Be or Not to Be, 256, 262
To Kill a Mockingbird, 270
The Tonight Show, 274
True Confessions, 270
V, 280
Vertigo, 263
Victor/Victoria 263
The Virgin Spring, 262, 270
Viridiana, 263
Wall Street Week, 274
Waltons, 280
The Way We Were, 258
Webster, 280
The Wiz, 255
The Wizard of Oz, 255
The Yellow Submarine, 258

Index of Names

Abbott, Walter, 159
Abel, 267
Abeles, Ronald P., 188
Adams, John, 269
Ahumada, Enrique Garcia, 39
Allen, Woody, 262
Alvez, Ruben, 8
Amos, 105
Andriole, Stephen J., 192
Angelica, Mother, 220
Aquinas, St. Thomas, 8, 21, 80
Aristotle, 8, 21, 39, 106, 138, 139
Armstrong, Ben, 219, 230, 231
Arthur, king of England, 266
Attenborough, Richard, 262
Augustine of Hippo, St., 8, 21, 160

Babin, Pierre, viii, xiii, 7, 37, 38, 68, 87, 125, 130, 132, 133, 134, 138, 150, 151, 159, 163, 164, 165
Badia, Len, 82
Barabbas, 266
Barbour, Ian C., 81
Bathsheeba, 267
Baum, Gregory, 160
Becket, St. Thomas, 266

Behrendt, Bill, 192
Bennet, Harve 264
Benny, Jack, 256
Bergman, Ingmar, 262, 268, 269
Bernadette, St., 269
Betts, George Herbert, 40
Bill, J. Brent, 188
Birrell, N.D., 192
Bishop, J., 190
Blake, William, 88
Blaukopf, K., 185
Bombeck, E. S., 182
Bower, Robert T., 188
Bower, William Clayton, 7, 26, 37, 39, 40, 127, 163
Braziller, George, 103
Brooks, Mel, 255-256, 262
Brown, Les, 188
Brown, Robert McAfee, 161
Brownlee, Fred L., 125, 163
Brubaker, Robert, 187
Buckland, Gail, 182
Bultmann, Rudolph, 65, 83
Bunuel, Luis, 263
Burgess, Harold William, 24, 38, 39, 86, 101, 158, 163
Burghardt, Walter J., 37
Burns, George, 268
Bushnell, Horace, 10, 38
Butterick, George, 161

286

Index of Names

Cain, 267
Caligari, Marc, 160
Calvin, John, 76
Campion, Donald, 161, 162
Camras, M., 182
Capra, Frank, 263
Castro, Fidel, 165
Chaplin, Charlie, 263
Chardin, Pierre Teilhard de, 8, 58, 59-61, 70, 81, 82, 94, 114, 126-127, 160, 162, 163
Chipman, Robert, 182
Chorafas, Dimitris N., 192, 193
Christ, Jesus, viii, ix-xi, 6, 21, 24, 25, 29, 32, 59, 71, 81, 84, 88-90, 108, 109, 114, 115, 120, 133, 136, 140, 155, 160, 203, 215-218, 225-227, 230, 237, 238, 261, 266-269.
Claire, St., 266
Clancy, Thomas H., 216, 219-224, 228, 230-232.
Clarke, Peter, 193
Coe, George A., 10, 25-28, 39, 87, 125-128, 151, 159, 163
Conrod, John, 193
Cook, Charles, 87, 125, 129-132, 151, 159, 163
Coppola, Frank, 263
Cosby, Bill, 279
Cristol, A., 190
Culkin, John, 237, 238, 250
Cullingford, Cedric, 189
Curtiss, Ernst Robert, 84
Czitrom, David, 250

Daly, Mary, 37
Darwin, Charles, 8, 58-60, 88
David, King of Israel, 267
Delmalge, Lewis, 164
DeMille, Cecil B., 263, 268, 269
Dennis, Everette E., 250
Denver, John, 268
Dewey, John, 10, 11

Dick, Bernard F., 187
Dickins, Charles, 240
Disney, Walt, 264
Dolan, Jr. Edward F., 191
Douglas, Michael, 263
Drucker, Marla, 188
Dulles, Avery, 19, 39, 68, 71, 76, 87, 118, 119, 130
Dygert, Warren, 185

Edwards, Blake, 263
Eliade, Mircea, 83
Eliot, George P., 80
Eliot, T. S., 83
Elizabeth I of England, 76
Ellul, Jacques, 41, 42, 46-47, 76, 77, 81-83, 103, 162
Erickson, Fritz J., 193
Esquivel, Jose, 164, 165
Evans, Susan, 193

Fellini, Frederico, 263
Ford, Brian J., 192
Ford, John, 263
Forey, Raymond, 182
Fosbroke, Hughell E. W., 161
Francis, St., of Assisi, 6, 266
Franklin, Benjamin, 269
Freeman, Michael, 184
Freire, Paulo, 142, 165
Freud, Sigmund, 61, 66, 114, 162, 163, 259
Fritts, William J., 86, 98-100, 159, 160
Frost, J. M., 185
Fuller, Buckminster, 103
Furnish, Dorothy Jean, 11

Gaebeline, Frank, 25, 39
Gandhi, 262
Geghardt-Seele, Peter A., 193
Gelalt, Robert, 182
Gershwin, George, 81
Gilmore, Susan, 185
Gleamer, Diana, 187

Goddard, Jean, 163
Goodman, Evelyn, 188
Graham, Billy, 215, 217, 218, 230, 231
Greeley, Andrew, 150, 250
Green, Verdant, 161
Grimes, Howard, 20, 40
Grob, Bernard, 182
Groome, Thomas, 87, 125, 135-143, 152, 164, 165
Gutenberg, Johannes, viii

Habermas, Jürgen, 139, 164
Halliwell, Leslie, 187
Hardy, Oliver, 260
Hardy, Thomas, 269
Harper, Dennis O., 192
Harris, Maria, 11, 28
Harrison, G.B., 83
Hart, Corinne, 130
Harwood, Don, 190
Hastings, Adrain, 161, 162
Havelock, Eric A., 18, 37, 38
Hegel, Georg Wilhelm, Friedrich, 8, 42, 46-49, 72, 135, 137, 139, 142, 143, 155
Hemingway, Ernest, 268
Henry II of England, 266
Henry V of England, 267
Henry VIII of England, 268
Hillind, Robert, 188
Hitchcock, Alfred, 263
Hitchcock, James, 86, 92-94, 119, 159, 160
Hitler, Adolf, 50
Hofinger, Johannes, 25, 39
Holland, Daniel W., 190
Horenstein, Henry, 184
Houston, Jean, 250
Howard, Jack C., 192
Howe, M., 188

Ignatius of Loyola, St., 140, 164
Innis, Harold Adams, 41, 42, 47-51, 72, 77, 82, 98, 142
Irvine, Mat, 188, 190

Jacobs, Lewis, 187
Jakobson, Roman, 23, 24, 39
James I of England, 76
Janur, Elizabeth, 188
Jarvie, Ian C., 187
Jefferson, Thomas, 269
John, the Evangelist, St., 8
John XXIII, 86, 106-108, 161
John Paul II, 81, 221
Johnson, Deborah C., 193
Jorgensen, Finn, 191
Joseph, St., 203
Jung, Carl, 61

Kaplan, Don, 191
Kass, Jerome, 182
Kelley, Michael R., 188
Kelly, George A., 86, 94-97, 159, 160
Kevane, Eugene, 160
Kierkegaard, Søren, 8
Kieser, Ellwood, 216, 224-227, 229, 231, 232
Knox, Ian P., 39, 86, 87, 126, 128, 152, 153, 155, 158, 160, 163, 165
Koury, Philip A., 187
Kuhns, William, 103, 130, 161

Lachensbruch, David, 191
Lake, Sara, 189
Landry, Carey, 222
Lanzendorf, Peter, 190
Laurel, Stan, 260
Lawrence, Jerome, 160
Lebaron, John, 190, 191
LeBar, Lois, 25
Leder, Jane M., 185, 191
LeDu, Jean, 165
Lee, James Michael, 11, 19, 31-34, 38-40, 55, 64, 71, 87, 100, 124, 125, 137-139, 142-150, 152, 158-161, 163, 165, 166, 238
Lee, Robert E., 160
Levenson, William B., 186, 188

Index of Names

Lewis, C. S., 260, 268
Lincoln, Abraham, 245
Logan, Ben, 188
Lonergan, Bernard, J. F., 80
Lucas, George, 264
Luke, St., 38
Lumpp, Randolph Franklin, 164
Luther, Martin, 6, 47

Marcel, Gabriel, 8
Marcus, Abraham, 182
Marcus, W., 182
Marino, Joseph S., 40
Maritain, Jacques, 8
Maruyama, Allen, 86, 87, 102-105, 159, 161
Marx, Karl, 8, 135, 139-141, 152, 165
Mary, 203
Masters, Robert, 250
Matthew, St., 267
Mattewson, 191
Mattingly, Paul, xiii
McCafferty, Richard Basil, 82
McInnis, James, 191
McKenzie, John L., 37
McLeish, Robert, 186
McLuhan, Marshall (Herbert), xiii, 4, 19, 32, 40, 42, 54, 58, 59-65, 76, 77, 80, 82, 83, 86-89, 98-100, 102-109, 120, 125, 127, 129, 130, 132-134, 138, 143-147, 149-152, 158-165, 236, 238, 239, 250
McNulty, Edward N., 188
McSweeney, William, 20, 39, 161
Melanchton, Philip, 76
Merrill, John C., 250
Miller, Philip, 190
Miller, Randolph Crump, 9, 30, 38, 40, 87, 154-156, 165
Mills, C. W., 103
Milton, John, 76
Montessori, Maria, 38

Moody, Kate, 188, 189
Mooney, Christopher, 82
Moran, Gabriel, xiii, 9, 29-31, 38, 40, 87, 119-123, 125, 127-130, 138, 141, 151, 159, 163
More, St. Thomas, 268
Morse, Samuel, 250
Moses, 268
Muggeridge, Malcolm, 66, 69, 81, 83, 86, 88-92, 119, 159, 160, 215-217, 226, 230, 231, 269
Muirhead, Bert, 185
Mumford, Lewis, 41, 43-44, 46, 76, 77, 81, 103
Murdoch, Rupert, 278
Murphy, John F., 163

Newton, Isaac, 238
Nichols, Mike, 264
Nineteen, K. W., 184
Nixon, Richard, 258
Novak, Michael, 162

Obbink, H. W., 165
O'Connor, Sandra Day, 251
O'Donnell, Bruce, 87, 125, 134, 135, 151, 159, 164
Olson, Harry F., 182
O'Meara, Thomas, 103, 161
Ong, Walter J., xiii, 3-6, 37-39, 41, 42, 54, 55, 58, 59, 65-77, 83, 87, 98, 114-118, 120, 121, 131, 133, 139, 140, 159, 162, 163, 164
Orne, Peter, 188
Ould, M. A., 192

Packard, Vance, 166, 281
Pantaleoni, Hewitt, 184
Paul, St., 8, 59, 222, 238
Paul VI, 96, 160
Perrotta, Kevin, 188
Peter, St., 269
Pfeiffer, Carl J., 83, 159, 163

Plato, 7, 8, 21
Postman, Neil, xiii, 5, 39, 41, 42, 50-54, 76, 77, 82, 83, 137, 164, 216-219, 230, 231, 271, 281

Quinlan, Paul, 206
Quint, Bert, 232

Ragosine, Victor E., 182
Rahner, Karl, 108, 136, 161, 164
Raines, H., 182
Ramos, Myra Bergman, 165
Ramus, Peter, 8, 18, 38, 74-76, 83
Rapoport, Diane, 185
Reagan, Ronald, 251
Richardson, Tony, 264
Robinson, Louis, 182
Rogers, Fred, 280
Rohrlich, Paula, 190, 191
Rosen, Frederick W., 191
Rousseau, Jean Jacques, 99
Ryder, Loren L., 182

Sabin, Louis, 186, 188
Sandman, Peter M., 250
Sarno, Ronald A., vii-viii, 39, 82
Satan, 88, 217
Savage, John E., 192
Schutz, Jill M., 189
Schwarz, Meg, 189
Schwarz, Tony, 250
Scopes, John Thomas, 88, 160, 267
Shakespeare, William, 262, 267
Shapiro, Jeremy, 164
Sherrill, Lewis Joseph, 29-30, 40
Siegel, Martin, 193
Silkwood, Karen, 259
Singleton, Ralph, 187
Sinyard, Neil, 187
Skinner, B. F., 38, 39, 41, 42, 54-59, 66, 76, 82
Sklar, Rick, 186
Sklar, Robert, 189

Sloan, Douglas, 193
Smart, James D., 29, 40
Smith, Albert E., 187
Smith, David F., 161, 193
Socrates, 7
Soukup, Paul A., 3, 37
Spielberg, Steven, 264
Stanhoff, Edward, 186, 188
Stanley, Robert H., 250
Stavins, R., 188
Stearne, Gerald Emmanuel, 80, 161
Stein, Robert, 250
Steinbeck, John, 267
Steinberg, Charles S., 250
Stevens, George, 261, 268
Stewart, James H., 192
Stokes, Olivia Pearl, 37
Stott, John, 215, 217, 231

Tavard, George, 20-21, 39
Teresa, Mother, 269
Theroux, James M., 186
Thomas, Ronald, 264
Thompson, Norma, xiii, 37
Thüsing, Wilhelm, 161, 164
Toffler, Alvin, 34-35, 40
Tracy, David, 20, 39
Trask, Willard, 83
Truffault, Francois, 264
Turow, Jospeh, 189

van Baaren, Th. P., 165
van Caster, Marcel, 87, 138, 153-156, 165
van Ruler, A. A., 165
van Unnik,. W. C., 165
von Galli, Mario, 161, 162
Vonk, John A., 193
von Ruiden, Otto, 188

Wakefield, George, 184, 187
Wallis, Jim, 82
Watson, Wilfred, 161
Weil, Simone, 89
Weisser, Donald, 103, 161

Welk, Lawrence, 275
Wesley, John, 76
Westerhoff III, John H., 7, 37
White, Robert, 164
Wiener, Norbert, 41, 44-46, 76, 77, 81, 82, 162
Wilkinson, John, 81, 83, 162
Williams, Gene B., 190
Williams, Kay, 190
Wilti, Paul E., 192

Winsor, Paul, 192
Witney, Stephen B., 188
Wyckoff, D. Campbell, 30, 40

Yurko, John, 190

Zbar, Paul, 188
Zeferelli, Franco, 168
Zwass, Vladimir, 182

Index of Subjects

ABC, 278
Abstract Christianity, 219, 230
Abstraction, 4
Advertising, 63-64, 223, 276
Affectivity, 4, 17, 32, 33
AM: Amplitude Modulation, 171-172
America, 10, 25, 269
Analogy, 81
Animation, 260
Anti-environment, 102-106, 129
Arbitron ratings, 274
Art, 26, 33, 244
Art, Christian, 6
Artificial intelligence, 44-46
Association, 236
Assumption, 9, 14, 21, 22
Audio (See Tape)
Audiovisual media, 9-12, 15-16, 26, 28, 35, 74-75, 91, 92, 131-135, 146, 157, 169-183, 195-214

Behavior, viii, 3-4, 12-13, 17, 23, 32-34, 38, 54-58
Behavior, religious, 18, 23
Behaviorialism, 19, 38
Behaviorism, 13, 23, 38, 54-58
Bible, 11, 23, 24, 28-30, 35-36, 121, 267

Black theology, 8
Book, 3, 4, 10, 15, 84-85
Brain, 150
   left-side hemisphere, 150
   right-side hemisphere, 150
Broadcast (See Radio broadcasting, Religious broadcasting and Television broadcasting)
Broadcast band, 112
Byzantine era, 6

Cable television (See Television: CATV)
Calvinism, 46-47
Camcorder, 198
Camera, 170-171, 173-177
Canada, 47-50
Carrier Wave, 171-173
Catechetics (Catechesis), 5-7, 9, 12, 19, 123-129, 154-156
Catechism, 6
Catholic Television Network, 220
Catholicism, 6, 14, 20, 24, 51-52, 154-156, 219-231
CBS, 227-228, 277-278
Century
   16th, 74-75
   18th, 93
   19th, 8-10, 25

Index of Subjects

20th, 8, 10-11, 25 (See Decades)
21st, 12
Christianity, 12, 20, 26
Christmas carols, 209-210
Church, ix, 6-8, 19-23, 25, 28-30, 50-51, 62-63, 71-74, 214
  Ancient, 6
  Catholic, 8, 11, 20, 22, 25, 92-98, 108-111, 219-231
  Christian, 20, 35, 77
  Medieval, 6, 8, 63
  Modern (See Theology, contemporary)
  Patristic, 6, 8
  Post-Vatican II, 8, 11, 97
  Reformed, 6
  Tridentine, 6
Cinema, 4, 236, 243, 245, (See also pictures)
Civil religion, 92-94
Clergy, 6, 9-11, 15, 22, 94-98
Code, 4, 24, 26, 30, 32
Co-determinism, 235
Co-expression, 131, 135
Cognition, ix, 3, 4, 17, 33, 69, 141-142, 149
Co-message, 236
Commercial, 52-54, 274-275
Commodore computer, 210-213
Communication model, 7
Communication theory (See Modern communication theory)
Communicative competence, 139
Community, ix, 5, 10, 19, 22, 25, 28, 30, 131
Community of faith, 7
Community, verbal, 23
Computer, personal, 5, 12, 13, 25, 36, 169, 178-181, 192-194, 199, 209-213, 237, 243-244, 246-247
Concept, 7, 232

Conscience, 20
Consciousness, xi, 29, 237
Content, xi, 14, 17, 18, 19, 22, 24, 26-28, 30, 33, 35
  lifestyle, 17, 33
  nonverbal, 17
  process, 17, 32-33, 107, 143-150, 237
  product, 17, 32, 107, 143-150, 156, 240
  structural, ix, 16, 17, 19, 32, 144-145, 237, 239, 241-249
  substantive, ix, 6, 16, 17, 19, 27, 32, 33, 107, 143-150, 237, 239-241
  unconscious, 17, 33
  verbal, 17
Context, 24, 26, 28, 29, 31
Creation, 25, 27, 213, 268
  divine, 44-47, 214
  human, 5, 44-47
Creation story, 8
Culture, 4-5, 7, 28 (See Literate culture, Print culture, and Oral culture)
Cybernetics, 44-46

Data Processing, 178-181
Decades (of the 20th century)
  1920s, 256-258
  1930s, 256-258
  1940s, 257-258
  1950s, 257-258
  1960s, 257-258
  1970s, 257-258
  1980s, 257
Democracy, 25, 27
Demographics, 224, 275-276, 277
Depression, 256-258
Determinism, 13, 46-47
  media, 41-80
  social, 111-112
  socio-media co-, 111-112
  technological, 46-47

Developmentalism (*See* Behavioralism)
Dialectic (*See* Hegelian dialectic)
Dialogue, 114
Dialogic Communication, 7, 114
Disc jockey, 207-208
Doctrine, viii, ix, 11, 24, 27, 31
Drugs, xi, 237

Ear, 169, 170, 236
Ecclesiology, 11, 19, 115, 118-119, 130
Ecumenism, 208
Education, 4-52, 8, 10, 12, 19, 26, 63-65
Educationist, 7, 9, 10, 11, 30, 31
Educator, 15
Effect,
    actual, 244-247
    intended, 244-247
Electric age, vii
Electro-magnetic spectrum, 171
Emotion, viii, 235-236
Empiricism, 17, 166
Emulsion, 170-171
Enlightenment, 93
English, 6, 23
Environment, x, 3-5, 10, 13, 15, 17-24, 34, 37
    media, 4, 12
Epistemology, 8, 18, 66
Eros, xi
Eroticism, xi
Eternal Word Television Network, 220
Europe, 6, 25, 269
Evaluation, 18, 34
Evangelical, 11, 87-92, 98-100
Evangelism, 215-231
Evil, 27, 88-92
Evolution, theory of, 8, 59-61
Existentialism, 8
Experience, vii, viii, 7, 11, 12, 20, 21, 26-28, 30, 32, 34, 36, 151, 155, 196, 236, 247

Extension,
    of calculation, 237
    of ear, 236-237
    of eye, 236-237
    of feet, 236
    of kinesthesia, 236-237
    of memory, 236-237
Eye, 169-170, 236

Faith, vii, xiv, 6-9, 13, 14, 16-20, 25-31, 130-131, 135-137, 269
Faith communication, vii, 4-19
Faith education, 13, 123-125
Faith story, 164-165
Fantasy, 88-92
Federal Communications Commission, 269
Feet, 169-170, 236
Fellowship, 30, 31
Feminist Theology, 8
Film, 197, 207
    feature film, 251-270
FM: Frequency Modulation, 173
Form, 17
Franchise, cable, 175-176
Free will, 46-47
Freedom, ix, 19, 29, 151, 240, 248-249
French, 6
Future Shock, 34

Global Consciousness, 9-10, 236
Global village, 10, 36
Gnosticism, 8
God, vii, ix, 15, 16, 18, 20-23, 25-31, 214, 217-218, 248, 267, 268
    God-question, 223
Good, 27
Good Friday, 203
Good Shepherd, 206-207
Gospel, ix-xi
    Gospel music, 221-222
Grace, x, 8, 16, 18, 239

Index of Subjects

Grades
  early primary, 200, 270
  middle primary, 200, 270
  secondary, 200
  collegian, 200-201
  adult, 201
Greek, 7, 8, 65, 139

Hegelian dialectic, 47-50, 135-143, 155
Hermeneutics, 139
Hierarchy, Catholic, 6, 94-98, 223-224
History, 4, 8
Holism, vii, 12-14, 17, 33, 36
  holistic knowledge, 237
Holy Spirit, 14, 31
Humanism, 13
  Christian, 102-106

Iconography, 51-52, 93
Idealism, 21, 25
Illiteracy, x, 12
Illusion (*See* Fantasy)
Image,
  latent, 170-171
  orthicon, 174
  television, 5
Immanentism, 8, 20-23, 28, 65-71, 86, 101-156, 158-159, 162, 218-231.
Immortality,
  artificial, 43-44
  divine, 43-44
Implosion, 59-60
Incarnation, 114-115
Independent VHF television stations, 175
Index of Forbidden Books, 51
Individualism, 20
Indoctrination, 6-7
Information, 23, 244
  Information environment, 35, 36
Integralism, 32, 152-158

Intelligence,
  artificial, 44-46
  human, 59-61
International Center for Study of Religious Education, 155

Jesse tree, 201
Judeo-Christian,
  lifestyle, 251-252, 260
  values, x
Justification by faith, 47

Kerygma, 6
Kerygmatic catechetics, 11
Kinesthesia, 169-170, 236
Kinetic imagery, 12
Kingdom of God, 217-218
Knowledge, 4, 18, 31-33

Laity, 6, 11, 22
Language, viii, xiii, 13, 22, 23, 26, 33, 62, 69
  audiovisual, vii, viii, 5
  intentional, 66
  Gutenberg, viii
  political, 135-143
  print, 51
  religious, 19, 22, 23, 134-135
  spoken, 6, 69
  theological, 23, 24, 77, 107
  verbal behavior, 22, 23
Laser beam, 10
Latin, 6, 21
Leader, Church (*See* Hierarchy)
Learned Latin, 73
Learning, ix, x, 7, 12-19, 26, 28, 33, 34, 36, 169, 183-184
  discovery, 25, 261
  programed, 5
Learner, ix-xi, xiii, 4-7, 9, 10, 12-15, 17-19, 22, 23, 26-34, 36, 37, 132, 135, 169, 181-182, 237, 239-249
  experience, 17-18
  media productions, 195-214

Lens, 170
Liberalism, 20, 21, 94
Liberation, 20
Liberation theology, 8
Life, 15, 16, 19, 26, 28-30, 32, 34
  artificial, 44-46
  human, 44-46
Lifestyle, ix, 15, 18, 32, 35, 36, 248
  Christian, 19, 22, 23, 36
  Judeo-Christian, 251-252, 260
  religious, 255, 260
Lighting, 198, 265
Linguistics, 19, 22
Listening room, 197
Literacy, 6
  media, 235-250
  print, x
Literate culture, 4, 5, 7-9, 13, 18, 28, 35, 36
Literature, 26, 153-154
Liturgy, 134
  liturgical renewal, 11
Logic, 18
Loudspeaker, 172, 197-199
Love, ix-xi, 16, 32, 33
  Christian xi, 160
  sexual xi, 160

McLuhanism, 59-65, 102-108, 134-135, 143-150, 151, 152
Macrotheory, 36, 65-71
Magisterium, 20, 24, 94-98, 128
Magnetic tape, 177-178
  audio, 202-210
  computer, 177-178
  video, 202-210
Mainframe computer, 178
Manuscript era, 6
Market research, 223
Marketing, 223
Marxism, 8, 20, 135-143
Mass media, 5, 10, 12, 13, 50-51, 225, 227
Mass-media culture, 4, 5

Master print, 254
Materialism, 19
Meaning, 56, 66-67
Mechanics, 43
Media, vii, xi, 4, 5, 15, 36, 131-132, 169, 235
Media bias, 47-50
Media commercials, 53
Media-congregation, 53, 92-93, 215-221
Media demand, 44
Media determination, 112
Media effect, 62-65, 71-76, 129, 214, 235-250
Media environment, 129, 135, 239
Media event, x, 236
Media experience, 213-214, 247
Media fantasy, 88-92
Media generation, 16, 35, 36
Media hype, 236
Media literacy, x, 37, 79, 129, 196, 235-250
Media preaching, 53, 54, 215-231
Media sports, 241-249
Media star, 236, 251, 253
Media world, vii, xiii, 5, 239
Meditation, xi, 237
Medium, viii, xi, 19
  hot, 146
  cool, 146
Meeting of minds, 208
Memory, 11, 170, 236-237
Message, ix, xi, 3, 4, 6, 7, 14, 22, 24, 25, 28, 29, 31, 32, 236
Metanoia, 222
Metaperspective, 85-86, 158-159
Metaphor, 66
Method, 18, 27, 31, 33, 36
Methodology, 5, 7, 22
Metromedia, 175
Microcomputer (See Computer)
Microphone, 178-181

Microprocessor, 178
Microwave relay, 173
Middle America, 277
Mime, 204, 262
Mini-computer, 178-181
Mini-laboratory, 5, 32
Mini-series, 266, 267
Mission, 30
Mixing, sound, 200
Modern communication theory, 3-40, 41-80, 101-158
Molar content, 17
Motion pictures, 169, 173-174, 186-187, 197-198
Motion picture appreciation, 186-187, 251-270
Multi-media, 196, 199
Music, 171, 184-185, 221-222, 262
Myth, 63, 72, 227

Narcissism, 90
National Religious Broadcasters, 189
Nature, 19, 21, 22
NBC, 277
Negative, photograph, 170-171
Neo-orthodoxy, 20
Neo-Platonism, 8, 21
Neo-Scholasticism, 8
Network, 173
  programing policy, 277-279
  radio, 173
  television, 175, 277-279
New Testament 8
News broadcast 88-92, 277-279
Newspapers, 9, 169
Nielsen Ratings System, 275
Nonverbal communication, 15, 26
Noosphere, 59-61

Operation, 54-58
Optical density recording, 174
Oral culture, 4-7, 9, 13, 25
Oral history, 205-206

Oral presentation, 14
Original sin, 27
Orthodoxy, 6
Orthopraxis, 136

Papacy, 106-108, 221
Parable, 6, 53
Participation, 12, 14, 16, 26, 27, 29, 31, 37, 61, 236
Passion, 236
Passion story, 203-204, 267, 268
Patriotism, 236, 248
PBS, 277-278
Pedagogy, 10, 19, 36, 117, 137
Perception, 61-62, 70, 100
Person, viii, ix, 3, 4, 10, 15-17, 23, 27-32, 34, 131-132
Personality development, 4
Personalism, 4
Persuasion, 52-53, 158, 276 (See also Advertising)
Philosophy, 7-9, 11, 20, 24, 25
  Aristotelian, 8, 21, 138
  Chardinian, 8, 59-61, 92-94
  existential, 8, 21-22
  Hegelian, 8, 47-50, 135-143, 155
  Marxist, 8, 20, 135-143
  Platonic, 7
  progressive, 46-47, 94
  scholastic, 8, 73-74
Phonograph, 9, 169, 171, 184-185, 197, 202-205, 236, 241, 244
Photocathode, 174
Photoelectric, 174
Photography, 169, 170-171, 184, 196-197, 201-202, 236, 240-242
Physics, 14
Plain meaning, 69
Pluralism, 20
Poetry, wit, 72
Polaroid, 171
Politics, 135-143
Political Christianity, 20, 135-143

Pope, 106-108, 221
Portrait, 203
Positive, photography, 170
Practice, 4, 32, 33, 37, 129-132
Praxis, 136-143
Preaching, 11, 52-54, 215-231
Pre-evangelization, 216
Press, 48-49, 51-52, 60-63, 74-76
Pride, 44-46, 236
Prime time, 273
Print, x, xiii, 11, 26, 35, 36, 83, 149
Print culture, x, 156, (See also Literate culture)
Print Language, xiii, 51
Probability, 44-46
Process, ix, 5, 12, 17, 19, 27, 28, 31, 33-35
  affective, 4, 17, 32, 33
  cognitive, ix, 3, 4, 17, 33, 69, 141-142, 149
  dialectic, 8, 47-50, 72-73, 135-143, 155
  dialogic, 72-73
Process content (See Content)
Proclamation, 6, 7
Production, 195-214
Program manual, 199
Programed Learning, 12-13, 181
Projector, 9, 173-174
Propaganda, 47
Protestantism, 6, 10, 11, 14, 22, 24, 25, 51-52, 76
  Evangelical, 22, 215-231
  mainline, 11, 20, 22, 219
Psychoanalysis, 61
  Freudian, 61, 66
  Jungian, 61
Public Service Announcement, 208-209

Radicalism, Catholic, 92-94
Radio, 4, 10, 185-186, 197, 207, 208, 236

Radio broadcasting, 169, 171-173, 185-186, 208-210, 215-231, 245-246
Radio effect, 245-246
Radio genre, 241
Radio receiver, 172-173, 197
Radio wave, 173-176
Ramism, 74-76
Ratings, 273-274
Reading, 6, 18, 50-54, 279-280
Reagent, 170-171
Reality, 21, 23, 33, 69, 74, 88-92
Records, phonograph, 171, 197, 202-205, 244
Reductionism, 49
Redemption, 25, 28-30, 214
Reel, film, 173-174
Reflection, 9, 11, 16
Reformation, Protestant, 49, 51-52, 74-76, 78
Reformers, Protestant, 8
  semi-Ramists, 76
Religion, x, 9, 14-17, 31, 32
Religious broadcasting, 215-231
Religious education, vii, x, xi, xiii, 3-40, 65-65, 75-76, 76-80, 119-123, 123-152, 169, 237-239
  contemporary, 28-31, 86-87, 101-123, 237-239
  profession of, vii, xi, 14
  religious education approach, 123-135
  social-cultural, 25-28, 123-135
  social science, 12-19, 21, 31-34, 143-150
  traditional, ix, xiii, 24-25, 86-101
  theological, 24-25, 28-31
Religious Education Association, 10, 125-127
Religious education themes, 213-214, 261, 266-268
Religious instruction, 4, 5, 10, 13, 14, 16-19, 22, 32, 33, 123-125, 150

Index of Subjects

Religious way of life, 19 (See also Lifestyle, religious)
Renaissance, 6, 8, 51-52, 63, 70, 74-76
Replication, 169-170, 236-237
Resurrection,
  artificial, 44
  of Jesus, 29, 267
  theological meaning of, 43-44
Reversal process, photography, 170-171
Revolution,
  American, 258, 269
  Catholic, 92-97
Rhetoric, 12

Sacrament, 19
Sacred, 8, 21
Salvation history, 164, 214
Satire, 241, 262, 263
Scholasticism, 8, 74-76
School, 42, 50-51
Science, 10, 21, 26, 33
Science fiction, 259
Scientific process, 4, 5, 10
Screen, 173-177, 197, 199
Script, film, 253
Secular, 8, 10, 13, 15, 16, 25, 48
Self, viii, 22, 29, 30, 69
  esteem, xi
Sex, x (See Eroticism)
Sexual promiscuity, 251
Shuttle, film, 173, 174
Sidebands, radio, 172
Sign, 24
Sin, x, 8, 20, 214
Slide projector, 10, 170-171, 196-197
Slides, film, 202-203
Social gospel, 25, 125-128
Social process, 125-129
Socialization, 5, 50-54
Society, 6, 25, 26, 28, 34, 135-143
  consumer, 46-47
  electronic, 5
  literate, 5
  mass media, 5
  print, 63
  oral, 5
  visual, 48
Software, computer, 179-181, 210-213
Soteriology, 8
Sound, 202-203, 206-208
  mixing, 200
  reproduction, 190-192, 237
  system, 200
  waves, 171-173
Speech, 3, 4, 18, 54-58, 114-117
Spirituality, medieval, 63
Stereophonic,
  phonograph, 10, 171
  radio, 17, 173
  recording, 171
Storyboard, 206-207, 214
Student, 10, 26, 27, 31, 33, 34, 36, 37
Studio,
  Multi-media, 199
  radio, 172
  television, 198
Stylus, phonograph, 171
Supernatural, 21-22
Symbol, ix, 23, 30, 134
Synchronized sound, 173-174, 199, 200
Synergy, 13
Synthesis, 20, 154-156

Talk show, 208
Tape,
  audio, 190-192, 203-210, 241, 242, 246
  video, 190-192, 207-210
Tape recorder, 10, 169, 177-178, 190-192
  audio (sound), 169, 177-178, 190-192, 198, 237
  video (visual), 177-178, 190-192, 198-199

Teacher, x, xiii, 3-7, 11-17, 19, 23, 24, 26, 27, 30-34, 36, 79-80, 148-149, 181-182
Teaching, ix-xi, 4, 9, 11-19, 21, 28, 31, 33, 34, 36, 84-166, 169, 180-184, 261
Technology, x, 9, 10, 12, 13, 43-50
Technological determinism, 41-80
Technological era, 5
Telegraph, 4, 5, 9, 169
Telephone, 5, 9, 169
Television, 4, 10, 188-190, 198, 236, 242-243, 246, 266-268
  appreciation, 188-190, 271-281
  broadcasting, 169, 174-177, 215, 231
  camera, 174-175
  environment, 52
  genre, 241-242, 279
  systems:
    cable, 175-177
    closed circuit 175-177
    SATV, 175-177
    UHF, 175-177
    VHF, 175-177
  Time slots, 273
Themes, religious education, 213-214, 262-264, 266-268
Theological imperialism, 22, 134
Theology, 5, 7-9, 12, 16, 19, 20-22, 30, 119-125
  cognitive verbal, 7-9
  contemporary, 28-31, 101-123, 132-134, 156-158
  dogmatic, 7-9
  immanentist, 28-31
  liberal, 20, 25
  liberation, 8
  orthodox, 20, 45
  neo-orthodox, 20
  radical, 20
  relational, 153-154
  revisionist, 20
  traditional, 24, 25, 28, 29, 45, 148
Theory, 16, 17, 33
Thinking,
  artificial, 44-46
  human, 44-46
Time, 4
Time line, 201
Tradition, ix, 7, 21, 28, 35, 154-156
Transcendism, 20-23, 86-101, 153-159, 162, 216-218
Transmitter, 17, 24, 26, 30, 31, 33
Transparency, film, 170-171
Truth, 23

UHF, 172, 175-176, 275
Unchurched, 225
Unconscious, 17, 33
University, 8, 11, 228-229

Value, 28, 33
  Christian, 24, 28, 31, 32, 34
Value clarification, 231-239
Value system, 237-239
Vatican II, 20, 108-114
Verbal Behavior, 54-58
Verbal environment, 54-58
VHF, 172, 175, 176
Video, 190-192
  cassette recorder, 177-178, 198-199, 207, 209-210
  display screen, 199
  games, 179-180
  tape, 190-192, 207-210
Viewing room, 198-199
Voice, 26, 33, 169, 170

Wisdom, x, 32
Witness, 24, 29
Writing, 4-7, 9, 18, 24
Word, viii, ix, 4, 5, 16, 33
Word processing, 181
World War II, 42, 244